The Debt Rescheduling Process

Marko Milivojević

Frances Pinter (Publishers), London

First published in Great Britain in 1985 by
Frances Pinter (Publishers) Limited
25 Floral Street, London WC2E 9DS

British Library Cataloguing in Publication Data
Milivojević, Marko
  The debt rescheduling process.
  1. Debts, External—Developing countries
  2. Payment—Developing countries
  I. Title
  336.3 '63 '091724 HJ8899
  ISBN 0-86187-575-3

Typeset by Joshua Associates Limited, Oxford
Printed and bound in Great Britain by
Biddles of Guildford Limited,
Guildford and King's Lynn

Contents

Tables

Figures

To my parents and my sister, Mila

Introduction

This study is based on the premiss that the debt problems of the developing countries, and the handling of those problems in the rescheduling process, is the most important issue in the area of international economic affairs at the present time. This is because the sheer size of the debt held by the developing countries, and the extensive disruption of normal debt servicing during the rescheduling process in the period 1982-4, has created all manner of possibly adverse implications for the stability of the international financial system, the viability of the large commercial banks that are the heart of that system, the continuation of co-operative relationships between debtor and creditor countries, and for the future economic and political evolution of the developing countries.

While the study is obviously concerned with the economic causes of debt growth, and the breakdown of normal debt servicing in the period 1982-4 in particular, it is also very concerned with the political aspects of these economic issues. In particular, the political consequences, both as regards the political evolution of developing countries and for political relations between such countries and creditor OECD countries, of the debt problem, and the economic adjustment process that took place in the developing countries in the period 1982-4 in particular.

It is the study's contention that though the international financial system, and the developing countries involved in the rescheduling/adjustment processes, have shown remarkable resilience to the shocks experienced since the debt crisis began in 1982, the debt problem of the developing countries has reached a critical turning-point at the beginning of 1985. That turning-point can be reduced to the following question: will relations between the developing countries and their foreign creditors continue to be co-operative, or will they become increasingly confrontational?

In the developing countries the political strains caused by economic adjustment are becoming intense enough to put the continuation of co-operative relations at risk in the future. In the creditor OECD countries there seems to be a political unwillingness to consider and construct, in co-operation with the developing countries, the sort of political programme necessary to solve the wider problem of how best to finance the economic development of the developing countries in the future, and thereby safeguard the political stability of such countries in the long term—a wider problem that could not be solved by the temporary and *ad hoc* remedial measures of the rescheduling process. Without such a general political solution to the problem, it is argued, the likelihood of increasing confrontation between debtor countries and their foreign creditors will increase in the future, which could create all manner of possibly adverse implications for the stability of the international financial system, and for the economic and political development of the developing countries in the future.

This study, being a general analysis of the debt rescheduling process in the developing countries, does not claim any originality as regards sources of data, and the analysis of such data. All the economic data used is from standard published sources published by the International Monetary Fund, the Bank for International Settlements, and commercial banks such as Morgan Guaranty. All the political data is from secondary published sources. Nor is the study concerned with econometric model-building, although models developed by others, and which are in the secondary sources, are used in the analysis.

The study's claim to analytical originality, therefore, primarily derives from its synthesis of economic and political analyses of the debt problems of the developing countries, and of the debt rescheduling process in particular. The political economy of the debt rescheduling process in the developing countries is the primary concern of the study. The choice of political economy, as opposed to conventional economic analysis, is based on the view that while the literature on the debt problems of the developing countries is very strong as regards economic and econometric analyses, the politics of the debt problem have not received the same sort of detailed attention in the literature. More generally, what political analysis does exist in the literature has tended to be compartmentalised, and separated from the purely economic analysis. The study's primary objective, in light of this compartmentalisation, has been to create an analytical synthesis of economic and political analyses, so as to produce a more meaningful insight into the debt problems of the developing countries, and the debt rescheduling process in particular.

The study is based on the premiss of classical political economy, which states that economics and politics cannot, in reality, be separated in the way they have been separated in the literature. The debt rescheduling process is not only an economic phenomenon; it has been highly politicised since it began in 1982. The same applies to the economic adjustment process, which also began in 1982. Being based on this premiss, the study, therefore, is greatly influenced by the classical theorists of international political economy. This mode of analysis, after years of neglect, is currently enjoying a revival in the literature on international economic affairs, as many commentators, disenchanted with purely economic and econometric analyses, have seen that international economic phenomena, of which the debt problem of the developing countries is but one example, cannot be adequately understood without analytical reference to the wider political framework within which all such economic phenomena exist.

The organisation of the study is based on the examination of themes, with reference to all developing countries, although three particular countries—Brazil, Mexico, and Yugoslavia—are given particular attention throughout the study. The inclusion of the two most important debtor countries, Brazil and Mexico, needs no justification. Yugoslavia, which has been neglected in the literature, is included because of that neglect. At various points in the text, in order to create the opportunity for comparative analysis, Poland, Nicaragua, Costa Rica, Argentina, and Venezuela are also examined in some detail. However, the case study approach is avoided, in order to create more opportunities for comparative analysis of differing rescheduling experiences in the various developing countries examined in the study.

Chapter 1 analyses the growth of the debt, and of debt service costs, of the developing countries in the period 1973–82. The causes of that debt growth, both exogenous and endogenous, are analysed, as are the causes of the 1982 South

American debt crisis. Brazil, Mexico, and Yugoslavia are given particular attention in this chapter.

Chapter 2 analyses the consequences of so large an amount of debt, and of the debt crisis of the period 1982-4, for both the international financial system, and the developing countries. The vulnerability (at the beginning of the debt crisis in 1982) of the international financial system, and the top nine US commercial banks in particular, to disruptions in normal debt servicing on the debt owed by the developing countries is analysed. The top nine US commercial banks are given particular attention because they dominate total Western commercial bank lending to developing countries, and to South American countries in particular. In addition, US banking laws demand that a great deal of data on banks is made public. This is not the case in Western Europe and Japan. Finally, the vulnerability of the top nine US banks is analysed as regards the situation at the end of 1984. A comparison is made with the situation in 1982.

The vulnerability of the developing countries is analysed, with regard to the macroeconomic consequences to their economies of the debt crisis of the period 1982-4. Because that crisis began (and was most serious) in South America, that region is given the most attention in this chapter. Aggregate analysis for all developing countries, and disaggregate analysis for particular South American countries and for Yugoslavia, is then used to examine the worsening economic situation of 1982-3, and the limited improvement in the economic situation in the period 1983-4. Lastly, the international financial system and the developing countries are examined as a whole, with reference to the overall consequences of the debt crisis during the period 1982-4.

Chapter 3 analyses the debt rescheduling process in its entirety, in the period 1982-4, and pays particular attention to the rescheduling of debt, and the imposition of economic adjustment in Brazil, Mexico, and Yugoslavia. Argentina, Venezuela, Poland, Hungary, Nicaragua, and Costa Rica are also given special attention because of their important, though different, roles in the rescheduling process.

The significance, and respective *modus operandi*, of the various economic and political institutions involved in the rescheduling process are analysed, with reference to various

developing countries to illustrate various aspects of their behaviour in different circumstances. Those institutions include
commercial banks (organised in advisory committees, and
outside such committees), the International Monetary Fund
(IMF), the Bank for International Settlements (BIS), Organisation for European Co-operation and Development (OECD)
country central banks, OECD Governments, the Paris Club,
and the Governments of the developing countries. Relations
between such institutions are examined with reference to
various differing circumstances in a number of developing
countries. The most important rescheduling/new loan agreements signed in the period 1982–4, and the agreements signed
by Brazil, Mexico, and Yugoslavia in particular, are examined
in detail.

Lastly, some generalisations are made about the behaviour
of the various economic and political institutions involved in
the rescheduling process, relations between such institutions,
how rescheduling agreements were reached, why rescheduling
agreements differed between countries, why agreements changed
in particular countries over time, and what factors—economic
and political—were common to all rescheduling and economic
adjustment experiences. Factors unique to particular developing countries involved in the rescheduling/adjustment processes
are also examined.

Chapter 4 analyses the most important implications, economic and political, of the rescheduling/adjustment processes.
Those processes are looked at in retrospect in order to identify
those important implications. On the creditor's side, because of
their great importance in the rescheduling/adjustment processes,
the commercial banks and the IMF are given particular attention in this chapter. As regards the IMF and the BIS regulatory
structure, the international and regulatory framework within
which commercial banks conduct their operations is examined
in detail. On the debtor's side, because of the importance of
this relationship for the future, the changing relationship
between developing countries and their foreign creditors is
given special attention in this chapter.

Chapter 5 analyses the politics of debt. The domestic political
consequences for developing countries of debt crisis, and of
economic adjustment in particular, are analysed. Special attention is given to South America. The connections between

domestic political conditions, and the changing relations between developing countries and their foreign creditors, are analysed. The development and significance of the first multilateral South American response to the debt crisis, the Cartagena Process, is analysed. These domestic political conditions, and the changing relations between developing countries and their foreign creditors, are then analysed with reference to international political factors, treating US–South American political relations in particular. US–Yugoslav political relations are also given special attention in this chapter. Lastly, varous prescriptive proposals that have been put forward to resolve the debt crisis are examined. Such proposals are then analysed, so as to come to a view as to how politically realistic, or unrealistic, each of the eight prescriptive proposals is.

Chapter 6 comes to some general conclusions about the debt crisis as it affected, and still affects, the international financial and political systems, the commercial banks, and the developing countries. Particular attention is given in this final chapter to the conclusions reached about the rescheduling process.

1 Growth of developing countries' debts 1973–1982

1.1 Extent of debt growth

From the first oil price increase in 1973–4 to the beginning of the current debt crisis in Mexico in August 1982, the total foreign debt of the non-oil developing countries (including new oil exporters such as Mexico) increased from $130 billion to $612 billion. In addition, if the debts ($80 billion) of five OPEC countries (Algeria, Ecuador, Indonesia, Nigeria, and Venezuela) are included, along with the debts ($53 billion) of Eastern Europe, then the total debt of the Third World stood at around $745 billion at the end of 1982.[1]

This almost fivefold increase of the debt, as shown in Table 1, represents an average annual growth rate of 19 per cent. Adjusted to take account of inflation, however, the real debt of the non-oil developing countries grew at an average annual growth rate of 8.7 per cent over the 1973–82 period. Relative to the growth of total Gross Domestic Product (GDP) of these countries, which averaged 4.5 per cent annually over this period, the burden of foreign debt increased from 22 per cent of total GDP in 1973 to 35 per cent of total GDP in 1982. However, because these countries experienced export growth that was greater than GDP growth, foreign debt as a percentage of total exports of goods and services increased far less. Foreign debt as a percentage of exports increased from 115 per cent in 1973 to 143 per cent in 1982 (see Table 1).

This increase in exports, however, did not fully compensate for the worsening position as regards the debt service ratio (ratio of debt service costs to exports of goods and services), which increased from an average of 15.4 per cent of exports in 1973–7 to 18.5 per cent of exports in 1978–80 and 22.2 per cent of exports in 1981–2. Rising interest rates were primarily responsible for this worsening debt service ratio, as an increase

Table 1 External debt of non-oil developing countries, 1973–1982: selected indicators (billions of US dollars and percentages)

	1973	1974	1975	1976	1977	1978	1979	1980	1981	1982
Total debt ($bn.)	130.1	160.8	190.8	228.0	278.5	336.3	396.9	474.0	550.0	612.4
Total debt, 1975 prices ($bn.)*	169.0	175.7	190.8	218.0	250.9	281.0	294.7	308.6	331.3	357.8
Long-term debt ($bn.)†	118.8	138.1	163.5	194.9	235.9	286.6	338.1	338.5	452.8	499.6
Total exports ($bn.)	112.7	153.7	155.9	181.7	220.3	258.3	333.0	419.8	444.4	427.4
Total debt as a percentage of total exports	115.4	104.6	122.4	125.5	126.4	130.2	119.2	121.9	124.9	143.3
Total debt service costs as a percentage of total exports	15.9	14.4	16.1	15.3	15.4	19.0	19.0	17.6	20.4	23.9
Above adjusted to take account of inflationary erosion of debt (%)	n.a.	−1.6	6.5	10.5	9.4	11.0	6.9	4.9	11.7	22.3
Total debt as a percentage of total GDP	22.4	21.8	23.8	25.7	27.4	28.5	27.5	27.6	31.0	34.7

Note: For a general discussion of statistical sources used in this study, see Appendix 1.
* Deflated by the US inflation rate.
† All debt above one year in maturity.
Source: IMF, *World Economic Outlook*, 1982 and 1983.

in interest rates, such as took place in the early 1980s, led automatically to an increase in the debt service ratio. This was because 70 per cent of the total debt by 1982 had floating interest rates tied to the London Interbank Offered Rate (LIBOR).

So while high inflation, which the floating interest rates tied to LIBOR are designed to compensate for, tends to erode the outstanding total debt to be repaid, it also tends to push up interest rates. Most First World Governments have increased interest rates in order to bring down inflation. Increasing interest rates tend, in turn, significantly to increase the debt service ratios of the non-oil developing countries. The increase in those ratios, especially after interest rates began to rise in 1980, is shown in Table 1.

However, if the nominal debt service ratio is adjusted to take account of the inflationary erosion of the total debt, the real debt service ratio is considerably lower than the nominal ratio. As shown in Table 1, throughout much of the period, the real debt service ratio was not as much of a burden as the nominal figure would have suggested. By 1981–2, when nominal interest rates were very high and inflation was declining, the real debt service ratio increased sharply—from 4.9 per cent in 1980 to 11.7 per cent in 1981 and 22.3 per cent in 1982.

This problem was compounded by the problem of short-term debt. By looking at the 'long-term debt' section of Table 1,[2] it is clear that short-term debt (with a maturity of one year or less) has risen sharply from 8.7 per cent of total debt in 1973 to an average of 14.6 per cent in 1974–9 and an average of 18.1 per cent in 1980–2. Such short-term debt, especially in the form of interbank lines (usually renewed on a daily basis) made available to local banks, is highly vulnerable to rapid withdrawal by creditor banks. When creditor bank confidence evaporated in 1982 this sort of short-term credit was the first to be withdrawn.

The general picutre, as revealed in Table 1, is that while total debt accelerated during the 1970s, the speed at which the debt grew was much more moderate than the nominal growth figures would suggest. When inflation is taken into account, and when real debt and debt service costs are compared to the growth of GDP and exports, then the general picture of increasing debt is not so alarming. As long as exports grew faster than did debt

Table 2 External debt of ten largest debtor countries, 1973–1982: selected indicators (billions of US dollars and percentages)

Country	1973	1974	1975	1976	1977	1978	1979	1980	1981	1982
Total debt*										
Brazil	13.8	18.9	23.3	28.6	35.2	48.4	57.4	66.1	75.7	88.2
Mexico	8.6	12.8	16.9	21.8	27.1	33.6	40.8	53.8	67.0	82.0
Argentina	6.4	8.0	7.9	8.3	9.7	12.5	19.0	27.2	35.7	38.0
Spain	5.7	8.6	10.7	13.5	16.3	18.4	22.2	27.4	33.2	n.a.
Korea (S.)	4.6	6.0	7.3	8.9	11.2	14.8	20.5	26.4	31.2	35.8
Venezuela	4.6	5.3	5.7	8.7	12.3	16.3	23.7	27.5	29.3	31.3
India	10.5	11.6	12.4	13.4	14.7	15.6	15.9	17.7	18.5	n.a.
Yugoslavia	4.6	5.4	6.3	7.7	9.6	11.8	14.9	17.6	18.5	n.a.
Indonesia	5.7	7.1	8.9	11.0	12.8	14.5	14.9	17.0	18.0	21.0
Israel	5.9	6.9	7.8	9.0	10.0	11.6	13.2	15.6	17.9	20.4
Debt service†/ exports (%)‡										
Brazil	36.7	36.0	40.8	45.3	48.7	59.3	65.6	60.8	66.9	87.1
Mexico	28.7	21.9	30.3	40.7	53.6	64.9	67.7	36.4	48.5	58.5
Argentina	19.9	21.3	31.9	26.2	19.1	41.6	21.3	32.2	37.5	102.9
Spain	5.2	4.2	9.3	10.7	13.3	19.5	15.7	15.5	19.0	n.a.
Korea (S.)	11.5	11.8	12.5	9.8	10.2	12.0	13.9	17.3	18.8	21.1
Venezuela	3.8	3.3	3.5	8.4	10.0	15.6	16.4	15.6	19.0	20.7
India	23.6	63.7	14.0	11.5	12.3	11.4	11.2	n.a.	n.a.	n.a.
Indonesia	3.4	2.1	6.2	7.2	8.3	9.7	7.4	4.9	5.2	11.3
Yugoslavia	21.7	21.7	21.1	18.3	19.4	21.0	20.8	20.0	n.a.	30.3
Israel	21.7	22.4	26.8	24.5	22.2	22.9	22.0	24.6	26.0	23.7

Debt§/exports (%)‡										
Brazil	106.2	145.9	194.3	195.8	207.6	252.5	269.3	259.1	256.6	365.3
Mexico	154.6	182.0	243.8	286.5	309.7	278.2	241.7	205.7	209.0	248.6
Argentina	140.8	145.2	211.5	145.7	96.8	96.1	97.3	182.5	275.3	353.5
Spain	−4.1	21.0	37.7	60.3	60.3	37.4	30.0	46.0	66.2	n.a.
Korea (S.)	88.9	106.5	110.2	73.4	63.0	70.2	89.8	103.8	103.9	104.5
Venezuela	51.2	−5.9	−37.3	−32.9	−8.7	35.6	41.5	33.2	29.3	104.2
India	290.7	248.0	200.8	159.9	125.7	107.9	81.1	n.a.	n.a.	n.a.
Yugoslavia	76.0·	75.6	88.8	81.8	100.1	110.4	133.6	118.8	99.8	n.a.
Indonesia	146.9	75.2	118.0	108.9	94.6	104.7	69.8	52.2	54.9	86.2
Israel	145.5	154.8	173.3	168.9	150.3	131.6	121.8	120.7	132.6	180.9

* Including short-term debt.
† Interest on long- and short-term debt plus amortisation of principal.
‡ Exports includes services.
§ Debt minus official assets, non-gold.
Source: World Bank, *World Debt Tables*; Bank of International Settlement (BIS), *The Maturity Distribution of International Bank Lending*; IMF, *International Financial Statistics*, and *Balance of Payments Yearbook*, various issues.

service costs, and as long as new borrowings continued to increase, the situation was manageable.

By 1981–2 things began to go wrong. In 1981, for example, the real debt service ratio increased sharply in relation to the 1980 figure. By 1982 the ratio stood at 22.3 per cent. This is above what the International Monetary Fund (IMF) considers prudent: for the IMF 20 per cent is the danger point. While the debt service ratio increased, along with the amount of total debt outstanding, there was an actual decline in the nominal value of exports (down 3.8 per cent on the 1981 figure) in 1982 (see Table 1). This fall in exports was caused by both the global recession and the deteriorating terms of trade experienced by the non-oil developing countries as the price of primary commodities fell. Even the price of oil began to fall from 1981 onwards. This fall in exports, along with a rising debt service ratio caused by increased interest rates, are the two most important factors that lay behind the crisis of 1982.

The general picture revealed in Table 1 is, however, an aggregate view. Such a view, while useful as a general background, is somewhat misleading in that it cannot, by its very nature, indicate what kind of situation individual countries find themselves in. Table 2, therefore, shows some of the indicators given in Table 1 for the ten developing and East European countries with the largest external debts. It also illustrates that the growth in the debts of the three largest debtors, Argentina, Brazil, and Mexico, was far greater than the fivefold nominal increase in debt for all the non-oil developing countries in the period 1973–82. For the same period, and in nominal terms, Brazil's debt increased sixfold, Mexico's tenfold, and Argentina's sixfold. As regards the debt service ratio, the difference between the aggregate view of Table 1 and the individual view of Table 2 is even greater.

Compared with a rise from 16 per cent in 1973–4 to 24 per cent in 1982 for all non-oil developing countries, Brazil's debt service ratio increased from 36 per cent to 87 per cent, Mexico's from 25 per cent to 58 per cent, and Argentina's from 21 per cent to 103 per cent, as shown in Table 2. With such high debt service ratios it is hardly surprising that the debt crisis began in South America in 1982.

Other countries, such as South Korea, did not have any problems, despite having very large debts in 1982. South Korea, because of its very strong export performance, only had a debt service ratio of 21 per cent in 1982. The experience of South Korea shows that, in the last analysis, it is export performance that determines whether or not any debtor country experiences a debt crisis. As Table 2 shows, the ratio of net debt (total debt minus official non-gold assets held by the Central Bank) to exports of goods and services increased from 257 per cent in 1981 to 365 per cent in 1982 in Brazil, from 209 per cent to 249 per cent in Mexico, and from 275 per cent to 354 per cent in Argentina. This deteriorating export performance in South America can be compared with strong export performance in South Korea. South Korea had a ratio of net debt to exports of only 104 per cent in 1982: about the same as the ratio in 1981 and 1982 (103 per cent).

1.2 Cutback in new lending

In this context of increasing debt service costs and stagnating exports, another negative variable began to be important in its consequences from 1981 onwards: creditor banks, worried about the rising level of debt and the ability of debtor countries to service their debts, began to cut back on new lending. This is shown in Figure 1. The consequence of reduced inflows, in a context of increasing interest rates and the amortisation of principal, was a net outflow scenario for fully half of the twenty-four countries in 1981. The net outflow scenario is shown in Figure 2. This was one full year before the debt crisis broke in Mexico in 1982. However, going into a new outflow situation is not necessarily a sign of crisis. Algeria, for example, deliberately slowed down its external borrowing programme and allowed debts to mature, without replacing the old debts 'with new loans. By 1982 the net outflow for the twenty-four countries was around $25 billion, as shown in Figure 1. Such an outflow from countries that are short of capital to countries of capital abundance is not a viable proposition in the long term. Historically, all developing countries have been net importers of capital, as one definition of underdevelopment is being short of capital for the development process.

Ironically, creditor banks, when they cut the amount of new

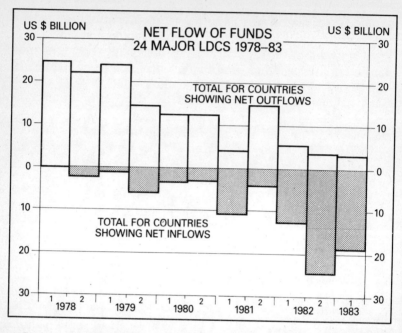

Source: American Express International Banking Corporation, *International Debt: Banks and the LDCs*, AMEX Bank Review Special Paper No. 10 (London, 1984), p. 10.

© 1984 American Express International Banking Corporation. Reproduced by permission from *International Debt: Banks and the LDCs*.

Figure 1　Net flow of funds, twenty-four major LDCs, 1978–1983.

lending, precipitated the very crisis that the cut in lending had sought to avoid. If new lending falls off, as it did, then the debt service ratio must rise, especially if interest rates are also rising and exports falling. Some countries, and Argentina in particular, found themselves in an impossible situation. Their debt service costs were larger than their entire export earnings. In the real world, of course, not all such exports earnings can go to debt service purposes, given the large import requirements of all developing countries. This cut in new lending had the effect of precipitating, albeit unintentionally, a general liquidity crisis in the Third World. The cut in the provision of short-term debt, and especially the sudden withdrawal of inter-bank lines to local banks, was particularly harmful to the cash-flow position of all developing countries.

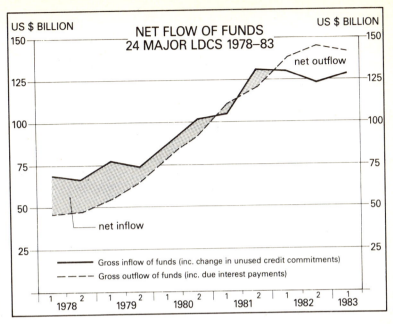

US $ BILLION

**NET FLOW OF FUNDS
24 MAJOR LDCS 1978–83**

net outflow

net inflow

—————— Gross inflow of funds (inc. change in unused credit commitments)
– – – – – Gross outflow of funds (inc. due interest payments)

Source: American Express International Banking Corporation, *International Debt: Banks and the LDCs*, AMEX Bank Review Special Paper No. 10 (London, 1984), p. 10.

© 1984 American Express International Banking Corporation. Reproduced by permission from *International Debt: Banks and the LDCs*.

Figure 2   Net flow of funds, twenty-four major LDCs, 1978–1983.

Like all aggregate data, the above cannot distinguish between individual countries. The position of the largest debtor, Brazil, is shown in Figure 3. Brazil was in a net outflow situation as early as the second oil price increase in 1979, but went back into a net inflow situation in 1981. The country found it much harder to obtain long-term credit, and so was forced into obtaining large amounts of short-term credit. Creditor banks thought that debt that quickly matured was less of a risk than was long-term debt. This may have been true, but in the short-term the consequence of so much short-term debt was to make Brazil vulnerable to the quick withdrawal of such short-term credit facilities. It was the withdrawal of inter-bank facilities to Brazilian banks, after Mexico went into crisis in August 1982, that led to crisis in Brazil later in that same year, although

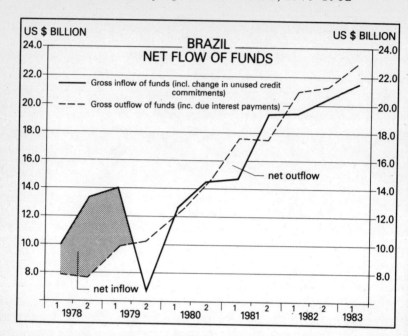

Source: American Express International Banking Corporation, *International Debt: Banks and the LDCs*, AMEX Bank Review Special Paper No. 10 (London, 1984), p. 56.

Figure 3   Brazil, net flow of funds, 1978–1983

the Brazilian Government did not formally ask for a debt rescheduling until 1983. Reasons of national pride were responsible for the latter delay in asking for a debt rescheduling.

Yugoslavia, as Figure 4 shows, was in a net outflow situation as early as 1980. Though not a member of COMECON, creditor banks refused to lend money once Poland's debt crisis began in 1980. Despite the insistence of the Yugoslav Government that Yugoslavia's debt problems were not comparable with those of Poland, what happened in Poland directly affected what happened in Yugoslavia—just as what happened in Mexico affected what happened in Brazil.

In Mexico, as Figure 5 shows, what was happening in Brazil and Yugoslavia—a net outflow situation long before crisis began—did not take place. Yet crisis came to Mexico first.

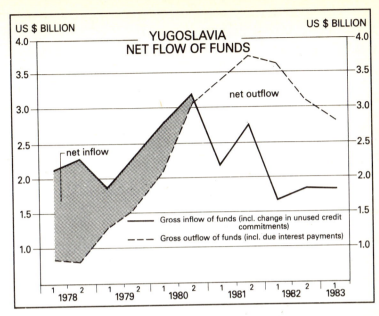

Source: American Express International Banking Corporation, *International Debt: Banks and the LDCs*, AMEX Bank Review Special Paper No. 10 (London, 1984), p. 182.
© 1984 American Express International Banking Corporation. Reproduced by permission from *International Debt: Banks and the LDCs*.

Figure 4   Yugoslavia, net flow of funds, 1978–1983.

The example of Mexico illustrates the dangers of generalising about the origins, and timing, of the debt crisis. Mexico was in a net inflow situation up to the very last moment—up to the very day in August 1982 when the Mexican Government invited its creditors to reschedule part of its foreign debt. From 1979 to 1981, while Brazil was borrowing less and while Yugoslavia was unable to borrow anything, Mexico borrowed $23 billion. In other words, almost 25 per cent of its foreign debt in 1982 was contracted for from 1979 onwards. As with Brazil, a great deal of this borrowing was in the form of short-term debt.

As in the case of Brazil later in 1982, the run-down of short-term credit precipitated the liquidity crisis in August 1982. Figure 5 shows how sharp, drastic, and extensive that run-down was. It began during the spring of 1982, precipitated the liquidity

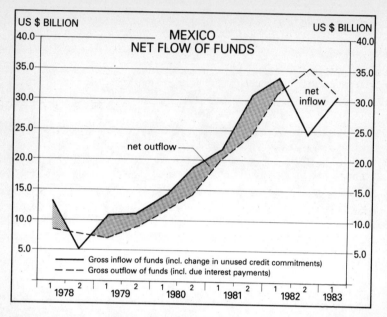

Source: American Express International Banking Corporation, *International Debt: Banks and the LDCs*, AMEX Bank Review Special Paper No. 10 (London, 1984), p. 116.
© 1984 American Express International Banking Corporation. Reproduced by permission from *International Debt: Banks and the LDCs*.

Figure 5   Mexico, net flow of funds, 1978–1983.

crisis in the summer that prompted the Mexican Government to ask its creditor banks to reschedule $19.5 billion[3] of principal due in 1982–3, and only began to bottom out in the autumn of 1982.

The fact that Mexico's bank creditors were lending to Mexico up to the spring of 1982 indicates that they had confidence in the Mexican economy, despite its large foreign debt. Mexico's oil exports were responsible for that confidence. In retrospect that confidence was misplaced, as the Mexican Government's request to reschedule took everybody by surprise—including the banks.

1.3 Exogenous causes of debt growth

Having examined the growth of debt during the 1970s, and having looked at the circumstances which led to crisis for three countries (and Mexico in particular) during the early 1980s, the next question to be answered is: why did the debt grow so fast in the 1970s?

The single most important cause of debt growth was the rise in oil prices in 1973–4 and 1979–80. Only a few debtor countries, such as Mexico, Indonesia, Venezuela, and Ecuador, benefited from the rise in oil prices. Table 3 shows the difference between what was paid for oil and what would have been paid for oil had its price not gone up more than the US inflation rate.

The additional cumulative cost of oil over the decade was, therefore, $260 billion. This massive transfer of resources between Third World countries could not have taken place without equally massive borrowing from Western banks. As

Table 3 Impact of oil prices on the debt of non-oil developing countries, 1973–1982 (billions of US dollars)

Year	A. Actual cost of oil.	B. Cost of oil if its price has not increased beyond US inflation rate.	A.–B. Additional cost of oil.
1973	4.8	4.8	0.0
1974	16.1	5.3	10.8
1975	17.3	5.7	11.6
1976	21.3	6.8	14.5
1977	23.8	7.5	16.3
1978	26.0	8.6	17.4
1979	39.0	10.9	28.1
1980	63.2	11.9	51.3
1981	66.7	12.1	54.6
1982	66.7	11.9	54.8
Total	344.9	85.5	259.5

Source: IMF, *World Economic Outlook*, and *International Financial Statistics*, various issues.

regards the latter, they were only too happy to lend to sovereign states whose export performance looked promising. Such lending was also more profitable than lending in First World markets. Moreover, demand for credit in the First World was stagnant. The Third World was regarded as a growth area for new lending by Western banks.

Ironically, the first South American country that declared it wanted to reschedule its foreign debt was also a large exporter of oil. This was Mexico. Oil, in a most strange way, was responsible for Mexico's large debt. Large loans were required to develop oil production facilities, and Mexico's creditors were willing to lend far more than was prudent on the basis of increasing oil prices. The Mexican Government, because it had oil exports, neglected the development of exports of manufactured goods. Other oil exporters with large debts, such as Venezuela, Nigeria, Indonesia, and Ecuador, experienced similar problems.

Nor would the debt problem be solved, or even ameliorated, by a fall in the price of oil. The largest debtors, such as Mexico, have come to rely on a high oil price. Any fall in the price, such as took place in 1984, means immediate damage to Mexico's debt servicing capacity. Should the world oil price collapse (a possibility) in 1985, the damage to the world financial system, caused by the plight of countries such as Mexico, would be far greater than any gain that would accrue to the balance of payments and foreign debt positions of the non-oil developing countries.

The increases in the price of oil were the prime cause of debt growth in the 1970s, but the combination of high inflation, nominal interest rates, and rapid export growth meant the burden of debt was manageable for the non-oil developing countries. There were exceptions, such as Zaïre in 1976 and Turkey in 1978,[4] but they were very few.

Yet after the second major oil price increase in 1979–80, it was rising real interest rates in the 1980–2 period that became the prime cause of debt growth, increasing debt service costs, and leading to the events of 1982. For the period 1973–80 real interest rates (nominal rate minus inflation rate) were, on the whole, negative. It made sense to borrow in such conditions. By 1979–80, nominal interests rates were high (LIBOR,—London Interbank Offered Rate—averaged 13.2 per cent), but US inflation was about equal to LIBOR. It was the last time interest rates were to be negative. By 1981–2, inflation fell sharply, but nominal interest rates remained high. This meant very high real interest rates of 7.5 per cent in 1981 and 11 per cent in 1982. It did not make sense to borrow in such conditions, but by then most non-oil developing countries had no choice in the matter. They had to borrow more in order to pay off old debts, and the interest due on them. These high interest rates had an immediate effect on debt growth.

Had real interest rates remained negative, as was the case for most of the 1960s and 1970s, the total debt of the non-oil developing countries would have been lower than it was during the 1980s. Bearing in mind that around 70 per cent of the debt has floating interest rates indexed to LIBOR, the total floating rate debt was $240 billion in 1980, $293 billion in 1981, and $329 billion in 1982. If the interest rate payable on that floating rate debt had been negative (as during the 1960s and 1970s) then, according to one authoritative estimate,[5] the total debt would have been $41 billion less than in fact it was in 1982.

Instead, in an effort to reduce inflation, Western Governments increased interest rates and/or adopted tight fiscal policies. The non-oil developing countries paid the price of that interest rate rise in 1981–2. For debtors inflation is a good thing, as it erodes the debt they have to pay off. For creditors, who wanted to reduce inflation, increased interest rates were a worthwhile price to pay for lower inflation.

The problem of this anti-inflationary policy, however, was that higher interest rates tended to aggravate the world recession that began in the 1979–80 period. Growth rates in the OECD countries fell from an average of 3.2 per cent during the 1973–9 period to an average of 1.2 per cent during the 1980–1 period. By 1982, for the first time since the end of World War II, there was no growth, only a decline of −0.3 per cent. This negative development had an immediate effect on the exports of the non-oil developing countries. If the export unit value of 1980 is assigned the index number of 100, it falls to 94 in 1981 and 90 in 1982 for the non-oil developing countries. Falling demand in the OECD countries, especially for primary commodities, was responsible for this fall in export values.

Table 4 Impact of exogenous vairables in the external debt of the
non-oil developing countries, 1973–1982 (billions of
US dollars)

Effect	Amount
Oil price increase in excess of US inflation, 1973–82	$260 billion
Real interest rate in excess of 1961–82 average, 1981–2	$41 billion
Terms of trade loss, 1981–2	$79 billion
Export volume loss caused by world recession, 1981–2	$21 billion
Non-oil effects subtotal	$141 billion
Overall total	$401 billion

Source: William R. Cline, *International Debt and the Stability of the World
Economy*, Policy Studies in International Economics No. 4 (Washington, DC: Institute for International Economics, 1983), p. 25.
  © Institute for International Economics. Reproduced by permission from *International Debt and the Stability of the World Economy*, William R. Cline.

Overall, it has been estimated[6] that the effect of higher
interest payments, lower export receipts, and higher import
costs (though US inflation fell, the developing countries still
had to pay more for their imports due to OPEC and to devaluations of their currencies against the US dollar) represented
around $141 billion in extra debt for the 1973–82 period.
Table 4 shows this estimate. The immensity of the $401 billion
figure indicates, as nothing else can, the importance of exogenous variables over the destinies of non-oil developing countries.
This interdependence between the developing countries and
OECD countries is undeniable, but its effects are not only
harmful to the developing countries. Given the importance of
developing countries as consumers of OECD countries' exports,
then any deterioration of their economic position reduces
growth in the OECD countries themselves. In 1982, 28 per cent
of OECD exports (4 per cent of total OECD GNP), and 40 per
cent of US exports (3 per cent of GNP), went to developing
countries. Morgan Guaranty estimated that if non-oil developing countries' growth fell by 3 per cent in 1983 (which did
take place, for example, in Brazil and Mexico in 1983), then
OECD growth would fall by 0.8 per cent and US growth would
fall by 0.5 per cent in 1983. Negative developments in the
First World can significantly harm the Third World, but the

eventual consequences of this process will, in time, damage the growth prospects of the First World. A mutually harmful circle of effect and counter-effect has been created between the developing countries and the OECD countries.

1.4 Endogenous causes of debt growth

Despite the importance of exogenous variables, it would be wrong to assume that the reasons for debt growth were purely exogenous. While South America went into crisis in 1982, the Pacific Rim economies (and South Korea in particular), which had been exposed to the same negative exogenous variables as had South America, did not go into crisis. South Korea, for example, had a foreign debt of $35 billion (fourth largest in the world) in 1982. Yet there was no crisis. It was, therefore, clear that endogenous factors were responsible for the lack of any crisis among the Pacific Rim economies.

In Mexico, for example, the Government adhered to a high growth (8.2 per cent average annual growth in 1978–81), large debt strategy, that rested on the assumption that oil prices would always keep rising. Even when this assumption proved to be wrong, from 1981 onwards, the Government still adhered to its old strategy. The same strategy prevailed in Brazil. The country had no oil exports, but it was assumed that export growth, which had been spectacular in the 1970s, would remain high in the 1980s. World recession, and the fact that Brazil still relied heavily on primary commodity exports (such as coffee) whose prices were falling, invalidated this assumption from 1981 onwards.

A further problem was the growing reliance on very short-term debt, which was very prevalent in Brazil, Mexico, Argentina, and Venezuela. In 1982, Brazil's short-term debt stood at $21.3 billion (total debt to banks: $62.7 billion); Mexico's stood at $31.2 billion (total: $62.7 billion); Argentina's stood at $13.5 billion (total: $25.5 billion), and Venezuela's stood at $15.3 billion (total: $26.7 billion).[8] Such over-reliance was most undesirable.[9] Over 50 per cent of Mexican and Venezuelan debts to Western banks had maturities of one year or less. The assumption was that such short-term debt facilities would be always available: yet another incorrect assumption.

These problems were, in turn, aggravated by the further problem of capital flight from South America. Throughout South America, and especially in Mexico and Venezuela, Government policy maintained an over-valued exchange rate on a fully convertible basis, combined with domestic interest rates that failed to provide any incentive to retain capital domestically. The result was capital flight on a massive scale. The Bank for International Settlements, in its 1983 *Annual Report*,[10] estimated repatriation of capital from South America at around $55 billion in the period 1978-83. Mexico lost $17 billion in 1981 and 1982—almost as much as it had borrowed in the same period. This capital flight was stopped only by the nationalisation of the private banking system, and the imposition of exchange controls by the Mexican Government in September 1982.[11] The South American rich, by repatirating such large amounts of capital (mostly to the USA), clearly have little faith in their own economies and political systems.

In Yugoslavia,[12] which has always had exchange controls and a non-convertible currency, there was no problem of capital flight. There was, however, the problem of short-term debt. Of the $9.5 billion Yugoslavia owed to Western banks, around $2.8 billion was in the form of short-term debt. Like Brazil and Mexico, Yugoslavia assumed that such short-term credits would always be available. However, as early as 1980-1, when Poland's debt problems became clear for all to see, such short-term credit dried up for Yugoslavia. Indeed, such was the lack of faith of Western creditors in the Yugoslav economy, that the country was denied all types of credit for most of 1981 and 1982. There had been a great deal of irresponsible borrowing by Yugoslavia, and no real thought had been given to boosting the export sector of the economy. The Yugoslav economy was plagued by high inflation, low productivity, a primitive technological base, and an artificially over-valued exchange rate. Consequently, its goods were not competitive on world markets.

Yugoslavia, in fact, is the most extreme example of a country that failed to make exports, and exports of high-value manufactured goods in particular, a top priority. Mexico, because of its oil exports, was also complacent as regards such exports. Only Brazil was successful in increasing its exports of manufactured goods, although it is still heavily dependent on the export of primary commodities. Yet all these countries, in comparison with countries like South Korea, were not very successful in increasing exports of high-value manufactured goods. The South Korean experience proves that a high growth (compound annual growth rate approaching 10 per cent in real terms during the 1960s and 1970s),[13] large debt ($35 billion in 1982), and fast export growth (South Korea's exports of manufactured goods grew at an astonishing 30 per cent annual rate throughout the 1970s)[14] strategy need not lead to a debt crisis.

Yet there was no intrinsic reason why South Korea, and not Brazil, Mexico, or Yugoslavia, was so stunning a success at boosting its exports of manufactured goods. Indeed, in terms of natural resources, South Korea was poorly endowed when compared to its South American and Balkan competitors. In the final analysis, it is a question of political will and cultural background whether or not a country is a success at exporting goods. Back in the 1950s and 1960s, the South Korean Government, seeing the rapid industrialisation of communist North Korea and the export-led economic boom in nearby Japan, made the development of its ability to export manufactured goods a top priority. In Mexico and Yugoslavia, though for different reasons, developing exports of manufactured goods was never a top priority. Brazil did make it a priority, and was successful, but it never had the sort of success that South Korea had, and has.

It can be said, by way of summary, that the growth in debt since 1973, and the events leading up to the debt crisis in 1982, can be attributed to higher oil prices in 1973–4 and 1979–80, higher interest rates in 1980–2, declining export income due to world recession and worsening terms of trade in 1981–2, and endogenous economic problems such as the inability of most debtor countries to keep their exports, and their exports of manufactured goods in particular, growing faster than total debt, debt service costs, and import costs.

Notes

1. While the controversy over statistical sources has, on the whole, been resolved (see Appendix 1), the controversies over why, how, and with what consequences the debt grew so fast from 1973 to 1982, have not

been resolved. The number of books on the subject is too large to list here. The most useful books used in this study are as follows: George Abbott, *International Indebtedness and the Developing Countries* (London: Croom Helm, 1979); J. C. Sánchez (ed.), *Debt and Development* (New York: Praeger, 1982); Jonathan Aronson (ed.), *Debt and the Less Developed Countries* (Boulder, Colorado: Westview Press, 1979); Graham Bird, *The International Monetary System and the Less Developed Countries* (London: Macmillan, 1978); Pierre Dhonte, *Clockwork Debt: Trade and the External Debt of Developing Countries* (Lexington, Mass.: Lexington Books, 1979); L. G. Franko and M. J. Seiber (eds), *Developing Country Debt* (New York: Pergamon Press, 1979); Marilyn Seiber, *International Borrowing By Developing Countries* (New York: Pergamon Press, 1982); Paul A. Wellons, *Borrowing By Developing Countries in the Euro-Currency Market* (Paris: OECD, 1977); and, Miguel S. Wionczek (ed.), *LDC External Debt and the World Economy* (Mexico City: El Colegio de Mexico, 1978).

2. And also at the data in Bank of International Settlements, *The Maturity Distribution of International Bank Lending* (Basle: BIS), various issues, 1977–84.

3. M. S. Mendelsohn, *Commercial Banks and the Restructuring of Cross-Border Debt* (New York: Group of Thirty, 1983), p. 23.

4. Turkey is discussed at length in Franko and Seiber, op. cit., Chapter 8; Zaïre is discussed, in similar detail, in Irving S. Friedman, 'Country Risk: The Lessons of Zaïre', *The Banker*, February 1978. Both studies suggest that political chaos (civil war in Turkey, curruption in Zaïre), and not any intrinsic lack of economic viability, was responsible for the debt problems faced by Turkey and Zaïre.

5. William R. Cline, *International Debt and the Stability of the World Economy* (Washington, DC: Institute For International Economics, 1983), p. 23.

6. Ibid., p. 24.

7. Morgan Guaranty, *World Financial Markets*, June 1983, p. 7.

8. Short-term debt data, by country, from American Express International Banking Corporation, *International Debt: Banks and the LDCs*, AMEX Bank Review Special Paper No. 10 (London: American Express International Banking Corporation, 1984); hereafter referred to as AMEX Report.

9. The problem of the growth in such credits is discussed in Azizali F. Mohammed and Fabrizio Saccomanni, 'Short-term Banking and Euro-Currency Credits to Developing Countries', *IMF Staff Papers*, September 1973. Creditor banks' reluctance to commit themselves to long maturities rather than debtor country preference for short maturities seems to be the reason for this growth, according to this study.

10. BIS, *Annual Report* (Basle: 1983), p. 101. In contrast to the situation in South America, there was no capital flight out of the Pacific Rim economies.
11. Mendelsohn, op. cit., p. 23.
12. For a more detailed discussion of Yugoslavia's debt problems, see Marko Milivojević, *The Yugoslav Hard Currency Debt and the Process of Economic Reform Since 1948*, Bradford Studies on Yugoslavia No. 9 (Bradford: Postgraduate School of Yugoslav Studies, 1985).
13. Morgan Guaranty, *World Financial Markets*, March 1984, p. 1.
14. Ibid., p. 2.

2 Consequences of developing countries' debts, 1982–1984

2.1 International financial system

By 1982, the international financial system[1] was vulnerable to the potential impact of default or disruption in the servicing of debt of the developing countries. By 1982, 50 per cent of the total debt of these countries was owed to commercial banks. The assets such banks had tied up in developing countries was large relative to their capital, and the write-off of such assets, in the event of default, would entail a significant loss of capital for those banks.

Given the importance of commercial banks in the international financial system, and given the importance of that system to the world economy as a whole, this vulnerability was of concern to governments, banks, and the IMF. This vulnerability can be best measured by looking at the extent of commercial bank exposure, relative to bank capital, in the developing countries. Table 5 shows the extent of that exposure. It is clear that the exposure of US banks is very high. For all US banks exposure rose from 131.6 per cent of capital in 1977 to 155 per cent of capital in 1982. For the nine largest US banks exposure rose from 188.2 per cent of capital in 1977 to 235.2 per cent of capital in 1982. Moreover, such high exposure is very concentrated in a few countries. Brazil and Mexico, the two largest debtors, each accounted for 30 per cent of the capital of all US banks, and 45 per cent of the capital of the nine largest US banks in 1982. For the top nine US banks, their collective exposure in Brazil and Mexico represented 90 per cent of their collected capital in 1982, if their equity is defined on the broadest possible basis to include debentures and reserves against losses.

As regards European and Japanese banks, their ratio of assets in developing countries to capital is less than is the case for US

Table 5 Exposure of US banks in non-oil developing countries
and Eastern Europe, relative to capital (percentages,
year end)

	1977	1978	1979	1980	1981	1982
All banks						
Eastern Europe	16.7	15.8	16.1	13.9	12.9	8.9
Non-oil LDCs	114.9	114.4	124.2	132.3	148.3	146.1
Total	131.6	130.2	140.3	146.2	163.5	155.0
Mexico	27.4	23.4	23.0	27.6	34.3	34.5
Brazil	29.4	28.6	27.3	25.4	26.9	28.9
Nine largest US banks						
Eastern Europe	25.0	23.5	23.9	21.8	19.5	13.9
Non-oil LDCs	163.2	166.8	182.1	199.3	220.6	221.2
Total	188.2	190.3	206.0	221.1	240.1	235.2
Mexico	32.9	30.4	29.6	37.8	44.4	44.4
Brazil	41.9	42.4	40.3	39.3	40.8	45.8

Source: US Federal Reserve Board, *Country Exposure Lending Survey*, various
issues.

banks. Lending to the developing countries is more important
(as a percentage of assets and as a source of profits) to US
banks than it is to non-US banks. Around 50 per cent of commercial bank lending to developing countries in 1982 was by
US banks. In 1982, 40 per cent of all US banks's foreign lending
went to developing countries. In 1982, 40 per cent of the total
assets of the nine largest US banks were located outside the
United States, which has consistently played the most important role in lending to the developing countries.

That lending was profitable. As early as 1977, Citicorp's
assets in Brazil yielded 35 per cent of Citicorp's net income for
that year. Citicorp was the second largest bank in the United
States in 1977. For the nine largest US banks, earnings from
developing countries accounted for 50 per cent of total profits
in 1982.[2] Traditionally, the highly competitive US domestic
financial services market caused relatively low profits for US
banks. In the 1970s it was saturated, as the demand for credit
was stagnant. Lending to developing countries, which grew
very fast in the 1970s, increased the profits and profitability
(return on capital invested) of US banks, and the top nine banks

in particular. However, the worsening assets/capital ratios of US banks and the potential threat to bank profits from disruptions to debt servicing in developing countries, made US investors wary of US bank equity. Lending to the developing countries was perceived as a high-risk business. Consequently, the demand for bank equity was not great—certainly not great enough to increase the value of that equity, and thereby to increase the assets/capital ratio. In 1982, only the stock of Citicorp and Morgan Guaranty was selling at a premium of around 20 per cent to book value on the US stock market. For the other seven largest US banks, their stock was selling at a discount to book value. Low equity values, in turn, had the effect of discouraging new equity issues by banks so as to avoid further dilutions in the value of existing equity. Yet new equity issues were required to improve the assets/capital ration.

In the United States, bank profits are published quarterly (in Europe and Japan it is an annual event), which makes US banks' equity highly vulnerable to the perceptions and concerns of investors. A potential scenario is lower profits in one quarter, caused by difficulties with assets in developing countries, which would lower the book value of bank stock, which would, in turn, erode the capital base, and so worsen the asset/capital ratio. In the event, the efficacy of the rescheduling process of 1982–4, ensured that this scenario did not become a reality for US banks.

Though US banks are heavily exposed in terms of assets to capital, and in terms of sources of profit, the picture is not so alarming when assets in developing countries are examined in relation to total assets. Thus, although the nine largest US banks had assets equal to 235.2 per cent of their total capital tied up in developing countries in 1982, those assets were only equal to 13.9 per cent of their total assets, both in and outside the United States. More generally, the $350 billion owed by developing countries to the commercial banks in 1982 represented only 20 per cent of the $1.8 trillion Eurocurrency market in that year.[3]

However, such aggregate data fail to indicate the degree of individual bank exposure in the most indebted developing countries. Since the largest US banks, which are the very heart of the international financial system, are the most heavily exposed in the indebted developing countries, disaggregated data tend to show that if only a small number of banks and developing countries run into trouble, then the vulnerability of the entire international financial system will increase. Given the importance of the nine largest US banks in the international financial system, any serious problems they encounter become problems for the entire system, and not just US problems.

Table 6 shows the exposure, relative to capital, of the nine largest US banks in five South American countries that have all experienced debt servicing difficulties of one sort or another. Exposure in Brazil, for example, equalled around 75 per cent of the capital of Citicorp and Manufacturers Hanover; exposure in Mexico equalled or exceeded 60 per cent of the capital of Manufacturers Hanover and Chemical Bank. Exposure in these five South American countries alone exceeds 150 per cent of capital for Citicorp, Bank of America, Chase Manhattan, Manufacturers Hanover and Chemical Bank.

Though US banks are the most vulnerable, given the extent of their exposure in the developing countries, it would be misleading to think that non-US banks did not face any problems. Table 7 lists total debt, by developing country, to all commercial banks, and indicates (again by developing country) whether or not normal debt servicing has been interrupted during 1982–3. European commercial banks were the most important creditors of Poland, Yugoslavia, East Germany, Hungary, and Nigeria, Malaysia, Egypt, and Algeria—nearly half the problem countries listed in Table 7. The Eastern European debt crisis, for example, was as big a problem for West European banks as South America was to US banks. Of the major commercial banks, only those of Japan did not face any regional debt crisis. This is because none of the Pacific Rim economies, where Japanese banks are important creditors, had any debt problems.

Table 7 shows that around 60 per cent of the debt owed by developing and East European countries to commercial banks is problem debt on which debt service was disrupted in the period 1982–3. However, the rescheduling process enabled all the assets of the commercial banks in these countries to be carried at book value on the banks' books, even though a significant proportion of those assets were either yielding no income, or the income was delayed for long periods of time. Because of the rescheduling process no such assets were publicly

Table 6 Exposure as a percentage of capital, nine largest US banks, end–1982

	Argentina	Brazil	Mexico	Venezuela	Chile	Total	Capital*
Citicorp	18.2	73.5	54.6	18.2	10.0	174.5	5,989
Bank of America	10.2	47.9	52.1	41.7	6.3	158.2	4,799
Chase Manhattan	21.3	56.9	40.0	24.0	11.8	154.0	4,221
Morgan Guaranty	24.4	54.3	34.8	17.5	9.7	140.7	3,107
Manufacturers Hanover	47.5	77.7	66.7	42.4	28.4	262.8	2,592
Chemical Bank	14.9	52.0	60.0	28.0	14.8	169.7	2,449
Continental Illinois	17.8	22.9	32.4	21.6	12.8	107.5	2,143
Bankers Trust	13.2	46.2	46.2	25.1	10.6	141.2	1,895
First National Chicago	14.5	40.6	50.1	17.4	11.6	134.2	1,725

Source: 1982 Annual Reports
* In millions of dollars. Bank capital includes equity, debentures, and reserves against possible losses.

Table 7 Debt owed to industrial-country* banks by developing and
East European Countries, June 1982

	Debt ($bn.)	Debt service ratio†	Disruption‖
Mexico	64.4	58.5	Yes
Brazil	55.3	87.1	Yes
Venezuela	27.2	20.7	Yes
Argentina	25.3	102.9	Yes
South Korea	20.0	21.1	No
Poland	13.8	90.3	Yes
Chile	11.8	60.4	Yes
Philippines	11.4	36.1	No
Yugoslavia	10.0	30.3	Yes
East Germany	9.4	29.0	No
Algeria	7.7	41.0	No
Hungary	6.4	33.0	Yes
Indonesia	8.2	11.3	No
Nigeria	6.7	25.0	Yes
Taiwan	6.4	18.3	No
Israel	6.1	23.7	No
Colombia	5.5	23.9	No
Egypt	5.4	39.0	Yes
Malaysia	5.3	5.0	No
Peru	5.2	53.4	Yes
Subtotal	311.5		
Of which debt disruption	213.0		
Total, LDCs‡ and Eastern Europe§	374.9		

Source: Bank for International Settlements, *The Maturity Structure of International Bank Lending*, 1982.

 * Group of Ten plus Switzerland, Austria, Denmark, and Eire.
 † Debt service as a percentage (ratio) of exports of goods and services in 1982; excluding short-term principal, including short-term interest.
 ‡ Including Yugoslavia; excluding Middle Eastern capital-surplus, oil-exporting countries.
 § Excluding USSR.
 ‖ Debt servicing disruption in 1982–3.

written off by banks. Such public write-offs of assets would mean, in effect, that the banks concerned had given up hope of ever recovering those assets. No bank was prepared to do such a thing. The level of write-offs made in private is a closely guarded secret, especially in Western Europe.

What, then, would be the consequences of any extended disruption of normal debt servicing? Outright repudiation of debt is most unlikely, given the adverse consequences to the countries concerned if they did repudiate their debts. Only Cuba and North Korea have repudiated their foreign debts since world War II.[4] However, the delays in debt service payments, which were so prevalent in the 1982–3 period, did represent *de facto* default. No bank declared any debtor country to be in formal, *de jure* default, as such a drastic move would have meant that the assets of all banks concerned in the debtor country would have had to be written off, due to the existence of cross-default clauses in all syndicated loan contracts.[5]

These delays did, however, represent a loss to banks in that debt service income from their assets was deferred into the future. The whole rescheduling process of 1982–4 was designed to ensure that debt service income, however delayed, would eventually be paid in the future. To compensate for that loss on deferred income, and in order to give banks an incentive to continue lending in circumstances of increased risk, the terms of the rescheduling agreements of 1982–4 were very profitable for the banks concerned. The entire rescheduling process was based on the assumption (in public at least) that all bank assets were, despite all the problems of the developing countries, performing assets.

Such an assumption, though no bank would admit as much in public, is somewhat unrealistic, especially as regards hopeless debtor countries such as Poland, where income was delayed for months. Debt service payments were not paid for years on Paris Club Governments' debts. The question of how much debt was non-performing, and what provisions were made by banks to cover such non-performing assets, was a key question in the debt crisis. It is in the area of provisions[6] to cover non-performing assets that the banks, and US banks in particular, were very vulnerable to any sharp increase in the proportion of their assets that were non-performing.

In the United States a provision of 1 per cent of total assets is considered adequate in normal times. In 1982, which was an abnormal time, Citicorp had an exposure of $10 billion in South America, but only made a provision of $680 million for its total assets (1 per cent). For Manufacturers Hanover, which had the largest relative exposure (as a percentage of capital) in South America, provisions were only $371 million for all its assets—a mere $47 million increase on its provisions for 1981. These small provisions, relative to total assets and to problem (potentially non-performing) assets in South America, were made in 1982 when the gross profits of the nine largest US banks amounted to $5.5 billion in that same year.[7] For US banks a high dividend pay-out to keep their equity high on the stock market was considered more important than setting aside adequate provisions for potential non-performing assets in conditions of debt crisis in the developing world.

The case of Continental Illinois,[8] the only major bank to go banrkupt in recent times, is instructive. By the end of 1982, 5.9 per cent of its loan portfolio of $2 billion was non-performing. That was twice the average for the top nine US banks in the same year. Bad loans to the amount of $286 million had to be written off in 1982—nearly 15 per cent of total assets. Yet in 1981, provisions amounted to only 1 per cent of total assets. The 1982 provision of $387 million had to be taken out of profits, which entailed a net loss in that year. The example of Continental Illinois, though extreme, illustrates the low and clearly inadequate level of provisions by US banks.

In Western Europe, and especially in West Germany and Switzerland, provisions are much higher than in the United States: 5 per cent of total assets is considered the norm in Switzerland; between 2 per cent and 3 per cent is the norm elsewhere. The whole question of provisions policy has created a great deal of controversy. The West Europeans accuse the Americans of irresponsibility. The Americans accuse the Europeans of being too cautious. Banking secrecy, as well as different regulatory environments in which banks operate, has made it difficult to come to some sort of agreement as to what bank assets, by country, are non-performing, and what constitutes an 'adequate' level of provision to be set aside by all banks concerned to cover non-performing assets.

US banks face a dilemma. The US regulatory authorities

have told them to increase provisions, but the only way they can do that is either to cut asset growth (thereby increasing provisions as a percentage of total assets) or to take provisions out of gross profits, which could cut net profits. Some sort of tax relief would yield little extra, as in 1981 the twenty largest US banks paid only 2.7 per cent tax on domestic income.[9] Taxes are not paid on offshore transactions. To increase provisions out of gross profits, in a very competitive financial services domestic market, would have an immediate adverse effect on US bank equity values on the stock market. In Western Europe, where there is far less competition and where stock markets do not work on the basis of quarterly declarations of bank profits, larger provisions out of gross profits are far easier to make.

Recently, however, the US regulatory authorities have taken steps[10] to bring the provision policies of US banks more into line with the situation in Western Europe and Japan. The International Lending and Supervision Act of 1983, for example, makes higher provisions for certain designated, high-risk debtor countries legally compulsory, and calls for a higher assets/capital ratio, by issues of new equity, sale of bonds, and a slower rate of total asset growth.

Another way to examine the international financial system's potential vulnerability is to ask a hypothetical question: what would happen if a number of South American countries (Argentina, Brazil, and Mexico) were to miss one year's payments of principal and interest? This did not, of course, happen in the 1982–3 period because of the efficacious rescue effort that took place, but it was a real possibility at one time.

US banking laws, enforced by the regulatory authorities, stipulate that if debt service income due to banks is delayed for over ninety days after it should have been paid, then the assets concerned should be written off. It was hardly surprising, therefore, that a great deal of the activity in the rescheduling process of 1982–4 was concerned with raising enough money from banks, lending such money to the concerned countries, who would then pay the arrears of interest that had built up. In this way the ninety-day deadline was rarely breached in South America.

One estimate stated that the loss of one year's payments from these three countries would cause losses equal to 28 per cent of the combined capital of the nine largest US banks.[11] By so reducing income from assets, the banks concerned would have been forced to liquidate their reserves, and could have found themselves in the position of not being able to service some of their liabilities. In addition, rumours could start a run on the banks concerned. The end result of such a scenario would be bankruptcy. However, the scenario is unlikely as the US regulatory authorities would step in before illiquidity became insolvency for the banks involed in such a scenario.

The cut in capital caused by the losses in this scenario would mean a sharp cut in new loan disbursement, as the banks concerned struggled to re-establish the 5 per cent ratio of capital to loans outstanding demanded by the US regulatory authorities. According to one estimate, a loss of $8 billion in capital, caused by one year's loss of income from the three countries, would mean that the nine largest US banks would have to cut loans outstanding by around $160 billion, in order to re-establish the 5 per cent capital/loans outstanding ratio.[12]

The economic dislocation of such a severe credit squeeze, in conditions of recession, could then push the United States into a 1930s-style depression. Certainly, in the absence of prompt regulatory authority action, crisis in one part of the US banking system would spread quickly throughout the entire international banking system, given the high level of interdependence that exists in that system. This sequence of events is hypothetical, but the scenario is not entirely incredible.

The precedent of 1929–33 is always remembered.[13] At that time, though for very different reasons and when the US regulatory authorities were rather inept, a crisis in the financial system was responsible for the development of a severe depression in the real economy. Moreover, by 1931, the effects of the financial crisis in the United States spread to Europe, with disastrous consequences for every country in Europe. In addition, the effect of that collapse in South America was even more traumatic than it was for Europe. Every South American country defaulted on its debts (mainly bonds) to US and European creditors. Though co-operation between central banks in 1931 was very limited by today's standards (which aided the spread of the crisis), the level of interdependence between banks in the United States and Europe was well developed. Such interdependence, in a political context of poor regulatory authority co-operation, ensured that the US crisis quickly became a global crisis.

Now the position is reversed. There was, and is, a possibility that a crisis in South America could, if left unchecked or handled ineptly, spread to the United States and Europe. The extent of interdependence now is far more developed than was the case in 1931, but the amount of co-operation between central banks, in the forums of the Bank for International Settlements and the IMF, is far greater than was the case in 1931. That co-operation means that this scenario is improbable, but it cannot be said the scenario is totally impossible. The fact that such a scenario was a possibility, however improbable it seemed, ensured that Governments (creditors and debtors), commercial banks, and the IMF took the debt problems of the developing countries very seriously during the debt rescheduling process of 1982-4.

2.2 Developing countries

If really serious economic dislocation, arising from the debt problems of developing countries, has only been a hypothetical possibility for the OECD countries, such dislocation has been a reality in virtually all developing countries since the debt crisis began in earnest in 1982. The economic consequences of the disruption in normal debt servicing and contracting relationships with creditors, and of the economic adjustment process debtors had to implement to regain the confidence of their creditors, have been severe. That severity, however, has been somewhat ameliorated by the debt rescheduling process of 1982-4. If that process had not taken place, and if the debt crisis faced by the developing countries had developed into a general collapse of the international financial system, then the economic consequences to the developing countries of such a scenario would have been disastrous. As it was, disaster was avoided.

In South America, where the consequences of the debt crisis were the most severe, the region's GDP fell by 3.3 per cent in 1983, after falling by 1 per cent in 1982. The GDP per head of the rapidly growing population fell by 5.6 per cent in 1983. The GDP per head in 1983 was about the same, in real terms, as it was in 1977. Instead of growing, the region's GDP is contracting. Imports fell by 29 per cent in 1983, after a 20 per cent fall in 1982. The poorest countries in South America have stopped importing altogether. This contraction of economic activity, and especially import-dependent economic activity, had the effect of reducing the region's balance of payments deficit on current account from $36.4 billion in 1982 to $8.5 billion in 1983. By 1983 the region was also a net exporter of capital, to the tune of $30 billion in that year. The overall effect of this painful economic adjustment was that the region's total foreign debt increased by only 7 per cent in 1983, compared with an average of 23 per cent per annum in the period from 1977 to 1981.[14]

While the economic adjustment process was ultimately caused by the region's inability to service its debts, the major consequences of that process was the drastic cut in imports. Since South America's economies are very import-dependent, the effects of this fall in imports were very severe.

These aggregate data do, however, tend to present a somewhat misleading picture, as some countries suffered far greater economic dislocation than did others. Table 8 reveals these differences as regards GDP growth. While the Pacific Rim economies continued to grow, the economies of South America contracted from 1982 to 1983. The rates at which they contracted, as Table 8 shows, were very uneven. While Chile's GDP contracted by 7.8 per cent from 1982 to 1983, and Peru's GDP contracted by 5.8 per cent for the same period, the contraction rate rarely exceeded 3 per cent for the remaining countries for the same period. By 1984, when the worst of the economic dislocation was over, all the countries had begun to grow again, though at different rates.

As regards current account, Table 9 shows that while deficits were still the norm in 1984, Mexico and Venezuela had been in surplus since 1983. For the deficit countries, however, deficits fell sharply from 1981 to 1984, with the exception of Colombia and Indonesia. Although these cuts in deficits were primarily caused by sharp cuts in imports from 1981 to 1983, a systematic policy of import substitution and a concurrent improved export performance during the same period led to an increase in imports from 1983 to 1984.

Table 10 shows the import and export positions of various

Table 8   Real GDP growth for selected countries, 1982–1984
(per cent per annum)

	1982–3	1984
Argentina	−1.3	3.0
Brazil	−1.1	2.5
Chile	−7.8	5.5
Colombia	0.9	2.0
Ecuador	−0.8	1.0
Mexico	−2.6	1.5
Peru	−5.8	2.0
Venezuela	−2.1	1.0
Average	−1.9	2.2
Nigeria	−3.3	−2.0
Philippines	2.0	−5.0
Indonesia	3.6	5.0
South Korea	7.6	8.0
Malaysia	5.7	6.5
Taiwan	5.5	9.5
Thailand	3.9	4.5
Turkey	3.9	4.5
Average	3.6	4.2

Source: Morgan Guaranty, *World Financial Markets*, October/November 1984, p. 4.

© Morgan Guaranty Trust Company of New York. Reproduced by permission from *World Financial Markets*.

countries for the period 1981–4, and imports increased in Chile, Ecuador, Mexico, and Venezuela from 1983 to 1984. From 1981 to 1983, imports fell dramatically in every South American country. The same was true in Nigeria, whereas the stronger Pacific Rim economies such as South Korea continued to increase their imports from 1981 to 1983. From 1983 to 1984, imports increased by 7.1 per cent for the whole of South America. Mexico, which is the strongest economy in South America, increased its imports by 36 per cent from 1983 to 1984.

Table 10 also illustrates that, with the exception of Mexico, whose exports grew at 10 per cent per annum from 1981 to 1984, exports fell by 7.9 per cent for the whole of South

Table 9 Current account balances for selected countries, 1981–1984
(billions of dollars)

	1981	1983	1984
Argentina	−4.7	−2.4	−2.0
Brazil	−11.7	−6.9	−2.3
Chile	−4.7	−1.1	−2.0
Colombia	−1.9	−2.7	−2.2
Ecuador	−1.0	−0.1	−0.2
Mexico	−12.5	5.5	3.9
Peru	−1.6	−0.9	−0.8
Venezuela	4.0	3.7	0.5
Subtotal	−34.3	−4.8	−5.0
Nigeria	−6.0	−4.8	−0.5
Philippines	−2.3	−3.2	−1.6
Indonesia	−0.6	−6.3	−3.5
South Korea	−4.6	−1.6	−1.8
Malaysia	−2.4	−2.8	−2.2
Taiwan	0.5	4.5	6.4
Thailand	−2.6	−2.9	−2.0
Turkey	−2.3	−2.3	−1.6
Subtotal	−20.4	−19.4	−6.7
Total	−54.6	−24.2	−11.8

Source: Morgan Guaranty, *World Financial Markets*, October/November 1984, p. 2.

America in the period 1981–3. In the Pacific Rim economies exports continued to rise during this period. From 1983 to 1984, exports increased in every South American country with the sole exception of Chile. Brazilian exports grew by 21 per cent in the period 1983–4, after a sharp fall in the period 1981–3.

The overall effect of such improvements in the current account position, for the stronger economies such as Mexico and Venezuela, is that they were earning enough from exports in 1984 to service their debts without any further increase in new borrowing. If Brazil's improved export performance is sustained into 1985, it should be in the same position as Mexico

Table 10   Merchandise imports and exports for selected countries, 1981–1984 (per cent changes based on balance of payments data in US dollars)

	Imports		Exports	
	1981–3	1983–4	1981–3	1983–4
Argentina	−51.1	−5.3	−14.3	11.0
Brazil	−30.2	−9.3	−6.0	21.0
Chile	−56.4	12.8	0.4	−1.3
Colombia	−0.1	−9.6	−6.7	8.3
Ecuador	−40.4	13.6	−7.0	7.8
Mexico	−67.7	36.0	10.2	10.3
Peru	−29.3	−7.0	−7.2	2.8
Venezuela	−44.1	32.8	−26.6	5.6
Subtotal	−45.6	7.1	−7.9	11.5
Nigeria	−35.8	−30.3	−41.8	6.6
Philippines	−4.5	−22.2	−13.2	8.7
Indonesia	7.2	−6.4	−20.0	10.2
South Korea	2.5	15.2	12.3	16.4
Malaysia	13.8	6.7	20.5	14.4
Taiwan	−7.3	20.6	11.7	23.9
Thailand	2.6	0.4	−8.6	14.1
Turkey	3.0	6.5	21.8	25.0
Subtotal	−4.6	2.1	−5.5	15.3
Total	−22.4	3.6	−6.5	13.7

Source: Morgan Guaranty, *World Financial Markets*, October/November 1984, p. 3.

and Venezuela by the end of 1985. Once a country is able to service debt without an increase in total debt, the worst of its debt crisis is over. In addition, official reserves are able to increase once the worst of the crisis is over. In 1984, Mexico's reserves, for example, were $7 billion, whereas they were $3.9 billion in 1983, and $800 million in 1982.

At the same time, debt growth has declined sharply in the period 1982–4. This is illustrated in Table 11. The total external debt of the eight largest South American countries listed in Table 11 grew by only 5.3 per cent in 1983 and 5 per cent in 1984. In real terms, after deducting the effects of inflation,

Table 11   Gross external debt and debt-to-export ratios for selected countries, 1982–1984 (billions of dollars for debt and percentages for ratios)

	External debt			Ratios		
	1982	1983	1984	1982	1983	1984
Argentina	41.7	43.4	45.0	385	435	405
Brazil	85.3	93.6	102.0	339	366	331
Chile	18.0	18.6	20.5	333	375	394
Colombia	10.6	11.2	11.7	193	247	259
Ecuador	6.3	6.9	7.1	235	246	241
Mexico	87.1	90.6	94.9	288	317	293
Peru	11.8	12.8	14.0	256	320	338
Venezuela	35.6	34.9	35.0	168	203	192
Subtotal	296.2	312.0	330.2	297*	327*	310*
Nigeria	13.8	18.2	19.0	75	146	160
Philippines	24.5	26.5	26.5	277	308	332
Indonesia	24.8	29.2	32.0	106	136	139
South Korea	37.3	40.1	44.0	121	125	120
Malaysia	11.5	14.8	17.0	68	80	83
Taiwan	9.7	10.0	10.3	37	34	29
Thailand	11.7	12.6	13.5	118	129	125
Turkey	22.3	23.9	25.3	235	267	243
Subtotal	155.6	175.3	187.6	119*	131*	124*
Total	451.8	487.3	517.8	196*	213*	200*

Source: Morgan Guaranty, *World Financial Markets*, October/November 1984, p. 5.

* Average.

© 1984 Morgan Guaranty Trust Company of New York. Reproduced by permission from *World Financial Markets*.

this is no growth at all. The debt total has stabilised itself. This compares with debt growth rates of 20 per cent per annum in countries like Mexico, prior to 1982.

As regards debt-to-export ratios, which are shown in Table 11, they fell in Argentina, Brazil, Ecuador, Mexico, and Venezuela from 1983 to 1984. This was a sign that both exports were increasing and debt growth had stopped in real terms. However, compared to the low ratios that were the norm in the Pacific Rim economies, the South American ratios were still very high.

In Yugoslavia events developed in a similar manner to what had happened in South America—severe economic dislocation from 1981 to 1983, followed by an improvement from 1983 to 1984. That improvement has been quite remarkable. By ruthlessly cutting imports (down from $13 billion in 1979 to $7.4 billion in 1984), the trade deficit was reduced from $6.4 billion in 1979 to $1.1 billion in 1984. The current account balance changed from a deficit of $3.7 billion in 1979 to a surplus of $800 million in 1984. Though exports stood at $6.3 billion in 1984 (a modest 1.3 per cent on the 1983 figure), increased invisible earnings were responsible for the surplus in 1984.

Despite this improvement, however, Yugoslavia was unable to pay its $5 billion debt servicing costs in 1984 from its non-borrowed income. Yugoslavia's weakness as an exporter, which cannot be easily improved in the short term, made it inevitable for Yugoslavia to seek further credit from commercial banks, OECD Governments, and the IMF in 1984 so as to be able to service its debt. Total debt, therefore, is rising in real terms, although it is the intention of the Government to see it fall from $20 billion in 1985 to $16 billion by 1990 at the latest.[15]

The improvement, though remarkable by Yugoslavia's past record, is relatively precarious compared to Mexico's performance since 1983. Unlike Mexico, export prospects are poor due to domestic economic problems that make Yugoslavia's products uncompetitive abroad. One measure of the relative precariousness of Yugoslavia's economic situation is revealed in the fact that official reserves stood at only $1.1 billion in 1984. There are projected debt service payments (principal and interest) of around $5 billion per annum in the period 1985-8. Further cuts in imports, increases in exports, and further new borrowing will be required to ensure that normal debt servicing prevails until 1988.

The economic dislocation caused by this major adjustment process was the most severe from 1982 to 1983, when GDP fell by 1.5 per cent.[16] This was the first time GDP had fallen in Yugoslavia since World War II. In addition, and again from 1982 to 1983, domestic demand fell by 4 per cent, real wages by 6 per cent, and industrial production just stagnated. It continued to stagnate in 1983, and only began to grow again in 1984. Finally, GDP fell by a further 1 per cent from 1983 to 1984.

2.3 Systemic resilience

If, for the sake of argument, the international financial system is compared to the human body, and the debt crisis experienced by the developing countries is compared to a disease, then it can be said this system, though vulnerable in 1982 to the disease, proved to be far more resilient than many observers imagined it to be at the time. The system proved able, through the rescheduling process of 1982–4, to come through the debt crisis relatively unscathed, and to ensure that the developing countries, which were the weakest part of the system, did not experience total disaster as a result of the debt crisis.

Since 1982, while continuing to lend profitably to the developing countries in the context of the rescheduling process (outside it in the Pacific Rim economies), commercial banks have progressively reduced their exposure in the developing countries.[17] Commercial banks in the BIS-reporting area increased their outstanding claims on all developing countries by $26 billion (a 5.7 per cent annual growth rate), between 1982 and 1984. Their claims on South America rose by $9 billion, or 3.4 per cent at an annual rate, over the same period. Most of the new lending was to Brazil and Mexico. For US banks the annual rate of increase was 2.2 per cent for all developing countries and 4.1 per cent for South America, for the same period. Figure 6 shows how lower asset growth had the effect of reducing the assets/capital ratio of the nine largest US banks.

The fall in the ratio has been quite remarkable, considering that the period of time involved (1982–4) has been short. In addition, the nine largest US banks increased their primary capital, including loan loss reserves, by 25 per cent over the 1982–4 period. In terms of assets/capital ratios, provisions, capitalisation, and profitability the nine largest US banks were stronger, and therefore less vulnerable in the event of future debt crises, in 1984 than they were in 1982.

With the developing countries it can be said, by way of summary, that the economic dislocation they had to endure

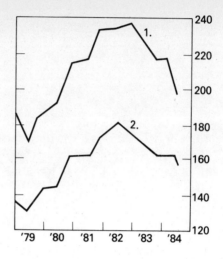

Source: Morgan Guaranty, *World Financial Markets*, October/November 1984, p. 6.

© 1984 Morgan Guaranty Trust Company of New York. Reproduced by permission from *World Financial Markets*.

Figure 6   Claims of nine largest US banks as per cent of primary capital, 1979–1984

from 1982 to 1983 was far more severe than anything the international financial system, and the OECD countries that dominate that system, had to go through. From 1982 to 1983, all the developing countries with a debt problem had to cut imports sharply, cut domestic investment, see industrial output fall, and tolerate falls in GDP. Conditions varied from country to country, but the basic reality of going down to lower levels of economic activity (GDP) was present in every country. The IMF insisted that external deficits had to be cut, debt growth slowed, domestic Government budgets had to be cut, inflation and monetary growth had to be cut, and exports increased. Once such economic adjustments were made during the rescheduling process, creditors were reassured, and economic recovery was then possible in the 1983–4 period. By 1983, the worst was over, especially in Mexico. By 1984, Mexico was back on the road to normal relations with its creditors and Brazil was likely to be on that road sometime in 1985. Weaker countries, such as Yugoslavia, experienced far more modest recoveries. However, no country experienced the sort of total economic disaster that some observers had expected in 1982.

Notes

1. For analyses of the vulnerability of the international commercial banks, and their position in the international financial system, see Anthony Angelini, *International Lending, Risk and the Euromarkets* (New York: Halstead Press, 1979); Edmar Lisboa Bacha and Carlos F. Diaz Alejandro, *International Financial Intermediation: A Long and Topical View*, Princeton Essays in International Finance No. 147 (Princeton, NJ: Princeton University Press, May 1982); W. H. Bruce Brittain, 'Developing Countries External Debt and the Private Banks', *Banca Nazionale de Lavoro Quarterly Review*, No. 123, December 1977; Irving S. Friedman, *The Emerging Role of Private Banks in the Developing World* (New York: Citicorp, 1977); W. P. Hogan and I. F. Pearce, *The Incredible Eurodollar: Or Why The World's Money System Is Collapsing* (London: Unwin Paperbacks, 1982); Anthony Sampson, *The Money Lenders: Bankers In A Dangerous World* (London: Hodder & Stoughton, 1981).

2. Chandra S. Hardy, 'Commercial Bank Lending to Developing Countries: Supply Constraints', *World Development*, Vol. 7, No. 2, February 1979, p. 190 (special issue on International Indebtedness and World Economic Stagnation).

3. John W. Dizard, 'International Banking: The End of Let's Pretend', *Fortune*, 29 November 1982, p. 78.

4. The repudiation issue is discussed at length in Jonathan Eaton and Mark Gersovitz, *Poor-Country Borrowing in Private Financial Markets and the Repudiation Issue*, Princeton Studies in International Finance No. 47 (Princeton, NJ: Princeton University Press, June 1981). This study suggests that only hostile communist Governments have, or are ever likely to, openly repudiated their foreign debts.

5. In 1981 Poland came the closest to being declared in default, as reported in *Economist Survey*, 'A Nightmare of Debt: A Survey of International Banking', *The Economist*, 20 March 1982, p. 21; hereafter referred to as *Economist Survey*. The Polish example further supports the view of Eaton and Gersovitz, op. cit., that communist Governments are the ones most likely to cause trouble for commercial banks in the future.

6. The provisions question is discussed in Colin Brown, 'The Problem of Provision Against Sovereign Debt', *The Banker*, February 1983. The case for a general harmonisation of provision policies in the OECD countries is made in Geoffrey Bell and Graeme Rutledge, 'How to Account for Problem Loans', *Euromoney*, January 1984.

7. Cline, op. cit., p. 37.
8. Examined at length in A. F. Ehrbar, 'Oil and Trouble at Continental Illinois', *Fortune*, 7 February 1982.
9. Cline, op. cit., p. 37.
10. Especially in the form of the International Lending and Supervision Act of 1983. This Act makes the establishment of reserves to offset losses in certain designated, very high-risk developing countries compulsory in law. See Bell/Rutledge, op. cit., for further details of this Act.
11. Cline, op. cit., p. 37.
12. Ibid., p. 38.
13. Discussed in Paul Bareau, 'The Lessons of an Earlier International Debt Crisis', *The Banker*, December 1983.
14. All data from Roland Dallas, 'Democracy and Debt in Latin America', *World Today*, April 1984.
15. All data from ABECOR Country Reports, *Yugoslavia*, various issues, 1983 and 1984 (Frankfurt: Dresdner Bank).
16. Discussed in more detail in Marko Milivojević, 'Anatomy of a Rescheduling: Yugoslavia, 1982–1983', *South Slav Journal*, Vol. 6, No. 2(20), summer 1983.
17. All data from Morgan Guaranty, *World Financial Markets*, October/November 1984, p. 4.

3 The debt rescheduling process, 1982–1984

3.1 Precursors of 1982

Although many commentators have discussed the debt rescheduling process, few have given as good a definition of it as William R. Cline, who defined debt rescheduling as 'at once an admission of debt servicing breakdown and a remedial measure for re-establishing more normal financial conditions'.[1] Though the 'remedial measures' of the 1982–4 period were, in many ways, unique, they did have precursors. For most of the post-war era OECD Governments, and multilateral institutions such as the IMF and the World Bank, have been the principal creditors of the developing countries. It was not until 1978 that 57 per cent of the total debt of the developing countries was owed to commercial banks.[2] By 1982, around 60 per cent of the total debt was owed to commercial banks.

Most of the post-war debt reschedulings were, therefore, reschedulings of official debt, which took place at meetings of creditor Governments, the debtor Government concerned, and multilateral institutions such as the World Bank in the so-called 'Paris Club'.[3] Since its creation in 1956, this creditor's club has chosen always to meet in Paris, and its meetings have always been chaired by a high ranking official of the French Treasury. Although commercial banks cannot attend such meetings, their interests have been protected. This was because a large proportion of 'official debt' was, in fact, credit made available to debtor countries by commercial banks, but such credit was insured by Western Government's export credit insurance agencies.

Appendix 2 shows the countries that came to the Paris Club to reschedule their debts, how much was rescheduled and when, for the period 1956–82. From 1956 to 1978, $5 billion of debt was rescheduled. Nine countries were involved. Some countries, such as India (seven reschedulings), came to the Paris Club many times. Other countries came only once. From 1978 to 1981, $9 billion of debt was rescheduled. Fifteen countries were involved. The extent of the difficulties faced by developing countries is revealed in the fact that nearly twice as much was rescheduled in three years (1978–81) than was rescheduled in twenty-two years (1956–81).

Though not a formal organisation in any sense, the Paris Club has built up a fund of expertise, has established certain rules, and has set many precedents to guide its operations over the years. The *modus operandi* of the Paris Club is as follows:

1. The Club will only agree to a meeting with a debtor if a default is imminent, so as to avoid creating a precedent by appearing to be willing to agree to such a meeting before all other available options have been exhausted by the debtor.
2. The Club will only agree to a meeting if the debtor has come to an agreement with the IMF to implement an economic adjustment programme prior to the meeting. This rule has been operative since 1966, and can only be waived if the debtor is not a member of the IMF. Poland, in 1981, was not a member of the IMF.
3. The Club will only negotiate with debtor Governments. Institutions such as the World Bank can only attend the meetings as observers.
4. The Club will only discuss government loans and/or government-insured suppliers' credits. All other forms of debt are excluded from the negotiations.
5. The Club insists that the Debtor Government views its official debts as wholly comparable with, and in no way inferior to, its commercial bank debts. The latter category of debt, in other words, is not to receive priority as regards the allocation of foreign exchange for debt-service purposes.
6. The Club insists it is a meeting of creditors and is not, nor can it ever seen to be, an aid donor.
7. The Club will only agree to the rescheduling of principal, and interest must be paid as normal, although delays in the payment of interest were tolerated in Poland recently.
8. The French Chairman of the Club imposes a time deadline on creditors and debtor alike to reach an agreement. The Chairman also acts as honest broker in the negotiations.

The Paris Club's *modus operandi* has frequently been criticised by debtor Governments. Rule 1, for example, suggests that the Club is more concerned with consequences (the debt crisis) of a high level of debt, rather than with trying to resolve the causes of the debt problem. The result of this rule is that the Paris Club, by delaying meetings with debtors until the very last minute, only faces a worse problem as a result of this delay.

After 1982, when commercial bank reschedulings became important, Rules 3 and 4 caused a great deal of confusion. Rule 3 means that the debtor Government must conduct two different, though concurrent, sets of rescheduling negotiations: one with the Paris Club, the other with commercial banks. The debtor Government is exposed to contradictory demands. Rule 4, which asks for strict 'comparability' between official and commercial bank debt, contradicts the position of commercial banks in their negotiations with the debtor Government. The banks insist that their debts be given priority by the debtor Government when it comes to the allocation of foreign exchange for debt servicing purposes. Such contradictory demands, as well as the lack of one forum for the rescheduling of all debt at one time, create needless confusion, put the debtor Government into an impossible position, and make the final objective of all reschedulings—re-establishment of normal financial conditions for the debtor—all that much more difficult to achieve.[4]

Despite these problems the actual meetings of the Paris Club, when compared to what occurred in commercial bank reschedulings in 1982, were relatively free of discord and confusion. The fact that very few people are involved in Paris Club meetings makes it easier for an agreement to be reached. The deadline imposed by the Chairman of the Paris Club means an agreement is reached relatively quickly. More generally, the accumulated expertise, clear rules, and established precedents of the Paris Club made the reaching of an agreement far more expeditious than was the case in the rescheduling negotiations between commercial banks and debtor Governments in 1982.

The Paris Club agreements were, and still are, of two types. Firstly, there are concessionary agreements, whereby the maturity of the principal is extended and a non-market interest rate is set on that rescheduled principal. The debt service burden of any debtor country, therefore, is considerably less after the rescheduling than before it. One World Bank estimate has put this debt relief, the cost of which is paid by Paris Club creditors, at $2 billion for the period 1956–81.[5] This relief, or debt write-off, has benefited a number of very poor countries a great deal. For example, 44.7 per cent of Ghana's total outstanding debt over the period 1966–74 was written off in this way; 56.1 per cent of Indonesia's total outstanding debt over the period 1966–70 was also written off in this way.[6]

However, such concessionary agreements were the exception. A total of $14 billion was rescheduled in the Paris Club from 1956 to 1981; only $2 billion was written off. The second category of market agreements was one in which the maturity of principal was extended, but the interest rate payable on that rescheduled principal would be the prevailing market interest rate. This was not debt relief, but it did represent an easing of the immediate debt servicing problems of the debtor Governments involved.

Prior to 1975, the average maturity extension on principal granted in Paris Club reschedulings was eight years. Since 1975 the average has been ten years.[7] Such long maturities were unique to the reschedulings of the Paris Club. Commercial banks, in their negotiations with debtor Governments, rarely granted such long maturities. Maturities of between five and eight years were the norm in commercial bank reschedulings. This was especially true of the 1982–3 period. It was not until 1984 that Mexico obtained a maturity of fourteen years in its rescheduling agreement in that year.

Prior to 1982, of the eighty debt rescheduling agreements signed in the period 1956–82, only twelve were agreements signed by debtor Governments and commercial banks. All the other agreements were signed in the Paris Club. Table 12 illustrates the debtor Government/commercial banks agreements of the period 1978–82 (spring of). The amounts rescheduled in these agreements are also given in Table 12, which should be examined in conjunction with Appendix 2 to put it into a wider context.

Table 12 shows that a total of $10.5 billion was rescheduled in four years, of which $7.7 billion was accounted for by only two countries: Turkey ($2.9 billion, 1979) and Poland ($4.8 billion, 1982). Though paltry by 1982 standards, such sums

Table 12 Debt rescheduling agreements signed with commercial
banks, 1978–1982

Year	Debtor countries	Amounts rescheduled (millions of US dollars)
1978	Jamaica	83
	Peru	821
		904
1979	Jamaica	149
	Turkey	2,930
		3,108
1980	Togo	69
	Zaïre	402
	Nicaragua	562
		1,033
1981	Jamaica	103
	Sudan	538
		641
1982	Poland	4,800
	Guyana	35

Source: M. S. Mendelsohn, *Commercial Banks and the Restructuring of Cross-Border-Debt* (New York: Group of Thirty, 1984), p. 5.
© 1984 Group of Thirty, Consultative Group on International Economic & Monetary Affairs, Inc. Reproduced by permission from *Commercial Banks and the Restructuring of Cross-Border-Debt*, Michael S. Mendelsohn.

dwarfed what had faced the Paris Club, and indeed the commercial banks themselves, in the past. The Polish rescheduling, involving $4.8 billion owed by a communist country that was not a member of the IMF, simply had no precedent.[8]

The Polish debt rescheduling negotiations, which went on from 1981 to 1982, were of great importance to the commercial banks involved in Poland. The negotiations set many important precedents, highlighted important differences between the Paris Club and the banks, led to many arguments between banks over tactics in the negotiations, and developed the organisational infrastructure (though *ad hoc*) with which the commercial banks would have to deal with the far larger debt reschedulings in South America in 1982.

Most important of all, perhaps, was that the Polish experience led to the development of co-operation between commercial banks existing in a competitive commercial environment that was not conducive to the development of co-operative inclinations among banks. The tension between competitive individualism, which is present in all banks, and the interests of the international financial system in which all banks exist, became very apparent in the Polish negotiations. This tension was to be even greater in the South American reschedulings of 1982.

Appendix 3 shows the progress of the Polish negotiations and provides background economic data on Poland's debt problems. The economic situation in the period 1979–81 was nothing short of catastrophic. Although political turmoil clearly aggravated the economic situation during this period, the ultimate cause of the catastrophe was highly irresponsible borrowing in the past by a Government that preferred not to think about how it was going to pay off its debts. Commercial banks, who believed in the existence of a so-called 'umbrella' in Poland (a politically naïve belief that the Soviet Union was the ultimate guarantor of COMECON's debts), were only too happy to lend to Poland. In the event, there was no 'umbrella' to help Poland in 1981. By 1981, on the eve of the rescheduling negotiations, Poland's total debt stood at $26 billion ($15 billion of which was owed to commercial banks; the rest to OECD Governments), its debt service ratio was 80 per cent, and total debt as a percentage of exports had reached 300 per cent.[9]

What, then, were the lessons of the Polish rescheduling negotiations, and what were the precedents created by them? Firstly, commercial bank creditors, in their negotiations with a debtor Government, are in a far weaker position than is the Paris Club. The Club is composed of some of the most powerful Governments in the world, which a debtor Government would be wary of alienating. Commercial banks, for all their economic power, are vulnerable economic entities whose ability to compel a sovereign state to do anything is, at best, very limited. In the case of Poland, which was not a member of the IMF, that ability was non-existent. After the Polish experience, the banks would forcibly insist that the debtor country come to an agreement with the IMF about implementing an economic adjustment programme. Such an agreement became a condition of the rescheduling. The only way banks could get a debtor country to adjust in this way was to support, and depend upon, the IMF, a political entity that has the power and influence, through debtor's membership of it and hence acceptance of its legitimacy, to ensure that economic adjustment takes place. Like the Paris Club, the IMF is dominated by the most powerful Governments in the world, and the US Government in particular.

Prior to Poland, the only other occasion when banks attempted to impose 'conditionality' (where the disbursement of credit is conditional upon staying within targets for various economic variables such as inflation) was in Peru in the period 1977–8, where a radical nationalist Government refused to come to an agreement with the IMF.[10] Various US banks, led by Citicorp, failed miserably to enforce 'conditionality'. The rescheduling negotiations became overtly politicised, as the Peruvian Government attacked the banks for interfering in Peru's internal affairs. The fact that the banks concerned were American infuriated the Peruvians even more. After nearly a year of discord, changes inside the Peruvian Government made it possible for the IMF to return and sort out the mess in 1978.

In Peru and Poland, where the IMF was not present to enforce 'conditionality', the only sanction was to declare the debtor Government to be in default. The trouble with this sanction was that it could only be used once, and if it was used then the banks concerned could forget about regaining the money they had lent. The ultimate sanction was never used, only the threat to use it. Such a threat, as Appendix 3 shows, was made to the Polish Government in September 1981, after months of lies, inexplicable delays, and brinksmanship from that Government in its dealings with its commercial bank creditors. In Poland the threat worked. The day after it was made the Polish Government signed a preliminary rescheduling agreement.

What if the threat is ignored? Such a threat, if it was carried out, would undoubtedly cause severe damage to the external trade and financial relationships of the debtor country concerned.

It could not destroy a sovereign state, especially if the state in question is allied to a powerful state. Cuba and North Korea, both allies of the Soviet Union, openly repudiated their debts during the 1970s. Both survived Western sanctions against them. Other than seizing the property of such countries outside their own borders, through the courts, creditors will not get their money back.

For commercial banks with very large exposures in a debtor country, such as the West German banks in Poland, to declare the debtor country concerned to be in default would be to risk their survival as viable commercial entities. Banks, unlike sovereign states, can go bankrupt and be liquidated. So, despite all the calls from certain political quarters for the banks to declare Poland to be in default after the military *coup d'état* in December 1981, the banks refused to do so. This was also true of the Paris Club Governments who did not declare Poland to be in default, even though relations with the Polish Government were very bad after the events of December 1981. For the banks their own survival, and not half-hearted political campaigns against an illegitimate regime, dictated their behaviour in Poland. If the Paris Club Governments, for all their anti-communist rhetoric, refused to declare Poland to be in default, why should the banks be expected to do so?

The relative weakness of bank creditors in their negotiations with debtor Governments was further aggravated by the problems caused by the presence of so many creditor banks in the rescheduling process. In the Paris Club, the fact that there are very few creditor Governments present in the negotiations, makes the reaching of a unified negotiating position, on the creditor's side of the table, relatively easy. In a commercial bank rescheduling the existence of hundreds of interested creditor banks makes the process of negotiation far more difficult, prolonged, and more liable to break down than is the case with the Paris Club negotiations.

The second lesson of the Polish rescheduling, therefore, was the great difficulty of reaching a consensus among creditor banks. This was to be true also of the South American reschedulings of 1982. A total of 501 banks were involved in Poland. A committee, through which the Polish Government negotiated with its bank creditors, was set up, but the position of the banks that comprised it was that of *primus inter pares* in

relation to the other banks not on the committee. The committee, in other words, could not agree to anything with the
Polish Government without first obtaining, via national task
forces for banks from West Germany, the United Kingdom,
France, the United States, Austria, Switzerland, Italy, and
Japan, the consent of all 501 banks involved in Poland. The
committee can only persuade. It cannot, nor has it any legal
power to, issue orders to those it represents, nor come to any
agreement with the debtor Government without the consent of
those it represents. Because of the existence of cross-default
clauses in all syndicated loan contracts, the committee also had
to ensure that every single bank refrained from declaring
Poland to be in default. These organisational problems complicated the negotiating process, although the organisational
modus operandi, though *ad hoc* by Paris Club standards, improved as banks gained more experience in the art of rescheduling debt.

The intra-creditor bank conflicts over Poland, as Appendix 3
shows, became quite bitter. This was, perhaps, inevitable given
the fact that banks had different levels of exposure in Poland,
had different perceptions of the Polish economy, and existed
in different national commercial and regulatory environments
at home. The West German banks, with the largest exposure
in Poland (17.3 per cent of the total owed by Poland to commercial banks),[11] consistently argued for a 'soft', or conciliatory,
approach to the Poles, in the interests of getting a quick agreement, and avoiding the possibility that Poland would be declared
to be in *de jure* default. It was in *de facto* default, but to have
admitted this in public would have been disastrous for the
West German banks. The Swiss and US banks, with far less
exposure in Poland than the Germans, demanded a 'tough'
approach which involved demanding prompt repayment of
short-term debt, activating penalty clause interest rates on
overdue payments, and trying to impose 'conditionality' on
the Poles. In the Polish context, where the IMF was not present
and given the 'soft' view of the German banks, the 'tough'
approach demanded by the Swiss and US banks was not a
realistic option. Though the advocates of the 'tough' approach
did, at one time (see Appendix 3), threaten to go for a separate
agreement with the Poles if the Germans continued to remain
'soft', a compromise position was eventually reached which was

nearer to the German position than to that of the Swiss and the Americans. It was soon realised by the committee that if these tactical differences were allowed to fester, then the Polish Government—ever ready to use such tactics—would ruthlessly exploit such differences to gain some tactical advantage for itself in the negotiations. The old game of divide-and-rule was attempted on many occasions by the Polish Government, but the committee never allowed the differences between its members to become so serious that such a game could actually have succeeded.

Intra-creditor bank differences over Poland were along national lines. In the end, however, they did not become so serious as to make a united creditor bank negotiating position impossible. It was to be in the Costa Rican rescheduling negotiations of June 1981–June 1982, that the most acrimonious intra-creditor bank differences emerged.

The total debt involved, at $2.7 billion (of which $1.1 billion was owed to commercial banks), was very large for so small an economy. What made the Costa Rican negotiations unique was that the commercial bank steering committee, representing the interests of creditor banks involved in syndicated lending, demanded that syndicated debt and bond debt held by Costa Rica receive *pari passu* treatment, although bond debt had traditionally received preferential treatment and had been kept out of the rescheduling process. Costa Rica serviced its bond debt as contractually agreed and never asked for such debts to be rescheduled, as it knew the rescheduling of bearer bonds was impossible. The holder of a bearer bond cannot be, nor desires to be, identified. The Costa Rican Government found the demand of the steering committee inexplicable, given the impossibility of rescheduling bond debt, but it seemed that the reason behind the demand was that the steering committee could not tolerate the fact that Costa Rica was servicing its bond debt normally, while being incapable of servicing its syndicated debt. This policy was, in the eyes of the steering committee, discrimination against syndicated debt. Therefore, the steering committee declared, *pari passu* treatment must prevail, or syndicated debt would not be rescheduled.

This demand put Costa Rica into an impossible position. Resisting this demand, which the Costa Rican Government did until January 1982, meant that Costa Rica was unable to reschedule its debt, and unable to raise money from its bank creditors. Costa Rica struggled hard to resist becoming the first country since World War II to reschedule publicly issued securities, but by January 1982 desperate economic circumstances forced it to accept the *pari passu* principle laid down by the steering committee in 1981.

By doing so, however, the Costa Rican Government put itself into immediate conflict with the holders of its bonds, and three bond issue managers—Banque Nationale de Paris, DG Bank, and European Banking Company—in particular. The European Banking Company, upon hearing of Costa Rica's decision of January 1982, reacted unfavourably in a long telex, which is the only communication in any rescheduling that has been openly published. It is set out in Appendix 4. The curious mixture of sympathetic understanding, patronising condescension, and blunt threats revealed in the telex infuriated the Costa Rican Government. Such crude threats, in the worlds of international politics and diplomacy, are rarely stated so bluntly. The European Banking Company, oblivious to such diplomatic niceties, bluntly stated that if Costa Rica failed to rescind its acceptance of the *pari passu* principle forthwith, then the European Banking Company would 'campaign vigorously to ensure that you become ineligible for any financing from the multilateral institutions' (see Appendix 4 for full text of telex). Such crude blackmail prompted the Costa Rican Government to leak the telex to the media.

In the end the demand for the *pari passu* principle was dropped by the steering committee, after it finally came to understand that rescheduling of bearer bonds is impossible, but not before months of needless acrimonious negotiations had passed. The Costa Rican negotiations are a prime example of the contradictory demands placed on a debtor country by its various creditors. As well as having to deal with the demands of the IMF and the Paris Club, the Costa Rican Government had to deal with the bank steering committee and the banks that had managed its issues of bonds.

Despite these intra-creditor bank differences, together with the organisational problems of rescheduling commercial bank debt, the terms under which debt was rescheduled were something upon which banks could easily agree. Broadly speaking, those terms were expensive for the debtor countries concerned.

The trend, in all the major reschedulings of the 1981–2 (summer) period (Poland, Romania, Costa Rica, Sudan), was in favour of relatively short maturities, high spreads above LIBOR, high renegotiation fees, and the inclusion of high-cost penalty clauses in all such agreements.

Poland, for example, rescheduled $2.4 billion in 1981 over seven and a half years, with a spread of $1\frac{3}{4}$ per cent over LIBOR and a penalty clause spread of $2\frac{3}{4}$ per cent over LIBOR, plus a renegotiation fee of 1 per cent. Such terms, and especially the high spreads on top of interest rates of 16 per cent in 1981, were criticised in some quarters, notably by the developing countries themselves that had to pay such terms.

Commercial banks, for their part, justified such terms on the grounds that the increased risk inherent in the rescheduling process justified the payment of a risk premium. It was also argued that in order to give banks an incentive to remain in the rescheduling process, and to commit new loans during that process, an increased rate of return on the rescheduled assets and on new loan assets was, therefore, essential. Such arguments were also used during the rescheduling negotiations of the 1982–3 period. Only during the 1983–4 period, during the consolidation phase of the rescheduling process, did terms improve for developing countries.

However, in the Nicaraguan rescheduling negotiations of 1980–1, the very reverse of what was demanded of Poland was granted to Nicaragua. The Nicaraguan rescheduling agreement, though exceptional as regards the terms obtained by the Nicaraguan Government, is a perfect example illustrating the dangers of making generalisations about the rescheduling experiences of so many different developing countries.

Full details of the Nicaraguan negotiations are set out in Appendix 5. The Nicaraguan debt rescheduling agreement, which involved $562 million of debt, was totally unprecedented. The maturity was twelve years with five years grace, past interest due was capitalised (to be paid off over five years), the interest rate payable was LIBOR plus a spread of 1.5 per cent (with a special rate of 7 per cent for the first five years of the agreement), no renegotiation fee was paid and the IMF (at the insistence of the Nicaraguan Government) was not involved.[12] Nicaragua had, in effect, negotiated an annual debt service ratio of 10 per cent for the period 1980–5, on a total debt of $1.5 billion. The principle of ability to pay had been conceded in *de facto* terms by the banks, but in *de jure* terms the banks insisted that the agreement was, given Nicaragua's exceptional circumstances, a 'market' agreement.

The agreement, according to the banks, was an exception, not a precedent for future rescheduling agreements. This, in fact, proved to be the case, although the agreement, innovative and realistic in every respect, could have served as a model for future action. The principle of ability to pay was forgotten in 1982. Instead of ability to pay, the banks insisted upon the 'market' approach in 1982. This approach increased the debt servicing costs of developing countries during the rescheduling process at a time when the developing countries concerned were least able to pay them. What appears to be rational for individual banks—increasing costs to compensate for the increased risk inherent in the rescheduling process—becomes irrational when every bank involved in the developing country concerned makes the same demand for higher costs. The cumulative effect of this process were demands that the developing country found difficult to pay.

3.2 Emergency response, 1982–1983

What distinguishes the reschedulings of 1982–3 from their precursors is the extent of the debts involved.[13] Table 13 shows the extent of the debt that was rescheduled in the period 1982–3. There was no precedent for the amounts involved. The amount of debt rescheduled in the ten months up to June 1983 was about twenty times larger than the amount rescheduled in any previous year. The $90 billion being rescheduled by the fifteen developing countries in Table 13 compares with total liabilities of $210 billion gross ($166.5 billion net) to international commercial banks. Nearly 50 per cent of what the developing countries owed to the commercial banks was being rescheduled during the period 1982–3.

Since rescheduled debt is problem debt, and given the extent of that debt, the international financial system, whose vulnerability was discussed in Chapter 2, was placed under great strain during the rescheduling process. The strain induced by the debt crisis, if it had been left to fester, carried with it the

Table 13 Debt rescheduling negotiations with commercial banks, 1982–1983

Countries	Amounts being rescheduled ($ bn.)		Total liabilities to international banks	
	Public sector	Private sector		
	Debt	Debt	Gross	Net
Mexico	19.5	15	59.0	48.5
Brazil	4.7	†	56.0	51.8
Argentina	5.5	6.0	22.2	16.4
Venezuela	16.3	n.a.	22.7	9.7
Peru	2.0	0.3	5.2	3.3
Chile	3.4	†	10.5	8.0
Uruguay	0.8	n.a.	1.2	0.0
Ecuador	1.2	1.3	4.1	3.3
Yugoslavia	3.4	n.a.*	9.3	7.3
Romania	0.6	n.a.*	4.0	3.7
Poland	7.0	n.a.*	13.4	12.4
Cuba, Costa Rica, Nicaragua, Honduras	2.1	n.a.	2.5	2.1
Total	66.5	22.6	210.0	166.5

n.a. Not available.
n.a.* Not applicable.
† Some private sector debt included in public sector total.
Source: M. S. Mendelsohn, *Commercial Banks and the Restructuring of Cross-Border-Debt* (New York: Group of Thirty, 1983), p. 4.
© 1984 Group of Thirty, Consultative Group on International Economic & Monetary Affairs, Inc. Reproduced by permission from *Commercial Banks and the Restructuring of Cross-Border-Debt*, Michael S. Mendelsohn.

potential to do great damage to the international financial system. This reality prompted the decisive emergency response of 1982–3 by Western Governments, the IMF, and the commercial banks. There were four major rescue operations: Argentina, Brazil, Mexico, and Yugoslavia. The IMF played a major role in all four. The US Government played the leading role in South America, while the Swiss Government played a similar role in Yugoslavia.

The Mexican rescheduling negotiations, which began in

August 1982 when the Mexican Government unilaterally suspended principal payments of $19.5 billion due in 1982, were the most important. The shock-wave caused by the Mexican move in August 1982 spread throughout South America, and the Mexican rescheduling negotiations were to become the pace-setters for all the other rescheduling negotiations in South America in the period 1982–4. Appendix 6 shows the course of the Mexican negotiations. They have received the most attention in the literature on the subject.[14] Appendix 7 shows the course of the Brazilian negotiations. These negotiations, which have received less attention in the literature,[15] are still (1985) going on. Appendix 8 shows the course of the Yugoslav negotiations, which have received the least attention in the literature.[16]

What, then, are the factors common to all these negotiations? What factors differentiate between them? Finally, what makes the negotiations of 1982–3 different from the negotiations of 1980–2? Table 14 is a comparative summary of the Brazilian, Mexican, and Yugoslavian rescue packages. For further details see Appendices 6, 7, and 8.

Perhaps the most distinctive factor, common to all three countries listed in Table 14, were the bridging loans provided by the US Government and the Bank for International Settlements (BIS) to cover the critically important period between the onset of crisis and the disbursement of loans by the IMF and the commercial banks. The US Government, through a variety of its agencies, provided $1.57 billion to Brazil and $2.925 billion to Mexico. $200 million was provided to Yugoslavia. This large and prompt commitment to Brazil and Mexico indicated both an awareness of the seriousness of the debt crisis these two countries faced, and the political importance of these two countries to the United States. As regards Yugoslavia, the US Government played an important role, via the $1.1 billion lent to that country by Paris Club Governments. The political importance of maintaining Yugoslavia's present neutrality was a major factor behind the efforts of the US Government to put together the rescue package for Yugoslavia. However, because Yugoslavia is neutral, it was thought appropriate to let another neutral country, Switzerland, head the rescue effort, although the US Government played the major role in putting the package together.

Table 14 The Brazilian, Mexican, and Yugoslavian rescue packages, 1982–1983 ($ bn.)

	Brazil	Mexico	Yugoslavia
1. Financial support			
IMF			
Stand-by facility	–	–	0.6
Extended fund	4.6	3.7	–
Compensatory finance/other	1.3	0.22	–
World Bank	–	–	0.3
BIS	1.2	0.925	0.5
Paris Club*	–	2.0	1.1
USA			
Oil payments†	–	1.0	–
Commodity credit‡	–	1.0	0.2
Federal Reserve	0.4	0.925	–
US Treasury	1.53	–	–
Commercial banks§	4.4	5.0	2.0
Total	13.4	14.7	4.7
2. Rescheduled debt‖			
Amount	4.9	19.5	1.8
Due	1983	1982–3	1983
Type	Public sector	Public sector	Public sector

Terms¶	8 years(m) 2.5 years(g) 2.5% LIBOR(s) 2¼% Prime(s) 1½% (f)	8 years(m) 4 years(g) 1⅞% LIBOR(s) 1¾% Prime(s) 1% (f)	5 years(m) 2 years(g) 1¾% LIBOR(s) 1% Fee(f)
3. New loan terms	Same as terms for rescheduled debt	6 years(m) 3 years(g) 2¼% LIBOR(s) 2⅝% Prime(s) 1¼% (f)	Same as terms for rescheduled debt
4. Total value of rescue package**	18.3	34.2	6.5

* New trade credits. Separate from rescheduling of Paris Club debt. Negotiations to reschedule Paris Club debt began in 1983.
† Prepayment for future oil deliveries to US strategic oil stores.
‡ For the purchase of agricultural commodities from US Government.
§ New loans, as opposed to rescheduled debt.
‖ Amounts refer to agreements signed 1982–3. Further amounts still the objects of negotiations. See Table 13.
¶ Amounts refer to agreements signed 1982–3.
** Total = financial support plus rescheduled debt.

Source: William R. Cline, *International Debt and the Stability of the World Economy* (Washington, DC: Institute for International Economics, 1983), p. 42; M. S. Mendelsohn, *Commercial Banks and the Restructuring of Cross-Border-Debt* (New York: Group of Thirty, 1983); Joseph Kraft, *The Mexican Rescue* (New York: Group of Thirty, 1984); Marko Milivojević, 'Anatomy of a Rescheduling: Yugoslavia, 1982–1983', *South Slav Journal*, Vol. 6, No. 2(20), Summer 1983.

Section 1: © 1983 Institute for International Economics. Reproduced by permission from *International Debt and the Stability of the World Economy*, William R. Cline.

Sections 2, 3 and 4: © 1984 Group of Thirty, Consultative Group on International Economic & Monetary Affairs, Inc. Reproduced by kind permission from *Commercial Banks and the Restructuring of Cross-Border-Debt*, M. S. Mendelsohn, and *The Mexican Rescue*, Joseph Kraft.
Material from the *South Slav Journal* reproduced by permission of the editor.

The most important US Government agency was the Federal Reserve Board. Its role, particularly in Mexico where it immediately provided a $925 million bridging loan, was of great importance, both in its unilateral actions and within the context of BIS, where the US Federal Reserve Board has observer status. The BIS itself, though loath to admit it in public, was far more important than its loans, though vital, would have suggested. The BIS lent $1.2 billion to Brazil, $925 million to Mexico, and $500 million to Yugoslavia. Its real importance resides in the fact that the BIS is a formal and informal forum for contacts and co-operation between the major central banks of the OECD countries.

The BIS, which was set up to handle transactions between central banks, was most unwilling to set a precedent by becoming, or by appearing to become, a source of long-term debt crisis assistance. Its bridging loans were for ninety days, but were rolled over many times in Brazil and Mexico. In *de facto* terms, these loans became medium-term, despite the protests of the BIS. In general, the BIS preferred to play a complementary role to the IMF in the rescue packages listed in Table 14. However, in Hungary[17] (not a member of the IMF at the time) in 1982, the BIS did play the leading role in rescuing the country from international bankruptcy.

Though a prudent borrower itself, Hungary was pushed into crisis by the withdrawal of its inter-bank facilities in 1982, a result of commercial banks' concern about events in Poland, Romania, Yugoslavia, and Mexico. This withdrawal put Hungary into immediate crisis. The BIS, though technically only an entity to handle transactions between central banks and with no authority or power to impose conditionality, provided a short-term bridging loan of $510 million, which in turn improved Hungary's standing among commercial banks. Once Hungary joined the IMF late in 1982, the BIS's short-term rescue operation enabled Hungary to recover quickly in 1983.

However, the most important factor common to the three reschedulings under discussion was the presence of the IMF. The IMF, it would be fair to say, played the leading role in all three reschedulings, and acquired unprecedented new powers and influence in the process of doing so. In addition, the IMF's activities created the most controversy in all three countries.

The IMF, because of its role in the implementation of economic adjustment programmes in the developing countries, has attracted a great deal of attention in the literature.[18] The consequences of these programmes, which are primarily designed to improve the debt servicing capabilities of debtors' economies and to stabilise their monetary systems, have attracted a certain amount of criticism in the literature.[19] In South America, where those consequences have been the most severe, the IMF serves as a useful whipping-boy for local politicians in public. In private, these same politicians accept the legitimacy of, and negotiate with, the IMF.

Only Argentina and Venezuela have had consistently poor relations with the IMF, and no developing country has pulled out of the IMF as a result of such poor relations. Mexico, Brazil, and Yugoslavia all enjoyed relatively good relations with the IMF. In public, Governments found it politically expedient to object to the demands of the IMF, given the political unpopularity of the consequences—lower growth, lower public spending, higher unemployment—of IMF-approved economic adjustment programmes. In private, however, relations were cordial as virtually all debtor Governments knew that economic adjustment, though politically unpopular, was necessary in order to resolve the debt crisis and to restore normal relations with creditors. Political expediency forced them not to admit this publicly. Relations were particularly cordial between the IMF and the Governments of Mexico and Yugoslavia. Brazil, though not deliberately unco-operative like Argentina and Venezuela, experienced difficulties with the IMF because it found it hard—as a result of deep structural economic problems—to reduce its very high inflation rate.

Most politicians and economists, however, recognise the importance of, and need for, the IMF; firstly, for leading the rescue operations of 1982–3, secondly, for enforcing economic adjustment, and thereby creating the conditions for the economic recovery of 1983–4 in Brazil, Mexico, and Yugoslavia.

As regards financial support Table 14 shows that the IMF lent $5.9 billion to Brazil, $3.92 billion to Mexico, and $600 million to Yugoslavia. The amount the IMF made available to these three countries ($10.42 billion) in the period 1982–3 constituted a substantial proportion of total IMF disbursements of $13.5 billion in the same period. The $13.5 billion lent in

1982–3 financed around 20 per cent of the combined current account deficits of the non-oil developing countries in that year. Table 15 shows that in the period 1979–82 IMF lending represented an average of less than 5 per cent of the combined current account deficits of the non-oil developing countries in that period. As a source of credit, and as Table 15 shows, the IMF was not very important throughout the 1970s. During normal times the IMF was content to let the commercial banks and official creditors do virtually all the lending to the developing countries. As a body authorised to oversee the international financial system, the IMF was important during the 1970s, although in the normal conditions of that decade its role was less overt in the developing countries than was the case in the abnormal conditions of 1982–3.

The credits disbursed by the IMF, though critically important in the context of the rescue packages, were not very significant in relation to the aggregate borrowing requirements of the non-oil developing countries, although after 1982 the IMF's credits became more significant than they had been in the 1970s and early 1980s. In addition, the IMF had more to lend. One of the more beneficial consequences of the debt crisis was the decision, taken by the member Governments of the IMF, to double the resources available to the IMF to $100 billion. This was done in 1983, after considerable opposition to the plan to increase the resources available to the IMF in the US Congress. Since the United States was the largest individual contributor to IMF resources, certain right-wing political forces in the US Congress felt it wrong for the IMF to 'bail out' the banks and the developing countries. In the end, however, political expediency triumphed over ideology: the IMF got its increased resources.

When conditionality is examined in reference to the 1982–3 debt crisis, it is clear that after the onset of that crisis in 1982 more of what the IMF lent was in the form of high-conditionality[20] credit disbursements. Table 16 shows the increasing importance of high-conditionality lending after 1982. In 1976, virtually all IMF credit was low-conditionality. Low-conditionality exceeded high-conditionality in 1976, 1977, and 1979. The reverse was true in 1978, and in every subsequent year up to 1983. However, it was not until 1982 that high-conditionality credits accounted for virtually all IMF lending

Table 15 Non-oil developing countries balance of payments: sources and uses of funds, 1973–1983
(billions of US dollars)

	1973	1974	1975	1976	1977	1978	1979	1980	1981	1982	1983
Use of funds:											
Current account deficit	11.3	37.0	46.3	32.6	28.9	41.3	61.0	89.0	107.7	86.8	67.8
Net reserve accumulation	10.4	2.7	–1.6	13.0	12.5	17.4	12.6	4.5	2.1	–7.1	7.2
Total	21.7	39.7	44.7	45.6	41.4	58.7	73.6	93.5	109.8	79.7	75.0
Sources of funds:											
Direct investment	4.2	5.3	5.3	5.0	5.4	7.3	8.9	10.1	13.9	11.4	10.9
Official transfers	5.5	8.7	7.1	7.5	8.2	8.2	11.6	12.5	13.8	13.2	13.1
NEB,* of which:											
Offical sources	4.9	6.8	11.7	10.5	11.4	13.8	13.3	17.6	23.0	19.5	23.8
Private banks	9.8	18.6	23.2	21.5	14.7	25.6	35.9	53.3	52.6	25.0	15.0
IMF credits	0.1	1.5	2.1	3.2	–	–	0.2	1.2	5.6	6.3	13.5
Miscellaneous	–2.8	–1.2	–4.7	–2.1	1.7	3.8	3.7	–1.2	0.9	4.3	–1.3
Total	21.7	39.7	44.7	45.6	41.4	58.7	73.6	93.4	109.8	79.7	75.0

* NEB—net external borrowing.
Source: IMF, *World Economic Outlook*, 1983.

Table 16 Low-conditionality and high-conditionality disbursements, 1976–1983 (billions of SDRs; all IMF members)

	Financial year ended April							
	1976	1977	1978	1979	1980	1981	1982	1983
1. Low-conditionality	5.09	2.97	0.41	0.64	1.05	1.56	1.65	4.12
First credit tranche	0.29	0.78	0.09	0.13	0.16	0.78	0.02	0.03
Oil facility	3.97	0.44	–	–	–	–	–	–
Compensatory financing facility	0.83	1.75	0.32	0.46	0.86	0.78	1.63	3.74
Buffer stock facility	–	–	–	0.05	0.03	–	–	0.35
2. High-conditionality	0.18	1.78	1.96	0.59	1.15	2.82	5.31	6.14
Credit tranche	0.17	1.59	1.85	0.35	0.93	1.90	2.73	3.68
Extended Fund facility	0.01	0.19	0.11	0.24	0.22	0.92	2.58	2.46
Total (1.+2.)	5.27	4.75	2.37	1.24	2.21	4.39	6.96	10.26

Source: IMF, *Annual Report*, 1983.

in that year. In 1983 it accounted for around 60 per cent of the total.

The disbursements to Brazil and Mexico all involved high-conditionality. All such disbursements were from the Extended Fund. The $600 million disbursed to Yugoslavia in 1983, which was the third tranche of a $1.8 billion IMF facility granted in 1981, involved low-conditionality. However, once that third tranche was disbursed, a high-conditionality agreement was agreed between the IMF and the Yugoslav Government.

It is these high-conditionality agreements, more than anything else, that give the IMF such power and influence in the rescheduling process. Only the IMF, a multilateral, political institution to which all the debtor countries belong, can enforce conditionality. Making the disbursement of credit conditional on the successful completion of a strictly verified economic adjustment programme is a politically sensitive activity.

The commercial banks, after their disastrous attempts to enforce conditionality in Peru in 1978 and Poland in 1981, were wise enough not to attempt to do so again in 1982. The commercial banks needed the IMF to enforce economic adjustment, but when the debt crisis began in 1982 they did not know that the assistance of the IMF would have its *quid pro quo*.

What distinguishes IMF policy in 1982 from its past activities in developing countries, was the imposition of conditionality on the commercial banks. Contrary to its previous practice, whereby the IMF merely hoped that the adoption of an economic adjustment programme by a developing country would act as a seal of approval to encourage the return of normal commercial bank lending, the IMF in 1982 explicitly told the commercial banks that the disbursement of IMF credits to debtor countries was conditional on the provision of new loans by the banks to the debtor countries. The somewhat brusque manner in which this condition was articulated (especially in Brazil and Mexico) by the IMF, made it sound like an order to many commercial banks.

Commercial banks were not used to taking orders from anybody, but in 1982 they had little choice in the matter. Without the IMF, they risked losing all their assets in the debtor countries concerned. The commercial banks needed the IMF, yet IMF support meant, in the last analysis, increasing political interference in the banking markets. This new role of the IMF was fully supported by the world's major central banks, within whose supervisory systems the commercial banks had to function, and whose views the banks could not afford to ignore.[21]

While various academic commentators[22] have long argued for this sort of IMF–commercial bank partnership as a rational solution to the problem of financing development in the developing countries, many commercial banks have tended to see the IMF's policies in the period 1982–3 as the cause of involuntary lending by commercial banks. The IMF was forcing banks to lend, but was unable to provide any formal guarantees to protect bank assets so committed in conditions of high country and sovereign risk.

Many banks resisted this pressure to lend. This was especially true of the smaller US banks, whose exposure was relatively small (in comparison to that of the top ten US banks), and who did not want to lend anything more to developing countries. This problem was particularly acute in the Brazilian rescheduling negotiations, where many small US banks refused to extend inter-bank facilities to Brazil. Their attitude was the cause of the most difficult problem in the Brazilian negotiations. Although Brazil and the IMF asked for $10 billion in interbank facilities from the commercial banks in 1982, only $6 billion was obtained from the banks by 1983 (see Appendix 8 for full details).

The entire rescheduling process was, in fact, a permanent struggle between the tendency to cut and run, ever present in every commercial bank that exists in a competitive environment, and to stay in the rescheduling/new loan process so as to safeguard the stability of the international financial system, and to restore the debtor countries concerned back to normal economic conditions. The IMF, whose primary consideration was the overall stability of the international financial system, went to great lengths to ensure that the cut-and-run option did not become endemic among banks. This option, while it may appear to be rational to an individual bank, becomes disastrous for both banks and the debtor country concerned if a large number of banks decide to follow it.

To sweeten the rather bitter pill of involuntary lending, which ended the illusion that large banks had any real freedom of choice in the rescheduling/new loan process, the IMF was sympathetic to the idea of a risk premium being levied on new loans and rescheduled debt by commercial banks. As Table 14 shows, the risk premium was high. For the three reschedulings under discussion, and with reference to the agreements signed in the period 1982–3, the average maturity on new loans was 6.3 years (average grace period was 2.5 years), the average spread over LIBOR was 2.1 per cent (average spread over US prime rate was 1.75 per cent), and the average renegotiation fee was 1.25 per cent. For rescheduled loans, and for the same period, the average maturity was 7 years (average grace period was 2.8 years), the average spread over LIBOR was 2 per cent (average spread over US prime rate was 1.9 per cent), and the average renegotiation fee was 1.5 per cent. Brazil paid the most; Mexico the least.

With such terms bank profits increased, and so provided an incentive for wary and reluctant commercial banks to lend new money to debtor countries during the rescheduling process. In Mexico, for example, the spread above LIBOR on new loans was 2.25 per cent. The pre-debt crisis spread was 1.75 per cent, a risk premium of 0.5 per cent, or $500 million extra to the banks. In Brazil, the spread above LIBOR on new loans was 2.5 per cent, which meant an extra $1 billion to the banks. The risk premium in Brazil was 1 per cent. The pre-debt crisis spread was 1.5 per cent in Brazil.

Yet despite these profitable incentives, and despite the success of the IMF in enforcing economic adjustment programmes in all three countries being discussed, the principal problem—especially in Brazil—for advisory committees was to persuade all creditor banks of the countries concerned to lend new money. Mexico, which had acted decisively when its debt crisis began in August 1982 and which subsequently implemented a successful economic adjustment programme, was the least troublesome example as regards raising new money. Even so, it took nearly eight months (November 1982–June 1983) for the Mexican advisory committee to raise $4.7 billion of new loans from 526 banks. Prior to 1982, 1,400 banks had lent money to Mexico on a regular basis. The most troublesome example as regards raising new money was Brazil, which failed to act decisively, delayed the implementation of economic adjustment, and failed to gain the confidence of its creditors until well into 1983. The result of all this was less new money in 1983—far less than Brazil needed. The result of that, in turn, was another debt crisis in the autumn of 1983. Which made it even more difficult to raise new money in 1984.

The organisational and logistical problems faced by the advisory committees were formidable. Appendix 9 illustrates the structure of the Mexican advisory committee. This sort of structure was, in all essential respects, also used in Brazil and Yugoslavia. US banks dominated the committees because they (the US banks) had the largest exposure in Brazil and Mexico, they had experience of large-scale corporate reschedulings in the United States (such as for Chrysler in the 1970s), and they had played the leading role in the commercial bank reschedulings of 1978–82 listed in Table 12. One US bank, Citicorp, was the most important. Indeed, William Rhodes,[23] a Citicorp Senior Vice-President, simultaneously held the chairmanships or co-chairmanships of the advisory committees for Mexico, Brazil (in 1983), Argentina, Peru, and Uruguay. In Yugoslavia an American bank, Manufacturers Hanover, chaired the advisory committee. The following sections set out the advisory committees' functions, as reflected in Appendix 9.

1. *Evaluation*

The macroeconomic subcommittee, reporting to the advisory committee (which in turn reports to all creditor banks via the regional communications networks), evaluates the state of the debtor's economy and its debt servicing capabilities in particular. This is a difficult task. The IMF is precluded by its Charter from sharing sensitive economic data given to its officers by debtor Governments with commercial banks. The macroeconomic subcommittee is, therefore, dependent on the debtor Government for basic data. The data so received can be misleading, as the debtor Government naturally wants to put over a good image of its economic position. Aside from macroeconomic analysis to determine country risk, the advisory committee (though not via a formal subcommittee) also receives the evaluation of political experts employed by large banks on the political situation inside the debtor country, and the inner workings of the Government in particular, so as to determine sovereign risk. Country risk analysis aims to answer the following question: can a given economy service a given level of debt? Sovereign risk analysis aims to answer the following question: is a given Government willing to service its debt? The advisory committee must then digest all this information, evaluate its significance, come to some sort of conclusion, and negotiate on the basis of that conclusion.

2. *Definition*

The task of determining, at the onset of the negotiations, who owes what to whom, and deciding what debt should be included in the rescheduling process, was the responsibility of the debt definition subcomittee—a very difficult task, given the fact that in many debtor countries the Governments had no clear idea of what they, or entities within their borders, owed to foreign banks. More generally, the advisory committee decided, in consultation with the debtor Government concerned, what debt was to be rescheduled. Finally, the advisory committee had to define the following: the status of debtor's bond liabilities, the relationship between bank and Paris Club debt, the relationship between rescheduled and non-rescheduled debt, the status of debts held by the private sector in developing countries, and the relationship between Government guaranteed and non-guaranteed debt.

3. *Negotiation*

The advisory committee must negotiate a mutually acceptable set of terms with the debtor Government for rescheduled debt and new loans. Maturity, grace period, spreads, and the fees are all negotiable. The advisory committee, drawing on the country risk evaluations of the macroeconomic subcommittee and the sovereign risk evaluations of the political experts, and determining the views of the banking market via the regional communications networks, must present the terms acceptable to all the banks it represents, and then get the debtor Government to accept them. This is a very difficult task, due to the fact that the opening negotiating positions of the advisory committee and the debtor Government are often very far apart.

4. *Communication*

This was, in many respects, the most important function of advisory committees. The advisory committee passes down, via the regional communications networks, evaluations of the debtor's economy, debt definitions arrived at, and opening negotiating positions as regards terms on rescheduled debt and new loans (i.e. persuading, via the same networks, banks to contribute to new syndicated loans—a very prolonged, difficult, and demanding activity). The inter-bank subcommittee, because inter-bank facilities are rolled over (or not) on a weekly basis, must go through this process of persuasion every week. More generally, the advisory committee must keep itself informed of what the banking market feels about terms for rescheduled debt and new loans. The fact that advisory committees have no formal powers over the banks on whose behalf they negotiate, but must rely on informal methods of persuasion and peer group pressure, means that the entire rescheduling process for commercial banks must be far more prolonged and difficult than is the case for the Paris Club.

5. *Liaison*

The advisory committee, and especially its chairman, liaises wih the IMF and the central bank authorities of OECD countries. The views of the IMF (in particular) and central banks, given the power of these institutions, must be given great attention by the advisory committee. Contacts with central banks can be used by the advisory committee to get such authorities to put pressure on banks they regulate to lend new money to debtor countries.

6. *Drafting*

The advisory committee, with the assistance of lawyers, must draft mutually acceptable rescheduling and new loan contracts. The wording of these long documents is not as straightforward as they would appear to be, given the sensitivity of debtor Governments as regards all documents they have to sign with foreign entities.

The problem of communication (or lack of it) between banks was a problem in all the three reschedulings under discussion, but it was the most acute in Brazil. Big US banks unsuccessfully urged smaller regional US banks to lend new money. It was a classic example of free riders in action: free-rider banks that wanted the advantages that a rescheduling agreement (the most important part of which are the new loans) would bring, but were unwilling to risk anything by way of lending new money to the country concerned. The obstinate attitude of some of these small banks was legendary. Joseph Kraft, in his study of the Mexican rescheduling negotiations, quotes the head of a small Florida bank as saying the following, with reference to the Mexican situation:

Citicorp and Bank of America negotiate the deal. They tell us to go along, and if we ask a question, they get sore. We had some bad risks, and we wanted out. We made trouble for the big banks on the theory that they might let us out of all the loans just to get us out of their hair. At one point we even made noises about a law suit against some of the Mexican banks. That turned out to be unwise. The threats came to the attention of the Federal Reserve Board. The Fed is our main regulator, and in fact we need approval for a merger. The bank examiners came around and started asking questions. That was enough for us. We dropped the suit, but in the end we didn't subscribe to the request for new money.[24] *

The smaller banks were profoundly irritating to advisory committees, but if they tried anything serious like a law suit (which would activate the cross-default clauses in all syndicated loan contracts) against the debtor country, then the relevant central bank authorities would put great pressure on the offending banks. Advisory committees, when informal methods had failed to persuade offending banks, resorted to more overt tactics. In January 1983, the Brazilian advisory committee, in an unprecedented move (see Appendix 7), publicly stated that it was prepared to publish the names of recalcitrant banks who refused to lend money to Brazil if they persisted in their refusals. In the final analysis, despite all the pressure from advisory committees, the IMF, and central banks, a small number of banks still refused to lend. Nothing could be done about it.

When looking at particular negotiations, and despite the fact

---

* © 1984 Group of Thirty. Consultative Group on International Economic & Monetary Affairs, Inc. Reproduced by permission from *The Mexican Rescue*, Joseph Kraft.

that many factors were common to all such negotiations, it is clear that each country had its own unique problems. In Brazil the failure of the advisory committee to raise the desired level of interbank facilities for the country, and the Brazilian Government's inability to implement its economic adjustment programme agreed with the IMF, were the major problems in the negotiations of 1982 and 1983.

In Mexico the status of the debts of the Mexican private sector was the major problem in the negotiations. At first, in 1982, the Mexican Government refused to accept liability for such non-guaranteed debts. Since around $15 billion was involved, the issue was very serious. Later in the negotiations, in deference to pressure from the advisory committee and the IMF, the Government agreed to accept the peso equivalent of the debt servicing payments due on this debt. By accepting such payments on these terms, and placing them in the central bank, the Government accepted in *de facto* terms that it was liable to service such debts in US dollars, as was contractually agreed in the original loan contracts signed by banks and private Mexican firms. This was because after the imposition of exchange controls in September 1982, no Mexican private firm could service its foreign debts in US dollars without permission from the Government.

However, actual disbursement of the US dollars out of the peso-equivalent account was delayed until the principal due on the entire private sector debt was itself rescheduled. The disagreements induced by this unilaterally declared policy of delay, which began in 1982, were not finally resolved until the end of 1983, but once Mexico's public sector debts had been satisfactorily rescheduled by the summer of 1983, the atmosphere was conducive to the solution of the private sector debt question.

In Yugoslavia, in a totally unexpected and unprecedented development, the major problem arose at the end of the negotiations when the advisory committee insisted that the new loan granted to Yugoslavia in 1983 be 'joint and severally' (see Appendix 8) in the names of the National Bank of Yugoslavia and the Socialist Federal Republic of Yugoslavia (SFRY). This insistent request, made in a climate of nervousness caused by the debt crisis, revealed a distinct lack of clarity on the part of the Yugoslav advisory committee as to which entity, in a highly decentralised political system, was ultimately responsible for the debts contracted by political and economic entities in Yugoslavia's constituent republics. The supreme political entity, the SFRY, had never actually borrowed in its own name, and legislation was required before it could do so. In the event, months of arguments followed until a mutually acceptable form of wording was agreed upon by the advisory committee and the Yugoslav Government. For Governments, the advisory committee discovered, the form of the wording of any agreement was as important as the actual contents of the agreement in question. This was certainly the case in Yugoslavia.

Despite these differences, however, the three rescheduling negotiations had more in common with one another than they had in terms of unique factors that separated them from each other. Common factors included the primacy of the IMF, the importance of BIS and OECD-country Governments' bridging loans, the high-risk premiums levied on rescheduled debt and new loans, the difficulties experienced by advisory committees in raising new loans, the development of involuntary lending, the existence of free riders, and the organisational problems faced by all advisory committees.

Broadly speaking, the rescue packages of 1982–3, and the three rescue packages discussed in this chapter in particular, were remarkably successful in preventing the development of circumstances in which the potential vulnerability of the international financial system, as it stood in 1982, could have developed into an actual collapse, or a severe weakening, of that system in 1983. By mid-1983, the feasibility and efficacity of the rescue packages was proven through long experience. A number of precedents had been set to guide future action, a fund of considerable expertise had developed to deal with future problems, and the *modus operandi* of advisory committees had been considerably improved. The question, in the period 1983–4, was: could the rescheduling process now develop in such a way as to consolidate, and develop further, the considerable achievements of the period 1982–3?

3.3 Consolidation, 1983–1984

While the construction of boundaries is inevitable in any written analysis of the rescheduling process, in the real world it was difficult, if not impossible, to say when the emergency response of the 1982–3 period ended, and the consolidation phase of the rescheduling process began.

Indeed, as Appendix 7 shows, the most difficult negotiations of the entire rescheduling process—in Brazil—took place from June 1983 to January 1984. In June 1983, when the IMF and the commercial banks had stopped the disbursement of credit to Brazil due to its inability to comply with the adjustment programme it had agreed with the IMF, William Rhodes (see Appendix 9), fresh from his triumph as chairman of the Mexican advisory committee, took over as Chairman of the Brazilian advisory committee. The rescue package for Brazil up to the summer of 1983, known as Phase I, had proved inadequate to resolve fully Brazil's debt servicing problems in 1983. This was not due to any major failing on the part of Phase I, but to Brazil's inability to adjust as agreed with the IMF. Since credit disbursements by the IMF and the banks were conditional on the successful implementation of Brazil's agreement with the IMF, Phase I was not as successful as the concurrent rescue package for Mexico, which did adjust as agreed with the IMF.

The fact that it appeared to be a genuine inability (especially as regards inflation) to adjust, and was not a political unwillingness to adjust (as in Argentina), persuaded William Rhodes's newly reorganised advisory committee to persevere with Phase II, which lasted from June 1983 to January 1984.

While the 1983 rescue package for Brazil had totalled $13.4 billion, the package for 1984, the IMF estimated, would have to total $11.5 billion. Yet Brazil's actual economic situation was worse in 1983, and was clearly perceived to be worse by the banks, than it had been in 1982. The banks had contributed $4.4 billion to the 1983 package. For the 1984 package the IMF requested the Brazilian advisory committee to raise $7 billion. Such a request, in a wider context of increasing doubt among banks about lending new money to Brazil, created a most difficult problem for the advisory committee during Phase II.

The first problem was that the structure of the Brazilian advisory committee, which had existed during Phase I and which was similar to the structure of the Mexican advisory committee as set out in Appendix 9, had attracted a certain amount of criticism during Phase I. William Rhodes, on his accession to the chairmanship of the Brazilian advisory committee, made the following organisational changes in response to these criticisms:

1. Many banks had complained about a lack of basic economic data on Brazil. An economic subcommittee was established to provide better economic data.
2. It was decided, at the outset of Phase II, to raise enough money for the whole of 1984, so as to avoid a repetition of the loan-raising process yet again during 1984.
3. Many small regional US banks had complained about being left out of the decision-making process, and they felt that the advisory committee only seemed to contact them when new money was required. In order to make US regional banks feel they were part of the decision-making process, several of them were placed on a special subcommittee, whose function was to liaise between the US regionals and the advisory committee.
4. Many non-US banks had complained that the rescheduling process in South America was totally dominated by large US banks (which it was), and they felt left out of the decision-making process. To deal with this criticism, Mr Guy Huntrods, director of Lloyds Bank International, was made a deputy chairman of the advisory committee. This move put a European banker close to the centre of decision-making power.
5. While recognising the importance of allowing discussions to diffuse tensions in the advisory committee, its new chairman decided to set objectives to be achieved within designated periods of time. This sort of discipline had long existed in the Paris Club, but it was not something that characterised the rather chaotic and prolonged proceedings of advisory committees. This important change speeded up the entire rescheduling process. Phase I in Brazil took nearly one year. Phase II was completed in six months.
6. While relations with the IMF had been rather strained during Phase I, the new chairman decided to improve liaison with that institution. In addition, he decided to make more systematic use of central banks, and the US Federal Reserve and the Bank of England in particular, to put pressure on the banks they regulated to lend more new money to Brazil during Phase II.

The cumulative effects of these organisational changes were to reduce tensions between banks, to put over the impression that some sort of strategic plan existed to deal with Brazil's problems, to speed up the rescheduling process, and to put the rescheduling problem into a longer-term time-frame than was the case in Phase I. Phase II, despite the formidable problems that existed in June 1983, raised more new money than did Phase I. Of the $7 billion requested by the IMF from the banks for Phase II, the advisory committee raised $6.5 billion by January 1984. By the spring of 1984 the entire rescue package was in place. This enabled debt service arrears to be cleared, and by the summer of 1984 Brazil's reserves stood at $5 billion.

The IMF, which had contributed $1.1 billion for Phase II, made an unprecedented concession to Brazil. The major problem during Phase I was Brazil's inability to stick to the targets agreed with the IMF. The principal target, for inflation, was not kept. However, other targets were kept. The budget deficit was cut from 6 per cent of GDP in 1982 to 2.7 per cent of GDP in 1983.[25] The current account deficit was reduced, exports increased, and total debt growth was reduced. During Phase II Brazil agreed to cut its inflation to 90 per cent. It proved unable to do so. Inflation was 211 per cent in 1984.[26] The concession was that the IMF did not make an issue of this failure during Phase II. Because of the great inflationary pressures in the Brazilian economy, the IMF decided, in effect, that the inflation rate would not be a performance criterion for Brazil during Phase II. In the long term, of course, the IMF wants to see lower inflation in Brazil, but during Phase II it recognised that the reduction of inflation would take far longer than it had assumed during Phase I.

The efficacity of the advisory committee, the concessions made by the IMF, and the considerable adjustment (other than inflation) made by Brazil ensured that Phase II was a success. By the summer of 1984, Brazil, while not into full consolidation like Mexico, was on the road to consolidation. Given its awesome economic and political problems, it was remarkable that it made even this much progress.

Mexico, meanwhile, was well into the period of consolidation by the summer of 1983. It had adjusted successfully, enjoyed good relations with the IMF, was relatively politically stable (by South American standards), and was, therefore, in a position to

Table 17   Terms of rescheduling and new loan agreements signed
by Mexico, 1983–1984

	Amount	Maturity	Grace	Spread	Fee
1983 Rescheduling	$19.5 bn.	8 years	4 years	1 7/8 ths.%/1.75% Prime LIBOR	1%
1984 Rescheduling	$49.0 bn.	14 years	6 years	1.11% LIBOR*	0.5%
1983 New loan	$5.0 bn.	3 years	3 years	2 1/8 ths.%/2.25% Prime LIBOR	1.25%
1984 New loan	$3.8 bn.	5 years	5 years	1.5% LIBOR*	0.5%

*In 1984 all above debt priced in LIBOR, with the exception of $6 billion of rescheduled debt that remained priced in US Prime Rate.

Source: Joseph Kraft, *The Mexican Rescue* (New York: Group of Thirty, 1984), for 1983; *Euromoney*, various issues, for 1984.

© 1984 Group of Thirty, Consultative Group on International Economic & Monetary Affairs, Inc. Reproduced by permission from *The Mexican Rescue*, Joseph Kraft.

change the very nature of the rescheduling process during its rescheduling negotiations of 1984. As in the emergency response period (1982–3), Mexico set the pace in the consolidation period (1983–4). Table 17 shows the extent of that change in 1984.

Whereas short maturities, short grace periods, high spreads, and high fees characterise the agreements of 1983, long maturities, long grace periods, low spreads, and low fees characterise the agreements of 1984. The banks, seeing the success of economic adjustment in Mexico in 1983, removed the high-risk premium in 1984. The 1984 new loan spread of 1.5 per cent over LIBOR, for example, is what Mexico was paying for new loans prior to its 1982 debt crisis. The 1984 new loan maturity, at nine years (five years grace), represents a considerable improvement on the 1983 new loan maturity of six years (three years grace). The fall in the fee, from 1.25 per cent in 1983 to 0.5 per cent in 1984, is a large one.

It is in the 1984 rescheduling agreement, however, that the most remarkable change takes place. The amount involved, $49 billion, is over half Mexico's total debt. Its fourteen-year maturity (compared to eight years in 1983) put the rescheduling process in Mexico into a long-term time-frame, and the fact that $49 billion was rescheduled at one go means that Mexico need not reschedule again for a long time. Prior to this agreement, rescheduling had been an annual exercise.

The greatest changes were for spreads and the move into LIBOR pricing. The 1984 rescheduled debt spread, at 1.11 per cent above LIBOR, is very low, and compares very well with a spread of 1.75 per cent over LIBOR in 1983 for the same type of debt. In 1983 most of the rescheduled debt was priced in US Prime Rate. This is traditionally higher than LIBOR. Of the $49 billion rescheduled in 1984, $43 billion was to be priced in LIBOR. In 1984 LIBOR was 12 per cent and US Prime Rate was 13 per cent. As regards new loan spreads, the fall from 2.25 per cent above LIBOR in 1983 to 1.5 per cent above LIBOR in 1984, was even greater (0.75 per cent) than the fall in spreads on rescheduled debt for the same period.

The IMF, clearly delighted at Mexico's success in adjusting in 1983, made a great concession in 1984. In 1982 and 1983, the IMF's agreements with Mexico were high-conditionality. In 1984 high-conditionality ended. The IMF agreed that Mexico need only consult with the IMF in a slightly more elaborate manner than all members do with the Fund under Article 4 of the IMF's Charter of Incorporation. This means, in practical terms, that IMF credit to Mexico is unconditional. This has never been given to a country in debt crisis. It was proof, if proof was needed, that Mexico was out of debt crisis. The fact that Mexico got this is also proof of the IMF's high regard for Mexico. It is significant that Brazil, Argentina, and Yugoslavia, who were immediately affected by the precedent set by the Mexican agreements of September 1984, asked for similar arrangements with the IMF: they were all refused.

While Brazil and Yugoslavia will probably get a long-term rescheduling of a large proportion of their total debt in 1985 or 1986, given the precedent set by Mexico and the realisation among creditors that putting the rescheduling process into a long-term time-frame is the most rational option to follow, it is most unlikely that the IMF will agree to end its high-conditionality agreements with them. The IMF's agreement with Brazil during Phase II was modified to take account of Brazil's unique inflation problem, but Yugoslavia is still in a high-conditionality agreement with the IMF.

The reason for this is that Yugoslavia, though it has made considerable progress in its economic adjustment since 1983, has some way to go before it fully consolidates that progress. In 1983 Yugoslavia required a $4.5 billion rescue package. In 1984 it required a $3 billion package. Of that 1984 package, the banks provided $1.5 billion in new money. The terms were an improvement on the terms demanded for the $1 billion lent by the banks in 1983. The spread paid in 1983, for example, was 1.75 per cent over LIBOR. The 1984 spread over LIBOR was 1.5 per cent. About the same as Yugoslavia was paying before it went into crisis in 1981.

The high-risk premium charged by banks in 1982 and 1983 was removed in 1984, and it has been accepted by Yugoslavia's creditors that a long-term rescheduling to cover the $3.5 billion of principal due every year from 1985 to 1988 should be negotiated in 1985.[27] The IMF, however, has insisted, despite the Yugoslavian Government's objections, that a further high-conditionality IMF stand-by agreement be signed after the current agreement expired on 31 March 1985. The IMF knows full well that if external IMF pressure to persuade Yugoslavia to adjust were removed, then the Yugoslav Government, for domestic political reasons, would revert to its irresponsible economic policies of the 1970s. The domestic economic costs of adjustment, in terms of lower GDP growth and lower living standards, have been high. The Government, acutely aware of these economic costs and their potential political implications, would like to rid itself of IMF agreements, but is realistic enough to know that such agreements are unavoidable if Yugoslavia is to retain the confidence of its foreign creditors.

In the rest of South America (other than Brazil and Mexico), the realisation that reaching an agreement with the IMF was unavoidable became very strong in 1984. Argentina, the supposed *enfant terrible* of the 1982–4 rescheduling process, came to an agreement with the IMF in December 1984 after over a year of prolonged, infuriating (to its creditors), and rather pointless negotiations—pointless in the sense that Argentina, despite all its radical rhetoric about the debt crisis and its constant brinkmanship in its negotiations with its creditors, had little substantive to show for its efforts since 1983. The negotiations, too byzantine in their complexity to present here, were even more difficult than Phase II in Brazil.

The main problem was that Argentina wanted to negotiate a deal on its own terms. Those terms, which were far removed from what the banking market wanted to charge Argentina, were unacceptable to the advisory committee. In the event the terms Argentina got in December 1984, despite its calculated policy of brinksmanship, bluff, and delay in the negotiations with the advisory committee, were those its creditors found acceptable. The pressure failed. Argentina's creditors could not, and did not submit, to such pressure, despite the risks they ran (to their assets in Argentina) by refusing to give in. To have done so would have created a precedent that would have plagued them in their concurrent negotiations with Brazil and Mexico.

In the end, Argentina obtained a rescheduling of $16.5 billion (out of a total debt of $45 billion) of public sector debt over twelve years, and $4.2 billion of new loans from the banks with a maturity of twelve years, and $1.4 billion from the IMF. The IMF credit is high-conditionality, whereby Argentina has agreed (among other things) to reduce its budget deficit, and to reduce its inflation rate of 675 per cent in 1984 to 300 per cent by mid-1985.

As regards the rescheduled debt and the new loans of 1984, the terms that Argentina received are an improvement on what the last military Government obtained in 1982, but not as good as Mexico obtained in 1984. In addition, and unlike Mexico, Argentina was obliged to accept a high-conditionality IMF agreement, upon which the disbursement of all new credit depends. Avoiding proper economic adjustment, which is what the Argentinian Government led by President Alfonsin wanted to achieve during its negotiations of 1983–4, is simply not possible in the real world. Brazil, Mexico, and Yugoslavia learnt that simple fact long before 1984. Argentina took until 1984 to learn it.

Only one country, Venezuela, managed to put together a rescheduling package without the formal participation of the IMF in 1984. The fact that the country is a member of OPEC with considerable oil revenues, that it is politically stable, and that its Government's domestic macroeconomic policies are very responsible (inflation, for example, was only 16 per cent in 1984), are the reasons for the absence of the IMF.

The Venezuelan Government, though it has avoided a

politically unpopular agreement with the IMF, is adjusting its economy by implementing a very tight monetary policy, cutting imports, and keeping the budget deficit to a very low (by South American standards) 2.5 per cent of GDP by implementing a tight fiscal policy. The IMF, though not formally involved, is reported to have informally supported the rescheduling package put together by the Venezuelan advisory committee. Without the informal IMF support, given the power of the IMF in the rescheduling process, it is improbable that the Venezuelan package could have been put together.

The package, agreed in September 1984, reschedules $20.7 billion of public sector debt due between 1983 and 1988, with a maturity of twelve years (no grace period). The long-term nature of the rescheduling, along with the fact that the rescheduled debt constitutes a significant proportion of Venezuela's total debt ($34 billion), makes it comparable to the Mexican agreement of 1984. However, the absence of a grace period and a high spread over LIBOR, makes it more costly than the Mexican agreement of 1984. Though Venezuela has adjusted, the absence of the IMF means that a risk premium was levied in 1984 on Venezuela by the banks. The Government's adversion to the IMF had to be paid for. Had the IMF been involved, and given Venezuela's good adjustment record, it seems unlikely that a risk premium would have been levied in 1984.

The absence of the IMF makes Venezuela unique in South America. An important precedent has been set, as Venezuela has shown that a country, given the right circumstances, can reschedule without the IMF being formally involved. However, Venezuela's circumstances do not, as yet, exist anywhere else in South America, and it seems therefore unlikely that any other country will be able to avoid the IMF at the present time. Peru, Chile, Bolivia, Ecuador, Uruguay, and Paraguay have rescheduled/adjusted, or are in the process of, rescheduling/ adjusting with the help of the IMF. Only Colombia, because of its highly lucrative illegal drug exports to the United States, has avoided rescheduling its debts. The example of Colombia seems to prove that crime does pay.

By the beginning of 1985, the period of consolidation was well advanced, although the consolidation process was somewhat tentative in countries like Brazil. It was at its strongest in Mexico, which was just about able to tap commercial banks for voluntary credits on terms that did not involve a high-risk premium being levied. If involuntary lending ends in Mexico in 1985, and if Brazil fully consolidates its tentative consolidation of 1984, then the term 'debt crisis' will no longer be applicable. These two countries are, and always have been, the most important problem cases. The rescheduling/adjustment process has brought Mexico out of crisis, and well on the way to recovery and normal relations with its foreign creditors. It may do the same for Brazil later in 1985. If Brazil and Mexico pull through, then the second-tier problem debtors such as Argentina, Venezuela, and Yugoslavia should not pose too much of a problem for the IMF and the advisory committees in 1985.

Notes

1. Cline, op. cit., p. 87.
2. Jeff Frieden, 'Third World Indebted Industrialization: International Finance and State Capitalism in Mexico, Brazil, Algeria and South Korea', *International Organisation*, Vol. 35, No. 3, summer 1981, p. 409.
3. The Paris Club reschedulings of the 1950s and 1960s are discussed in Henry J. Bitterman, *The Refunding of International Debt* (Durham, North Carolina: Duke University Press, 1973). The reschedulings of the 1970s are discussed in Chandra S. Hardy, *Rescheduling Developing-Country Debts, 1956–1981: Lessons and Recommednations* (Washington, DC: Overseas Development Council, 1982).
4. Discussed in more detail in Jeffrey E. Garten, 'Rescheduling Sovereign Debt: Is There a Better Approach?', *World Economy*, Vol. 5, No. 3, November 1982.
5. Hardy (1982), op. cit., p. 30
6. Ibid., p. 29.
7. Ibid., p. 25.
8. The origins of the Polish debt crisis are discussed in Richard Portes, 'East Europe's Debt: Interdependence is a Two-Way Street', *Foreign Affairs*, Vol. 55, No. 4, July 1977; the 1981 crisis and the subsequent rescheduling negotiations are discussed in Darrell Delamaide, *Debt Shock* (London: Weidenfeld & Nicolson, 1984), Chapter 4, and in *Economist Survey*, op. cit., pp. 10–22.
9. *Economist Survey*, op. cit., p. 16.
10. Discussed in more detail in Barbara Stallings and Julian Martel, 'Public Debt and Private Profit: International Finance in Peru and

Argentina', *NACLA Report*, Vol. XII, No. 4, July/August 1978 (New York: North American Congress on Latin America).

11. *Economist Survey*, op. cit., p. 16.

12. The Nicaraguan negotiations are discussed in Richard S. Weinert, 'Nicaragua's Debt Renegotiations', *Cambridge Journal of Economics*, No. 5, 1981, pp. 187–94.

13. The literature on the specific topic of commercial bank debt re-rescheduling negotiations is sparse (in comparison to what has been written on the Paris Club), but the following provide general discussions of the topic: Mendelsohn, op. cit.; Group of Thirty, *Rescheduling Techniques: Papers Presented to an International Conference on Sovereign Debt, London, 3 and 4 November, 1983* (London: OYEZ IBC Ltd. for the Group of Thirty, New York); Garten, op. cit.; John Mathis, 'Lessons Learned From International Debt Reschedulings', *Journal of Commercial Bank Lending*, January 1983; Peter E. Leslie, 'The Techniques For Debt Rescheduling', in *The Euromarkets in 1983: Papers Presented to an International Conference on The Euromarkets, London, 8 and 9 March, 1983* (London: Financial Times Conferences); W. G. Wickersham, 'Rescheduling of Sovereign Debt', *International Financial Law Review*, September 1982.

14. See Mendelsohn, op. cit., for a comparative analysis of the Mexican and Brazilian rescheduling experiences, and Joseph Kraft, *The Mexican Rescue* (New York: Group of Thirty, 1984), for a detailed analysis of the Mexican rescheduling experience.

15. See Mendelsohn, op. cit., for the Brazilian negotiations up to mid-1983.

16. For Yugoslavia, see Milivojević (1983), op. cit., for the period up to 1983. For the 1983–5 period, see Milivojević (1985), op. cit.

17. On Hungary, see Padraic Fallon and David Shireff, 'The Betrayal of Eastern Europe', *Euromoney*, September 1982.

18. The literature on the IMF is extensive. The following have been the most useful in this study: Graham Bird, 'A role for the IMF in Economic Development', *Banca Nazionale de Lavoro Quarterly Review*, December 1982, and 'The Banks and the IMF-Division of Labour', *Lloyds Bank Review*, No. 150, October 1983; Sidney Dell, *On Being Grandmotherly: The Evolution of IMF Conditionality*, Princeton Essays in International Finance No. 144 (Princeton, NJ: Princeton University Press, 1981); Martin Honeywell (ed.), *The Poverty Brokers: The IMF and Latin America* (London: Latin American Bureau, 1983); Karel Jansen (ed.), *Monetarism, Economic Crisis and the Third World* (London: Frank Cass, 1983); Tony Killick (ed.), *Adjustment and Financing in the Developing World: The Role of the IMF* (London/Washington, DC: Overseas Development Institute/IMF, 1982), and *The Quest For Economic Stabilization: The IMF and the Third World*

(London: Heinemann, 1984); Cheryl Payer, *The Debt Trap: The IMF and the Third World* (Harmondsworth: Penguin, 1974); Corrado Pirzio-Biroli, 'Making Sense of the IMF Conditionality Debate', *Journal of World Trade Law*, October 1983; John Williamson, *The Lending Policies of the IMF* (Washington, DC: Institute for International Economics, 1982), and *IMF Conditionality* (Washington, DC; IFIE, 1983).

19. Honeywell, op. cit., and Payer, op. cit., are representative of criticism coming from the left of the political spectrum. They criticise the IMF in terms of the North/South debtate. Like the extreme left, the extreme right is also against the IMF, though for very different reasons. Two representative right-wing views are as follows: Karl Brunner, 'International Debt, Insolvency and Illiquidity', *Journal of Economic Affairs*, Vol. 3, No. 3, April 1983, and Roland Vaubel, 'The Moral Hazard of IMF Lending', *World Economy*, September 1983. The right-wing view, which believes that the market should sort out the debt crisis, is against the bail-out of banks and developing countries by the IMF. Most observers and economists in the OECD countries, however, accept the need for the IMF to be involved with developing countries. In South America, though the left-wing does criticise the IMF, the issue is more in terms of foreigners (the IMF) infringing national sovereignty. A good critique of the IMF's activities in South America is in Réne Villarreal, *The Monetarist Counter-Revolution* (Mexico City: El Colegio de Mexico, 1983).

20. Fully discussed in Pirzio-Biroli, op. cit. Briefly, high-conditionality means placing greater demands (in terms of tougher targets for inflation, the budget deficit, etc.) on the debtor country in return for IMF credits, the disbursement of which is conditional upon staying within the targets agreed with the IMF. Low-conditionality means very few demands on the debtor country. To all intents and purposes, low-conditionality means no real conditionality at all—unconditional credit.

21. The increase in IMF power and influence after 1982 is discussed in Peter Field, 'The IMF and Central Banks, Flex Their Muscles', *Euromoney*, January 1983.

22. Most notably, William R. Cline, *International Monetary Reform and the Developing Countries* (Washington, DC: Brookings Institute, 1976); Jessica P. Einhorn, 'International Bank Lending: Expanding The Dialogue', *Columbia Journal of World Business*, Fall 1978, and 'Co-operation Between Public and Private Lenders To the Third World', *World Economy*, May 1979.

23. Profiled in Neil Osborn, 'The Rhodes Show Goes On and On', *Euromoney*, March 1984. His British equivalent, Mr Guy Huntrods of Lloyds Bank International, served as deputy chairman of the Brazilian

advisory committee under Rhodes. Huntrods is profiled in the *Guardian*, 17 December 1984.

24. Kraft, op. cit., p. 53.
25. Alan Robinson, 'One by One, They Come to Terms', *Euromoney*, March 1984.
26. Ibid.
27. David Buchan and Alexander Lebt, 'Yugoslavia Battles to Keep the IMF at Bay', *Financial Times*, 20 November 1984.

4 The implications of the debt rescheduling process, 1982–1984

4.1 Involuntary lending

The phenomenon of involuntary, or forced, lending may be defined as being the increase in banks' exposure in developing countries that are rescheduling their debts and that, because of the increase in country and sovereign risk inherent in the rescheduling process, are unable to attract voluntary lending from banks not already exposed in such countries. The phenomenon of involuntary lending was present in every developing country involved in the rescheduling process. Of the $30 billion lent to all non-oil developing countries by commercial banks in 1983, for example, $15 billion was involuntary lending to countries involved in the rescheduling process such as Brazil, Mexico, Argentina, and Yugoslavia.[1]

While the IMF's imposition of conditions on banks during the rescue packages of 1982–3 were obviously an important cause of involuntary lending by banks, it would be wrong to assume, therefore, that IMF pressure was the only cause of the involuntary lending that did take place.

J. M. Keynes[2] once remarked that if an individual owed £100 to a bank, then the individual had a problem; but if the individual owed £1 million to a bank, then the bank had a problem. The greater the exposure of a bank in a developing country with debt servicing problems, the more the bank in question sinks into the so-called 'lender's trap'. Such a trap means, in effect, that banks with large exposures in developing countries must lend new money during the rescheduling process in order to ensure that their outstanding assets in such countries remain performing, and, therefore, on the banks' books. New lending in such circumstances was induced by the desire to protect outstanding assets and to obey the demands of the IMF. Which of these two essentially negative reasons for new lending was more important is irrelevant. The point was that new lending was taking place in circumstances radically different from normal times, when creditors had real freedom of choice. During the rescheduling process, banks with very large exposures in developing countries lost their freedom of choice.

The literature[3] on Euromarket bank lending to developing countries, which grew very fast during the 1970s, sees such lending in terms that were invalidated by the rescheduling process. Banks, operating out of the unregulated Euromarket, assessed the creditworthiness of developing countries, found them creditworthy or otherwise, and priced their loans in accordance with the conclusions they had reached as regards the country and sovereign risk present in the countries concerned. Banks had real freedom of choice—especially during the early 1970s—as they could stop lending if they so wished. Despite the relatively high risks of lending to developing countries, high profits prompted banks to continue increasing their exposures in developing countries. Yet the larger that exposure became, the less control and freedom of choice the banks concerned really had. The rescheduling process, which revealed that many banks had no real freedom of choice in the developing countries concerned, was merely the culmination of that earlier (especially during the late 1970s) erosion of banks' real freedom of choice.

Ironically, the very dynamic of seeking to avoid political interference in the lending process, which was the *raison d'être* of the Euromarkets, led to a set of circumstances, during the rescheduling process, when such political interference in the lending process did reach large and totally unprecedented proportions. Moreover, the IMF was, in effect, ordering the banks to lend in circumstances that no bank, utilising normal creditworthiness criteria to assess country and sovereign risk, would have lent new money. Yet the IMF, despite its orders to banks, was unwilling, and unable under its own Articles of Agreement, to offer any sort of official guarantees or insurance for the security of the new assets committed by banks as a result of the IMF's orders.

The IMF said, in effect, either you (the banks) lend, and thereby ensure your outstanding assets remain performing, or you risk losing everything by not lending, because if you do not lend, neither will the IMF. The basic dynamic of involuntary lending, therefore, was one in which banks increased their out-standing exposure by providing new loans. This new dynamic would prevail as long as banks thought that such new lending would ensure that outstanding assets would remain performing, and would thereby lessen the risk of default, and that such new lending was not just a case of throwing new money after bad money.

At the beginning of the rescheduling process in 1982, when all the concerned countries were in *de facto* default (being in arrears on principal due), it was extremely difficult, if not impossible, to know whether or not it was just a case of throwing good money after bad money. Many small and medium-sized banks, with relatively small exposures in the countries concerned, thought it was a case of throwing good money after bad, and no amount of pressure from advisory committees and the IMF could induce them to increase their outstanding exposure by lending new money. For the large banks, who dominated the advisory committees, it was a choice between *de facto* default now (1982) or *de jure* default (if no new money was lent) in the future. Whereas *de facto* default was a possibility even if new loans were made, *de facto* and *de jure* default (as banks declared countries to be in default) would be inevitable if no new loans were made, given the attitude of the IMF, which would not lend to developing countries if banks refused to provide new loans.

The existing (1982) circumstances were obviously important factors that banks considered as they decided whether or not to provide new loans, but probable future circumstances were even more important in the decision-making process for new loan disbursement. The banks concerned would provide addi-tional new loans as long as the reduction in the probability of *de jure* default in the future thereby achieved exceeded the probability of *de facto* and *de jure* default after the disburse-ment of those new loans. During the rescheduling process, and especially in the period 1982–3, the reduction in the initial probability of *de jure* default did exceed the probability of future *de facto* and *de jure* default, as the new money disbursed by banks, the IMF, and OECD Governments proved sufficient to reduce the probability of future default by the developing countries involved in that process.

However, it was not until 1984 and the consolidation phase

of the rescheduling process, that the combination of new credit disbursement, local economic adjustment, and slower, local, total debt growth created the circumstances in which banks could again consider the possibility of voluntary lending. Only Mexico, and then only some time in 1985, is in a position to say that it is nearly able to attract voluntary lending from its creditor banks. For all other developing countries, however, all new credit disbursement is still involuntary and is at far lower levels than prevailed prior to 1982—a situation that is likely to prevail until well into 1985.

Overall, however, and especially after the successful completion of the major rescue operations of 1982–3, the risk inherent in the rescheduling process decreased. This lower risk was reflected in the improved terms—longer maturities, lower spreads, and lower fees—granted to developing countries for rescheduled debt and new loans in 1984. The improved terms of 1984, and especially the terms granted to Mexico in that year, indicated that no high-risk premium was being levied by banks in 1984. The terms granted to Mexico, for example, were about the same as when Mexico was paying prior to 1982. However, new loan disbursements were still low and involuntary: normal relations between commercial banks and developing countries remains a thing of the future.

4.2 Free riders

The phenomenon of involuntary lending is something that disproportionately affected large banks with large exposures in developing countries, as many small and medium-sized banks refused to lend any new money. These small banks are classic free riders, in that they took advantage of the increased quality of their outstanding assets in developing countries— a manœuvre made possible as a result of the new loans provided by the large banks—but at the same time failed to incur any additional risk themselves by extending new loans to developing countries.

The phenomenon of free riders is well known in international affairs,[4] but it was not something that was associated with international banking until the advent of the rescheduling process, when it became a major problem. It would not have been a problem if commercial bank lending had been the exclusive concern of the large banks. The top nine US banks, for example, accounted for around 60 per cent of all US bank lending to developing countries. As regards West European and Japanese banks, virtually all lending to developing countries from such banks was made by large banks. However, because of the importance of small banks in the US, the overall situation was one in which a large number of small and medium-sized banks accounted for a significant proportion of total commercial bank lending to developing countries. This fact made it very difficult to resolve the free-rider problem in the rescheduling process.

At first glance it seems strange why the free-rider problem emerged at all, as, despite existing in a highly competitive Euromarket, banks had developed techniques that had the effect of increasing interdependence and integration in that market. The inter-bank market, syndicated lending, consortium banking, and correspondent banking are all examples of interdependence and integration.[5] In addition, technical developments such as Electronic Funds Transfer (EFT) also contributed to the process of integration. However, despite such integration in the Euromarkets, the concept of co-operation to resolve crisis in a highly competitive environment was not well developed. Mutually beneficial integrative developments that increase profits, such as syndicated lending, are very different from collective co-operative action to safeguard the stability of the international financial system as a whole. Such action yields no profit in the short-term, and can involve a loss. So, while the stability of the overall system was a worthy objective in theory, its highly abstract and general nature was far removed from the individualistic, practical, and untheoretical mentality of banks operating in a highly competitive environment in which individual survival was the primary objective of every bank.

In normal times such arguments were, in any case, purely academic, but in the context of the rescheduling process they became very important. That process revealed that integrative developments among banks in normal times were no guarantee of co-operation between banks in times of crisis. Many small and medium-sized banks simply pulled out of the lending process to developing countries once the seriousness of that crisis had become apparent. Of the 1,400 banks that had lent to Mexico on a regular basis prior to 1982, only 562 banks lent new money to that country in 1982 and 1983. While the amounts such small individual banks could provide were small, the cumulative effect of many such banks refusing to lend new money was to place a greater burden on the larger banks who were lending new money. In both Brazil and Mexico, to take only the most important debtors, the raising of new loans by advisory committees became a central problem.

The problem was particularly acute in Brazil. As in Mexico, there was a limit (7 per cent of outstanding exposure) as regards the amount of new money banks involved in the process had to contribute. Despite the actions of the free riders, the large banks were unwilling to go over 7 per cent of outstanding exposure, and the end result of this was a gap between what the banks were prepared to lend and what Brazil required. One of the major tasks of the Brazilian advisory committee was to eliminate that gap. It failed to do so in 1983 during Phase I. While Brazil asked for $10 billion in inter-bank lines in late 1982, only $6 billion was raised by the advisory committee by mid-1983.

The advisory committees and the IMF never did solve the problem of free riders. With the help of Central Banks they did manage, however, to make the problem far less serious than it could have been, by exerting great pressure on many banks that may have been tempted to become free riders. Without that constant pressure, it seems certain that the free-rider problem would have been far worse than in fact it was.

How, then, did advisory committees and the IMF attempt to deal with free riders? Mancur Olson, in his classic study[6] of the free-rider phenomenon, identified the three options that were, in fact, used in the rescheduling process:

1. *Argument*

In arguing for the essential stability of the international financial system in the interest of all banks, it must follow that collective co-operative action by all such banks to safeguard that stability is the only rational course of action to take.

2. *Positive incentives*

Since argument, however rational, is rarely enough to convince people, then offering positive incentives to lend is the next step. In the rescheduling process this meant the levying of a high-risk premium on rescheduled debt and new loans, which meant higher profits and a higher rate of return on the new assets so committed. At this stage self-interest, coupled with friendly peer group pressure, is of primary importance.

3. *Negative incentives*

If the positive incentives fail, then negative incentives must be used. Threats to use punitive methods are the norm at this stage of the game. Advisory committees made overt threats to publish the names of recalcitrant banks. The IMF and Central Banks exerted covert pressure on recalcitrant banks. Central Bank pressure, in particular, became intense if recalcitrant banks attempted to begin legal proceedings against particular developing countries to have them declared to be in formal *de jure* default. At this stage unfriendly peer group pressure, coupled with threats of punitive action by official institutions, is of primary importance.

In the rescheduling process the first option, rational argument, was rarely enough of a reason in itself to ensure co-operation from determined free riders. For large banks, however, it was an important reason, for if their large assets in developing countries had to be written off, then the possible consequences for the system as a whole could be very serious. For the IMF, systemic stability was always the main reason for its actions in the rescheduling process. For free-rider banks, with relatively small exposures in developing countries, it was no argument at all. As long as they felt safer as a result of not providing new loans, as was certainly the case, then arguments about the hypothetical threats to the system as a whole in the future did not interest them. Each small recalcitrant bank, moreover, argued that its failure to provide a small sum of money could not possibly increase instability in the system as a whole. For individual banks this was indeed true, but if a large number of such banks did this then it was untrue.

The second option, positive incentives, did not unduly

impress the free riders, as the profits they could expect on small loans would be too small to justify further exposure in a high-risk environment. For large banks the positive incentives were most attractive. Their outstanding assets remained performing and they could look forward to large profits on the large new loans they disbursed to developing countries in the rescheduling process.

The third option, negative incentives, was reserved for those really determined free riders who had disregarded the first two options. These incentives were mostly threats to punish, in one way or another, the recalcitrant banks. However, there was a limit to such threats in free-market economic systems that existed in democratic countries.

As regards the developing countries, they were able to put forward a number of negative incentives to recalcitrant banks. Firstly, they made it clear that such banks would not be welcome in the future when normal times returned. Secondly, although it was a very risky option, they made it clear that the outstanding assets of recalcitrant banks would be treated less favourably than those of co-operative banks when it came to the allocation of foreign exchange for debt service purposes. This threat was openly articulated in Mexico, and there is some evidence[7] to suggest that the outstanding assets of recalcitrant banks were discriminated against by the Mexican Government. This discrimination consisted of allowing arrears of principal and interest payments that were due to build up, while paying the arrears of principal and interest on the assets of co-operative banks. Such tactics were risky, in that they could provoke legal proceedings by recalcitrant banks, which would have proved disastrous for the country concerned due to the existence of cross-default clauses in all syndicated loan contracts. Such legal proceedings—to have the debtor country concerned (in this case Mexico) declared to be in formal default —were only averted by great pressure from the US Federal Reserve Board on the US banks concerned.

Such great covert pressure was common in the United States, where there was no tradition of friendly co-operation between the Central Bank and commercial banks. In the United Kingdom, in complete contrast, there was a long tradition of Bank of England leadership in times of crisis. It was enough for the Bank of England informally to request the big UK banks to be co-operative in the rescheduling process. More generally, Central Bank authorities turned a blind eye to the use of a network of influence that large banks had among small recalcitrant banks. Threats were made to exclude such banks from future syndicated lending (with the full support of the developing country concerned), to terminate correspondent banking facilities provided to such banks, and to cut inter-bank lines to such banks.

However, despite the intensity of this tripartite (from banks, Central Banks/IMF, developing countries) pressure on free-rider banks, a certain number—especially in the United States —refused to co-operate. In the final analysis, nothing could be, nor was, done, to deal with such determined free riders.

4.3 Primacy of politics

One of the unintended consequences of the growth of com-mercial bank lending to developing countries during the 1970s, and the concurrent decline in official lending to such countries during the same period, was the unprecedented growth of political interference in the lending process during the re-scheduling process of 1982–4. The problems of the rescheduling process were not resolved through the market, but through political action by the IMF, Central Banks, and OECD Govern-ments, with advisory committees playing a complementary role to the leadership role of the IMF. That political action by official institutions raised many questions about the inter-national political and regulatory framework[8] within which commercial banks existed.

During the 1970s, when official lending to developing coun-tries declined, the IMF and Central Banks praised the com-mercial banks for their role in recycling OPEC surpluses to developing countries in the process of adjustment to the oil price increases of 1973–4 and 1979–80. Yet in the context of the rescheduling process of 1982–4, and by looking at the events of the 1970s retrospectively, many commentators,[9] and indeed some central bankers,[10] criticised the growth of com-mercial bank lending to developing countries during the 1970s. That debt growth was said to be irresponsible, unsustainable, and bound to lead to debt crisis eventually. Many banks felt such retrospective criticisms were unjust, given the fact that the IMF and Central Banks had not criticised that debt growth during the 1970s. On the contrary, they had praised it. Such criticisms, which blamed the banks for the mess they found themselves in and suggested they should not be bailed out by the IMF, were particularly strong in the United States. In the US Congress in 1983, for example, there was significant opposition to the Reagan Administration's plan to double the US quota to the IMF.[11]

While the commercial banks were criticised for excessive lending in the 1970s, they were also criticised—by the IMF— for not lending enough during the rescheduling process of 1982-4. It became clear that there was some deficiency in an international financial system that led to an excess of lending in the 1970s, yet resulted in a severe shortage of lending in the 1980s. Such oscillations, which tended to increase the instability of the system as a whole, were clearly undesirable.

Were the operations of the commercial banks the cause of these defects, or merely the consequences of them? In the 1970s, official creditors had been politically unwilling to lend the amounts of money required by developing countries. They had given the green light for banks to lend, they had praised the financial intermediatory activities of these banks in the developing countries, and they had not criticised the growth in total debt until the early 1980s. Commercial banks, faced with profitable opportunities in developing countries, were only too happy to replace official creditors and become the principal creditors of the developing countries. However, because of official encouragement for these developments in the 1970s, there was an implicit assumption among commercial banks that the IMF, Central Banks, and OECD Governments would come to the aid of developing countries that ran into trouble as a result of their debts. There was also an implicit assumption among commercial banks that a lender of last resort existed to safeguard the stability of the international financial system in general, and the assets of commercial banks tied up in developing countries in particular.

The high risks faced by banks in developing countries, if these implicit assumptions were accepted to be true (as they were), were thereby partly externalised[12] from the commercial banks to the international political and regulatory framework in which such banks existed. Without these assumptions being made, it is unlikely that bank lending to developing countries would have grown at the rate it did during the 1970s and early 1980s.

How valid were these implicit assumptions? The East European debt crisis, which was a prologue to the main debt crisis of 1982, badly damaged the validity of similar assumptions that had been made about bank lending in the communist world. In Eastern Europe the banks had assumed that the Soviet Union was the lender of last resort, and it would, therefore, bail out Poland, Romania, and Hungary in the early 1980s. This assumption was totally false. The Soviet Union did not provide an 'umbrella' to protect, aid, or in any way bail out these countries. Indeed, it was the West—the IMF in Romania and the BIS in Hungary—that provided the 'umbrella'. In Poland, although no official Western institutions were involved (other than the Paris Club), only the patience and indulgence of commercial banks prevented a total disaster in that country.

The assumption that a protective cocoon existed that somehow protected the assets of banks, and thereby reduced the risks faced by such banks, was proved to be false in Eastern Europe—as far as the Soviet Union was concerned. The same assumption also existed as regards commercial bank lending to developing countries. The big question after the sobering experience of Eastern Europe was whether that assumption was, or indeed ever had been, valid as regards developing countries.

The assumption is that a lender of last resort exists. Like all implicit assumptions, it is more an article of faith than a statement of provable fact. A great deal of ambiguity exists as to whether or not such a lender of last resort does, in fact, exist. In 1975, immediately after the shock caused by the Herstatt collapse in West Germany and the secondary banking crisis in the United Kingdom, the BIS issued a key document,[13] which stated that while supervisory responsibility for overseas branches of banks lies with parent-country Central Banks, the overseas subsidiaries of such banks were the supervisory responsibility of host-country Central Banks. Since many of the latter were either weak (developing countries), or purely nominal (offshore banking centres), in 1983—after the Ambrosiano collapse in Italy—the BIS issued another document,[14] which stated that banks should be solely supervised by parent-country central banks on a globally consolidated basis.

While this 1983 BIS document clarified who was responsible for what, as regards supervisory responsibilities, they did not even mention who, if anybody, was responsible for lender of last-resort responsibilities. Indeed, a top Bank of England official, who chaired the committee that produced the 1975 and 1983 BIS documents, stated that 'there should not necessarily be considered to be any automatic link between acceptance of responsibility for ongoing supervision and the assumption of a lender of last resort role'.[15]

In addition, both the BIS statements on supervisory responsibilities, make a sharp distinction between banks' illiquidity and insolvency. The relevant Central Bank authorities would provide assistance to illiquid banks so as to prevent them from becoming insolvent, but this sharp distinction means, in effect, that there is no official guarantee of survival for banks whose problems in developing countries become so serious as to render them insolvent. However, although insolvency is a possibility in such a situation, it is unlikely that if a bank became illiquid as a direct result of its operations in developing countries, the relevant Central Bank would probably step in to prevent illiquidity from developing into insolvency.

There is, in fact, no formal lender of last resort in the international financial system. There is, on the other hand, formal and informal co-operation between Central Banks in the BIS, and a mutual commitment among such Central Banks, along with the IMF, to take remedial action so as to ensure that a local problem (like the debt crisis faced by developing countries) does not develop into a general crisis in the international financial system.

Though there is a mutual commitment to take remedial action, and though co-operation is highly developed by Central Banks in the BIS, there is still much that divides Central Banks on such matters as provision levels, capital/assets ratios, and dividend retention levels. These differences in regulatory practices, born of different banking and regulatory systems, have, however, been lessened by the moves in the BIS to harmonise regulatory practices, and these differences are less important than the co-operative mechanisms that exist in the BIS and that exist between finance ministers in the IMF. That co-operation between official institutions proved its efficacity during the rescheduling process of 1982–4.

If there is considerable doubt as to whether Central Bank authorities are the elusive lenders of last resort, there is no doubt that the IMF, which played the leading role in the rescheduling process, is not the lender of last resort. This has raised many questions about the role of the IMF in the rescheduling process in general, and its role in the development of involuntary lending by banks to developing countries in particular.

Since the IMF did put great pressure on banks to provide new loans during the rescheduling process, it was argued by banks that it should take at least partial responsibility for, or in some way guarantee the security of, the new loans made available by banks in circumstances of high risk. However, despite exerting great pressure to lend, the IMF's Articles of Agreement precluded the Fund from offering any guarantee, be it *de facto* or *de jure*, for these new loans.

The IMF's policy of exerting pressure on banks to provide new loans, and the fact that the IMF was unable to guarantee the security of such new assets if something went badly wrong in the countries concerned, attracted a great deal of criticism, mostly from the banks. But this issue also prompted the only split between the IMF and the BIS during the rescheduling process, when the BIS's President, Dr Fritz Leutwiler, publicly criticised the IMF for urging banks to extend large inter-bank lines to Brazil during Phase I in 1983. He argued that such pressure on the part of the IMF—to do something that could prove damaging to the banks concerned, but for which the IMF was unable to accept responsibility—was morally wrong.

Though not a formal lender of last resort, the IMF did disburse loans to, and enforced economic adjustment programmes in, developing countries so as to reduce the likelihood of such countries defaulting, and it also ensured that the bank assets tied up in such countries remained performing. This reduction of overall risk, which took place in the rescheduling process, was a form of indirect aid to the banks from the IMF. However, during the emergency response stage of the rescheduling process (1982–4), it appeared to many banks that the IMF was increasing the risk for banks, by being the cause of involuntary lending. In the medium term, and especially towards the end of the consolidation phase of the rescheduling process (1984), it was clear that the cumulative effect of the IMF's policies was to lessen the risk for all banks involved in lending to developing countries.

Given the primacy of the IMF and the Central Banks in the rescheduling process, and given their overall primacy in the international financial system in so far as they set the basic rules of the game, the long-term implications of the IMF–Central Banks–OECD Governments/commercial banks partnership that developed in the rescheduling process are bound to be significant. The *status quo ante* of the 1970s, in which there was a distinct lack of symmetry between official and commercial bank lending to developing countries, was gone forever. Despite the tensions inherent in the IMF/commercial bank relationship, the sense of co-operation and co-ordination it engendered may lead to a more evenly balanced disbursement of new loans to developing countries by banks, the IMF, and other official creditors, without the undesirable oscillations in disbursement levels characteristic of the 1970s and early 1980s. A more rational, ordered, and efficient way of financing development in developing countries may emerge out of this partnership.

As regards the banks, one of the positive things to emerge out of the rescheduling process was a new spirit of co-operation, leaving aside the problem of free riders for the moment. This co-operation was particularly strong between banks that served on advisory committees. The tangible consequence of that co-operative spirit was the establishment of the Institute of International Finance in January 1983.[16] For full details see Appendix 10. The Institute aimed to collect and disseminate information on developing countries to member banks, to encourage contacts between the Governments of developing countries and banks, and to improve liaison between banks and institutions like the IMF and the World Bank.

4.4 Symbiosis and asymmetrical adjustment

From 1973 to 1982, the commercial bank/developing country relationship that developed into an important aspect of the international financial system, can be said to be symbiotic: a mutually beneficial relationship between two different kinds of entities. For the commercial banks, the relationship produced higher profits than could have been earned on assets invested in OECD countries. For the developing countries, the relationship resulted in higher rates of economic growth than would have been possible had no foreign borrowing taken place.

Although a controversy exists in the literature[17] as to whether so much foreign borrowing was desirable, the majority view in developing countries was that purely domestic savings were not adequate for the ambitious development programmes envisaged by the Governments of those countries. The relative merits of whether to put emphasis on economic development that primarily relies on foreign borrowing, or to rely primarily on domestic savings, are controversial issues, but it would be fair to say that most developing countries felt that a symbiotic relationship existed with their foreign creditors if the benefits (higher growth) accruing from that relationship exceeded the costs (debt service). In the 1973–82 period, the benefits did exceed the costs, as net resource transfer was favourable for developing countries, growth rates were consequently high, debt servicing costs were manageable due to rising exports and to nominal interest rates, and it was not, therefore, surprising that a consensus emerged in developing countries that large-scale foreign borrowing was desirable.

Historically, past events showed that foreign borrowing had always played an important role in economic development the world over. During the period 1820–1914, when the United Kingdom was the world's principal creditor nation, UK credit played a major role in financing economic development in the United States, South America, and in much of Western Europe.[18] In the inter-war years (1918–39), when the United States became the world's principal creditor nation, US credit played a major role in the economic development of South America.

During the 1973–82 period, the debate in developing countries and OECD countries alike was not over the desirability of large-scale foreign borrowing by developing countries, but over the debt servicing capacity of developing countries. It was assumed, and the literature on debt servicing capacity tended to confirm,[19] that if export earnings increased faster than debt servicing costs then there was no reason, in theory, why total debt could not grow indefinitely. That assumption was valid as long as export earnings rose and nominal interest rates kept debt servicing costs manageable, but it was invalidated by export stagnation and high real interest rates from 1980 onwards. These unfavourable developments, and the debt crisis of 1982, had the cumulative effect of raising all manner of questions that the earlier consensus on the desirability of large-scale foreign borrowing had removed from the arena of legitimate debate in developing countries.

That consensus, however, had never been total. A minority position existed in developing countries which came from nationalistic and left-wing political quarters, and which argued that large-scale foreign borrowing had the effect of increasing dependence on, and integration with, exogenous economic forces and institutions. Such critics argued that the more indebted a developing country became, the less real control it had over its economic and political destiny, and the more it became a hostage to external economic forces over which it had no control whatsoever.[20]

The events of the 1980s seemed to confirm, and made it difficult to refute, these criticisms, since unfavourable exogenous economic variables such as recession and protectionism in OECD countries, deteriorating terms of trade, and high real interest rates were the primary causes of the debt crisis of 1982. By 1982, developing countries found themselves in a very vulnerable position in relation to their creditors. They had, in fact, always been vulnerable to the consequences of a cutback in credit by their creditors, but as long as the debtor/creditor relationship was mutually beneficial the vulnerability was only potential. The increasing integration between the developing countries and the world economy, via increases in trade and borrowing from the Euromarket, made that potential vulnerability inevitable—inevitable in the sense that if developing countries wanted to increase their foreign trade and borrowing, then they had to be prepared to take the consequences (good and bad) of that integration with the world economy. Throughout the 1970s, the consequences were on the whole good, as benefits exceeded the costs of large-scale foreign borrowing. In the 1980s, and after 1982 in particular, the consequences turned bad, as the costs exceeded the benefits of large-scale foreign borrowing. Only in conditions of crisis, during the rescheduling process of 1982–4, did the developing countries involved in that process come to realise how vulnerable they had become to exogenous economic and political forces and institutions.

The critics of large-scale foreign borrowing had, in addition, always argued that the debtor/creditor relationship in the developing world was not one of equals. Although the events of 1982 revealed that creditor banks were vulnerable to the possible consequences of the debt crisis in the developing countries, they did not suffer greatly as a result of the efficacity of the rescue packages put together by the IMF during the rescheduling process. The developing countries, on the other hand, were far more vulnerable to the consequences of, and were less able to deal with, the breakdown of the normal debtor/creditor relationship than were the commercial banks.

In an international system in which economic and political power was unevenly distributed,[21] and in which the developing countries were in a weak economic position in relation to the rich creditor countries, it was inevitable that the economic adjustments that were made in the rescheduling process of 1982–4 were most asymmetrical. It was not evenly balanced adjustment by both developing and OECD countries. Instead, all the economic adjustment was done by the developing countries. The costs of adjustment were high, but only through adjustment would developing countries regain the confidence of their foreign creditors in general, and the commercial banks in particular. Table 18 shows the costs and benefits of foreign borrowing in normal and abnormal times.

Whereas during normal times foreign borrowing brought only benefits, during the abnormal times there were only costs and only one benefit. During the rescheduling process, and especially during the emergency response phase of that process (1982–3), the only benefit for developing countries was the realisation that successful economic adjustment would restore the confidence of foreign creditors. During the consolidation phase (1983–4) of the rescheduling process, however, the developing countries did benefit from improved terms on rescheduled debt and new loans, and the growing confidence of foreign creditors. Despite these small benefits, the overall situation in 1984 was one in which the costs exceeded the benefits of foreign borrowing. In particular, the very *raison d'être* of foreign borrowing, which was to transfer resources

Table 18   Costs and benefits of foreign borrowing for developing
countries in normal and abnormal times

Normal (1973–81/2)*	Abnormal (1981/2–84)*
Net resource transfer positive† (Benefit)	Net resource transfer negative‡ (Cost)
High GDP growth due to positive NRT (Benefit)	Contraction in GDP or zero GDP growth due to negative NRT and economic adjustment (Cost)
IMF absent (Benefit)	IMF present to enforce economic adjustment (Cost)
Have unconditional confidence of foreign creditors (Benefit)	Regaining confidence of foreign creditors conditional on successful economic adjustment (Benefit)
Relative political stability due to economic boom (Benefit)	Growing political instability due to economic recession (Cost)

   * Some developing countries in negative net resource transfer situation in 1981,
others in 1982. Therefore, transition from normal to abnormal times, in both 1981
and 1982.
   † Where total new loan disbursements *exceed* debt servicing costs.
   ‡ Where debt servicing costs *exceed* total new loan disbursements.

from areas of capital abundance (OECD countries) to areas of
capital scarcity (developing countries), was rendered null and
void by the existence of a negative net resource transfer situation in all the developing countries. Since the *raison d'être*
behind foreign borrowing no longer existed, the only beneficial
incentive for developing countries to tolerate the negative net
resource transfer situation they found themselves in was to
persevere in economic adjustment, in the hope of eventually
regaining the confidence of their foreign creditors. By 1984,
that confidence was strongest as regards Mexico, but even in
Mexico it was not yet strong enough to enable the resumption
of voluntary lending by banks.
   The big question raised, but not answered, by the rescheduling process for developing countries was a simple one: how long
could, or would, such countries tolerate this negative net
resource transfer situation and the concurrent recession caused
by economic adjustment programmes? Historically, developing
countries have been economically unable, and politically

unwilling, to tolerate such a negative net resource transfer situation, and its attendant consequences for any great length of time. A negative net resource transfer situation is unviable in the long term.

The basic reason for this is that if GDP growth is low or negative (as is now the case in most of South America) in a wider context of rapid population growth, then GDP per capita falls in real terms. This is certainly happening in South America at the present time. The possible social and political implications of such negative economic developments are what make a negative net resource transfer situation an unviable proposition in the long term. It is strictly a short-term proposition. The rescheduling process is that short-term period during which countries like Mexico have regained the confidence of their foreign creditors, but there is considerable doubt as to whether that confidence is sufficient to restore voluntary lending by banks to pre-1982 levels within the next few years, thereby putting such countries into a positive net resource transfer situation.

At the beginning of 1985, all lending to developing countries involved in the rescheduling process was involuntary and entirely connected with rescheduling process financing arrangements. Only Mexico is anywhere near being able to attract voluntary lending by commercial banks. Yet, only by increasing new loan disbursements by banks and official creditors will developing countries be able to go into a positive net resource transfer situation. The problem of who is going to lend the required amounts of money promises to become the most difficult to resolve over the new few years.

Although its total resources were doubled to around $100 billion in 1983, the IMF has only around $40 billion to disburse at any one time. This is because the IMF has a very conservative assets/capital ratio (around one to one), most of its primary capital is in the form of gold that cannot be sold, and it cannot borrow money from the Euromarkets. As a result of these institutional restraints, the disbursable resources of the IMF are limited. The resources are adequate to deal with the rescheduling/economic adjustment processes, but not enough to induce high-growth development in developing countries.

In 1983 the IMF disbursed $13.5 billion.[22] In 1984 the IMF disbursed $21 billion.[23] This latter figure, though large in absolute terms, was made in a wider context of low current-account deficits, low debt growth, and low commercial bank lending in the developing countries involved in the rescheduling process. However, compared to total net external borrowing of $75 billion[24] (of which the commercial banks lent $52.6 billion) by all developing countries in 1981 (the last normal year prior to the onset of crisis in 1982), then the $21 billion disbursed in 1984 looks less significant in relative terms. Though IMF disbursements increased in 1984, declining new lending by commercial banks in late 1984 meant that the total new resources available to developing countries in 1984 were far removed from the net external borrowing requirements that a high-growth economic development strategy would entail.

The commercial banks, who now insist that the IMF and other official creditors must lend more to developing countries, seem to assume that the IMF's resources are infinite. They are not, and given the strong resistance in the US Congress to the increase of the US quota to the IMF in 1983, it is clear that it is not politically possible to increase IMF resources again within the next few years. Also, it is often forgotten that the IMF is not a development institution. Under its Articles of Agreement the IMF was empowered, among other things, to provide short-term financial assistance to member countries facing temporary balance-of-payments problems. Although the Extended Fund has become more important, and the long-term maturity credits recently disbursed by the IMF are *de facto* development credits, the IMF's primary purpose is to disburse credit, in the context of high conditionality, economic adjustment programmes, so as to resolve short-term economic problems.

The World Bank, which *is* a development institution, is restricted by its own Articles of Agreement to lending no more than the equivalent of its own capital. In 1982, World Bank new loan commitments were $10.5 billion, but due to the multi-year lag in its disbursements, net disbursements in 1982 were only $4.5 billion.[25] Because of its Articles of Agreement, net disbursements did not increase significantly in 1983 and 1984, and even the higher disbursement levels in these two years were far removed from the borrowing requirements of developing countries. More generally, the World Bank has traditionally concentrated its lending to the poorest developing countries,[26] which the commercial banks were not interested in. If the World Bank began to increase its lending to the richer developing countries, such as those in South America, who would then lend to the poorest countries?

Which leaves OECD Governments and the BIS. The BIS has declared that it is not willing, nor is it able under its own rules, to provide long-term development finance for development purposes. OECD Governments, both unilaterally and in the context of the Paris Club, seem to be politically unwilling to disburse the sort of amounts of money required by developing countries. Nor are they, it seems, willing to adjust themselves by reducing interest rates and halting the rise in protectionist measures. This is especially true of the United States Government, which seems to be responsible, through its monetary and fiscal policies, for very high real interest rates. A significant cut in interest rates, and the return of nominal interest rates in particular, would significantly reduce the debt servicing costs of developing countries.

In 1984, while developing countries were ruthlessly adjusting their economies at the behest of the IMF, the OECD countries, and the United States in particular, were pursuing policies whose cumulative effect, though unintentional, was to make the process of adjustment all the more difficult to endure. The OECD countries were not, in fact, seriously adjusting their economies, while constantly preaching the virtues of economic adjustment to the developing countries. This most asymmetrical adjustment, in which all the real adjustment was carried out by the developing countries, produced a great deal of bitterness among developing countries in general, and the countries of South America in particular. If, as seems increasingly likely, this asymmetrical adjustment becomes a long-term phenomenon, then the symbiotic debtor/creditor relationship, which existed prior to the debt crisis of 1982, may never be reborn.

It seems clear that for that old symbiotic relationship to be reborn commercial bank lending to developing countries will have to increase significantly in the short and medium term. OECD Governments will also have to lend more. Given the fact that the Euromarket is the largest credit source in the world economy, and given the limited resources of the IMF and the World Bank, it is clear that only increased lending by commercial banks can enable developing countries to resume the high-growth strategy they pursued in the 1970s. Whether this new lending will, in fact, take place is the big question of 1985. In the long term, it is a question upon which a great deal depends—both for the continuing stability of the international financial system and for the economic development of the developing countries involved in the rescheduling process.

Notes

1. Cline, op. cit., p. 79.
2. Mentioned by John Williamson, 'Keynes and the International Economic Order', in David Worswick and James Trevithick (eds), *Keynes and the Modern World* (Cambridge: Cambridge University Press, 1983).
3. The literature depicts a constant struggle by banks to escape from political interference in the lending process: firstly, through the development of the unregulated Eurocurrency market, secondly, in the provision of totally unconditional (as regards use) loans to developing countries. Such loans, because they were unconditional (unlike those of the World Bank and other official creditors), proved highly popular with developing countries. For these matters see Angelini, op. cit.; Stephen I. Davis, 'How Risky is International Lending?', *Harvard Business Review*, January/February 1977; Ian Giddy and Russ Ray, 'The Eurodollar Market and the Third World', *University of Michigan Business Review*, March 1976; L. S. Goodman, 'Bank lending to Non-OPEC LDCs: Are Risks Diversifiable?', *Federal Reserve Board of New York Quarterly Review*, summer 1981; Institute of Bankers, *The Financing of Long-Term Development: Papers Presented to the 32nd International Banking School, Cambridge, August 1979* (London: Institute of Bankers, 1979); Ishan Kapur, 'An Analysis of the Supply of Eurocurrency Finance to Developing Countries', *Oxford Bulletin of Economics and Statistics*, Vol. 39, No. 3, August 1977; Mohammed and Saccomanni, op. cit.; and, Yoon-Dae Euh, *Commercial Banks and the Creditworthiness of Less Developed Countries* (Ann Arbor, Michigan: Michigan University Micro-Films International Research Press, 1978).
4. A classic example is the refusal of the West European countries in NATO and Japan to finance defence policies commensurate with their economic power. Instead, they prefer to let the United States (through NATO and the US–Japanese Security Treaty) pay the bulk of the cost of defending the free world against the Soviet Union. They get their security cheap. Like all free riders they gain benefits, but do not pay the costs of that which makes those benefits possible. The classic study of free-rider theory is Mancur Olson, *The Logic*

of Collective Action (Harvard, Mass.: Harvard University Press, 1965; 2nd edn., 1971).

5. For discussions of the integrative and competitive aspects of Euro-currency market bank operations, see Jerry Coakley and Laurence Harris, *The City of Capital: London's Role as a Financial Centre* (Oxford: Basil Blackwell, 1983); J. M. Gray and H. P. Gray, 'The Multinational Bank: A Financial MNC?', *Journal of Banking and Finance*, No. 5, 1981; M. S. Mendelsohn, *Money on the Move: The Modern International Capital Market* (New York: McGraw Hill, 1980); Eugene L. Versluysen, *The Political Economy of International Finance* (Farnborough: Gower, 1981).

6. Olson, op. cit.

7. Cline, op. cit., p. 80.

8. That framework, and the questions raised as to its ability to deal with the debt crisis of 1982–3, is examined in Peter Cooke, 'The International Banking Scene: A Supervisory Perspective', *Bank of England Quarterly Bulletin*, Vol. 23, No. 1, March 1983; Jack Gutentag and Richard Herring, *The Lender-of-Last-Resort-Function in an International Context*, Princeton Essays in International Finance No. 151 (Princeton, NJ: Princeton University Press, May 1983); Robert M. Solow, 'On the Lender of Last Resort', in Charles P. Kindleberger and Jean-Pierre Laffar-Gue (eds), *Financial Crises* (Cambridge: Cambridge University Press, 1982); Henry C. Wallich, 'Rescheduling as Seen by the Supervisor and the Lender of Last Resort', in Henry C. Wallich (ed.), *Crises in Economic and Financial Structure* (Lexington, Mass.: Lexington Books, 1982).

9. See Brunner, op. cit., and Vaubel, op. cit., for such views.

10. Henry C. Wallich, 'Banks, LDC's Share Concern for Viable System', *Journal of Commerce*, 30 July 1981, p. 4A. Unlike Brunner and Vaubel, who are academics (and therefore can be ignored, as they have no real power), Wallich was a member of the US Federal Reserve Board.

11. The US quota increase was approved, after many delays due to opposition in the Congress, but there was a *quid pro quo*: the International Lending and Supervision Act of 1983, which placed many restrictions on commercial banks as regards their lending to developing countries. See Note 10, Chapter 2, for full details of the Act.

12. A point made cogently by Sidney Weintraub and William R. Cline (eds), *Economic Stabilization in Developing Countries* (Washington, DC: Brookings Institution, 1981), pp. 40–1.

13. The BIS Committee on Banking Regulations and Supervisory Practices (the Cooke Committee), *Report on the Supervision of Banks' Foreign Establishments* (the Basle Concordat) (Basle: BIS, 1975).

14. The BIS Committee on Banking Regulations and Supervisory Practices,

Principles for the Supervision of Banks' Foreign Establishments (the revised Basle Concordat) (Basle: BIS, 1983).

15. Peter Cooke, 'Developments in Co-operation Among Banking Supervisory Authorities', *Bank of England Quarterly Bulletin*, Vol. 21, No. 2, June 1981, pp. 234-5.

16. Discussed in William Hall, 'The Ditchley Institute: Search for the right man as leader', *World Banking Survey (Part I), Financial Times*, 9 May 1983; Mendelsohn, op. cit., pp. 34-6; Charles Grant, 'How the Ditchley Initiative is Becoming Reality', *Euromoney*, July 1983.

17. Most commentators viewed foreign borrowing as most desirable for the development process, as in Kaj Areskoug, *External Public Borrowing: Its Role in Economic Development* (New York: Praeger, 1969); Dragoslav Avramović, *Economic Growth and External Debt* (Baltimore: Johns Hopkins University Press, 1964); Hollis B. Chenery, 'Foreign Assistance and Economic Development', *American Economic Review*, Vol. LVI, September 1966; Walter E. Robichek, 'Official Borrowing Abroad: Some Reflections', *Finance and Development*, March 1980; for a regional view, see Antonio Jorge (ed.), *Foreign Debt and Latin American Economic Development* (New York: Pergamon Press, 1983). A minority of commentators, on the other hand, argued that the high costs of foreign borrowing (in terms of debt service costs and changes in domestic economic priorities) exceeded the benefits, as in Gustav F. Papanek, 'The Effect of Aid and Other Resource Transfers on Savings and Growth in Less Developed Countries', *Economic Journal*, 82, September 1972, and 'Aid, Foreign Private Investment Savings, and Growth in Less Developed Countries', *Journal of Political Economy*, January/February 1973; Thomas E. Weisskopf, 'The Impact of Foreign Capital Inflow on Domestic Savings in Underdeveloped Countries', *Journal of International Ecnomics*, 2, 1972.

18. Helen Hughes, 'Debt and Development: The Role of Foreign Capital in Economic Growth', *World Development*, Vol. 7, No. 2, February 1979 (Special Issue on International Indebtedness and World Economic Stagnation).

19. See G. Feder and R. E. Just, 'A Study of Debt Servicing Capacity Applying Logic Analysis', *Journal of Development Economics*, Vol. 4, March 1977; G. Feder, R. E. Just, and K. Ross, 'Projecting Debt Servicing Capacity of Developing Countries', *Journal of Financial and Quantitative Analysis*, Vol. 16, December 1981; C. R. Frank and W. R. Cline, 'Measurement of Debt Servicing Capacity: An Application of Discriminant Analysis', *Journal of International Economics*, Vol. 1, August 1971; Gordon W. Smith, *The External Debt Prospects of the Non-oil Developing Countries: An Econometric Analysis*, New International Economic Order Series Monograph

No. 10 (Washington, DC: Overseas Development Council, 1977). Also see D. C. McDonald, 'Debt Capacity and Developing Country Borrowing: A Survey', *IMF Staff Papers*, September 1983.

20. These 'dependencia' theories are examined in Frieden, op. cit.; Honeywell, op. cit.; Payer, op. cit.; Howard Wachtel, *The New Gnomes: Multinational Banks in the Third World* (Washington, DC: Transnational Institute, 1977). For a South American perspective, where the controversies over dependent/independent methods of economic development have been the most intense, see André Gunder Frank, *Capitalism and Underdevelopment in Latin America* (New York: Monthly Review Press, 1967); Celso Furtado, *The Economic Development of Latin America: Historical Background and Contemporary Problems* (Cambridge: Cambridge University Press, 1976); and Villarreal, op. cit., for events in the 1980s.

21. These wider power relationships are rarely discussed in the development economics literature, but there are exceptions, as in Benjamin J. Cohen, *Organizing The World's Money: The Political Economy of International Monetary Relations* (London: Macmillan, 1977); Janet Kelly, 'International Capital Markets: Power and Security in the International System', *Orbis*, winter 1978; Charles Lipson, 'The International Organization of Third World Debt', *Orbis*, Vol. 35, No. 4, autumn 1981; Michael Moffit, *The World's Money: International Banking from Bretton Woods to the Brink of Insolvency* (London: Michael Joseph, 1984).

22. See Table 21, Chapter 3.

23. A. D. Bain, 'International Lenders and World Debt', *Midland Bank Review*, winter 1984, p. 19.

24. See Table 21, Chapter 3.

25. Cline, op. cit., p. 111.

26. See Cheryl Payer, *The World Bank* (New York: Monthly Review Press, 1982).

5 The politics of debt, 1982–1984

5.1 Domestic politics

In 1983, midway through the rescheduling process, a managing director of Morgan Stanley, Barton Biggs, stated that 'somehow the conventional wisdom of 200 million sullen South Americans sweating away in the hot sun for the next decade to earn interest on their debt so Citicorp can raise its dividend twice a year does not square with my image of political reality'.[1]

Mr Biggs, one of a small number of investment/merchant bankers acting as advisers[2] to the Governments of developing countries in their rescheduling negotiations with commercial banks (see Appendix 11), had been sceptical from the start of the debt crisis in 1982 about the premisses made by commercial banks and the IMF during the rescheduling process. Those premisses were as follows:

1. that the debt crisis was a purely economic phenomenon, to be resolved between debtors and creditors;
2. that economic adjustment, enforced by the IMF, was the necessary and desirable *quid pro quo* to restore the confidence of foreign creditors in the economies of developing countries;
3. that the consequences of economic adjustment, and negative net resource transfer, were sustainable in the short and medium term;
4. that the Governments of developing countries, being fully aware of the potentially disastrous consequences to their economies if they were unco-operative with their foreign creditors, would continue to be co-operative, to conduct their rescheduling negotiations in a purely bilateral context, and not allow domestic political considerations to lead them to abrogate their contractual commitments to their foreign creditors.

Mr Biggs, along with many other commentators,[3] felt that the debt crisis was not only an economic phenomenon, but that it had been highly politicised from its beginning in 1982, both in terms of the domestic political implications of the rescheduling/ adjustment processes for developing countries, and in the subsequent international political implications. He suggested that the demands of foreign creditors in the rescheduling/ adjustment processes were politically unrealistic, in that there were clear political limits to the amount of domestic recession, unemployment, low GDP growth, and negative net resource transfer, beyond which the Governments of developing countries dared not, and would not, go. Moreover, the social and political strains caused by these economic problems were only sustainable in the short term, and not in the medium and long term, as many foreign creditors assumed. Such assumptions, Mr Biggs suggested, were politically unrealistic and indicated an ignorance of the volatile political systems that existed in virtually all developing countries.

These domestic political strains could not but have an effect on relations between the Governments of developing countries and their foreign creditors. If those political strains became so intense that fear of revolution became greater than fear of creditors' reprisals, then the Governments of developing countries could turn away from co-operation with their foreign creditors and become hostile and confrontational in their attitudes to their foreign creditors.[4]

What, then, were the domestic political implications of the rescheduling/adjustment processes in developing countries? Table 19 shows the domestic political systems of the largest debtor countries involved in the rescheduling/adjustment processes. One of the more interesting trends in recent South American politics[5] is the passing away of the old military dictatorships, which were once synonymous with the region, and the return of democratic political systems. Currently Argentina, Bolivia, Colombia, the Dominican Republic, Ecuador, Mexico, Peru, Uruguay, and Venezuela are democracies, although many of them are flawed by comparison with the sort of democracies that exist in the United States and Western Europe. Brazil is in the process of becoming a democracy. The old military dictatorships only remain in Chile and Paraguay.

The general point about democracies, and newly emergent

democracies in particular, is that they generate high popular expectations, they ensure that such expectations cannot be ignored by elected Governments, and they rule out the option of large-scale repression by such Governments against the people they rule. Military dictatorships, which are repressive and authoritarian by definition, can ignore popular expectations, and do not hesitate to use violence against the people they rule.

In democratic political systems, therefore, the ability of elected Governments to enforce politically unpopular policies, in the face of organised political opposition to them, is far less than is the case for unelected military dictatorships. The limits of the politically possible, in other words, are reached relatively early in democratic political systems. In military dictatorships the limits of the politically possible, as regards the enforcement of politically unpopular policies, can be extended far more than is the case in democracies if enough ruthless repression is used. However, even military dictatorships cannot rule by repression alone. Without some legitimacy and popular support such dictatorships, as recent events in South America showed, cannot prevail in the long term.

In 1983, after only one year of economic adjustment in South America, the UN's Economic Commission for Latin America (ECLA) was worried about 'situations difficult to control, economically and socially'.[6] Table 19 shows that riots have taken place in Brazil, Chile, the Dominican Republic, and Peru. Peru, which is facing a communist guerrilla insurrection, is rapidly heading into a civil war situation, similar to the one that is presently raging in El Salvador and Guatemala.[7] Such serious disorders have, until the present time, been confined to the smaller and economically weak debtor countries such as Peru and the Dominican Republic, but the riots in Brazil are an ominous development for the future.

By 1984, in the words of two top US Government officials with special responsibility for South America, 'the risk may well be disorder rather than dictatorship'.[8] Since the old military dictatorships have expired, and the military élites of South America have no real desire to seize power at the present time, no military option exists in South America to deal with this spectre of disorder, anarchy, and revolutionary political turmoil.

Ironically, while the idea of military dictatorships as a possible

Table 19 Domestic politics, selected countries, 1982–1984

	Type of Government	Degree of political polarisation	Degree of popular expectations	Riots	Civil war	Relations with foreign creditors
Argentina	Prior to December 1983, overt right-wing military junta; thereafter, restoration of democracy, and rule of centre–left Radical Party of President Alfonsin.	High. Peronist Party main opposition. Strong in trade unions.	High. Democracy ruled by a radical party.	No	No	Confrontation
Brazil	Covert right-wing military junta in the process of overseeing a return to a limited form of democracy.	High, but since direct elections are still to come, the greatest pressure is for the restoration of full democracy.	High. Emerging democracy ruled by party committed to change.	Yes	No	Co-operation
Chile	Overt right-wing military junta.	High. However, political parties are banned.	High, due to insecure position of the junta, which is expected to go.	Yes	No	Co-operation

Dominican Republic	Democracy ruled by right-wing President Salvador Jorge Blanco.	High. Opposition: Dominican Liberation Party.	Low, but a long tradition of 'street politics', i.e. riots.	Yes	No	Co-operation
Mexico	Nominal democracy rule by the Institutional Revolutionary Party (PRI) for the last fifty years.	Low. National Action Party made a small impact in 1983 elections.	Low, as long tradition of politcal apathy in Mexico.	No	No	Co-operation
Peru	Democracy ruled by centre–right Popular Action Party of President Fernando Belaúnde.	High. Opposition: Apra Party. Also left getting more popular.	Low, although many are turning to the revolutionary path of the guerrillas.	Yes	Yes	Co-operation
Venezuela	Democracy ruled since 1983 by centre–left Democratic Action Party of President Jaime Lusinchi.	High. Opposition: Christian Democratic Party.	High. Old democracy ruled by radical party.	No	No	Confrontation
Yugoslavia	Communist dictatorship ruled by the League of Yugoslav Communists (LYC) since 1945.	No organised opposition allowed, but sharp divisions exist between contituent nations of Yugoslavia.	High, as regards living standards. Low, as regards political change.	Yes	No	Co-operation

solution to complex social problems has come to be completely discredited in South America, in communist Yugoslavia there is increasing talk of the need for a 'Yugoslav Jaruzelski'.[9] As Table 19 shows, there have been riots in the poorest area of the country, Kosovo, but the country is a long way from the political situation that prevailed in Poland on the eve of General Jaruzelski's *coup d'état* in December 1981. Although Yugoslavia is ruled by the League of Yugoslav Communists (LYC), the LYC is not united; it is ideologically confused, and has no clear political strategy to resolve Yugoslavia's problems other than its own survival as a bastion of power and privilege. These political problems exist in a wider society in which popular expectations are high with regard to living standards. However, as in Poland, there are no channels by which genuine popular feelings can be expressed. A situation in which popular expectations are not met, where the political establishment is confused and incompetent, where there are no free elections, and where there are serious conflicts between the constituent nations of Yugoslavia, is one that inevitably leads to spontaneous outbursts of anger (which is what riots are). Riots cannot, of course, overthrow the rule of the LYC, but the prospect of more disorders in the future is making the idea of a military solution to the problem increasingly attractive to more and more people in Yugoslavia. The Yugoslav military, whose main concern is the preservation of national unity and defence of the country's borders, may come to feel that internal disorders constitute a real threat to national unity and security. If this does happen, a *coup d'état* will follow.

The spectre of increasing disorder must, however, be qualified as a problem, as with so many issues in the rescheduling process, that varies in intensity from one developing country to another. Mexico,[10] for example, has undergone the most severe economic adjustment since 1982, but no riots have taken place, the ruling Institutional Revolutionary Party (PRI) easily fought off challenges from rival parties in the last election in 1983, and the country is remarkably politically stable given the present economic situation. It seems that the traditional political apathy of Mexicans, along with the iron grip of the PRI on all aspects of life in Mexico (the PRI has ruled the country for the last fifty years), is responsible for this remarkable, though unique, state of affairs.

Mexico's political stability, and its very co-operative attitude towards foreign creditors in the rescheduling process, is not typical of the rest of South America. Brazil,[11] for example, is in the process of changing its political system from a military dictatorship into a democracy. The popular pressure for the restoration of democracy, a change in domestic economic priorities, and for the rejection of IMF enforced economic adjustment programmes, is intense. The new Government is committed to change, and has questioned Brazil's previous co-operation with its foreign creditors, although that co-operation was gradually being eroded throughout 1984. Brazil, because of the political instability caused by the riots and by the political uncertainties surrounding the transition to democracy after twenty years of military dictatorship, is very much at the centre of concern with regard to the politics of debt. In 1983, like Mexico, it was fully co-operating with its foreign creditors, but political events in 1984 and 1985 have put a question mark against the future continuation of that co-operation with foreign creditors. This is not because the Government is radical (it is moderate), but because economic and political events inside Brazil are forcing that Government into confrontation with its foreign creditors, and the IMF in particular.

Brazil may, in fact, go the way of Argentina, its traditional rival in South America. Argentina[12] is the classic example of a newly democratic country, ruled by a centre–left Government, that decided not to put the interests of foreign creditors above those of the majority of its own people. Although it had signed agreements with the IMF in 1983 and 1984, the Argentinian Government failed to keep within the targets agreed with the IMF, and it has not adjusted its economy in a way that would satisfy IMF demands. Its whole attitude to its foreign creditors, and the IMF in particular, has been confrontational. It has, in addition, put itself forward as a desirable example for other South American countries, Brazil in particular, to emulate in their relations with their creditors.

Argentina's example has been influential. A country whose economic ability to service its debts was quite good, given its large official reserves (result of large grain exports), Argentina was politically unwilling to co-operate with its foreign creditors in its debt rescheduling negotiations of 1983–4. It is a classic example of political unwillingness to service debt, as opposed to economic inability to do so. Although its foreign creditors refused to grant Argentina the terms it wanted in the rescheduling negotiations for fear of setting a precedent that would have immediately affected the concurrent rescheduling negotiations in Brazil and Mexico, it was obvious to the rest of South America that Argentina was not harshly punished by its foreign creditors for its confrontational and recalcitrant attitudes. It was not, for example, called into formal default by its commercial bank creditors, although it deliberately delayed the payment of interest on its debt for six months during 1984.

In the end, of course, Argentina signed an agreement with the IMF in December 1984, and the terms it obtained from the advisory committee were far less accommodating than it had originally demanded, but there is still considerable doubt as to whether the sort of economic adjustment demanded by the IMF in Argentina is politically possible. President Alfonsin, if the removal (in February 1985) of his unpopular (with the IMF and the advisory committee) Economics Minister, Bernardo Grinspun, is anthing to go by, wants to adjust at the present (1985) time. His radicalism, in the period 1983–4 was more rhetorical than substantive, as the pressure his Government exerted on foreign creditors was designed to extract better terms for Argentina from its foreign creditors. Outright repudiation of the debt was never on the agenda.

However, because of the democratic political system in Argentina, and the great power of the Peronist Party (which controls the trade unions) in particular, there are great restraints on what President Alfonsin can attempt politically as regards economic adjustment. Argentina, in 1985, is both an example of the political restraints on the economic adjustment process and of calculated confrontation with foreign creditors as a tactic to extract better terms for rescheduled debt and new loans. By late 1984, it was clear that those tactics had failed, given the determination of the advisory committee and the IMF not to capitulate to Argentina's demands despite numerous provocations, but the reality of the political restraints on President Alfonsin in 1985 made it unclear whether the agreement his Government signed with the IMF in December 1984 is worth anything more than the paper it is written on. Argentina cannot, for example, keep its inflation rate below the target agreed with the IMF in 1984—300 per cent per annum. That inflation rate, which would be regarded as catastrophic in OECD countries, was regarded as low in Argentina, where inflation was raging at an annual rate of just over 700 per cent in early 1985.

Venezuela,[13] the other major example of a debtor country ruled by a democratic Government that decided to go into confrontation with its foreign creditors, has had a democratic political system since 1958, has been ruled by the centre–left Democratic Action Party since 1983, and has had a virtual political consensus on refusing to accept the dictates of the IMF. Because of its large oil reveneues, a relatively small population, political stability, and discipline in domestic macro-economic management, Venezuela was able to avoid having to come to an agreement with the IMF in 1984.

It was the first major debtor country to reschedule its debts without the participation of the IMF. Only Nicaragua, in 1981, had been able to do this prior to the historic Venezuelan agreement of 1984. Despite great pressure by commercial banks to accept an agreement with the IMF, the Venezuelan Government was able to withstand this pressure because of relatively favourable domestic economic and political circumstances. By withstanding that pressure, the Government set an important precedent. A rescheduling agreement is possible, though very difficult to achieve, without the participation of the IMF, because an advisory committee, faced with a choice between an agreement without the IMF or no agreement at all will, ultimately, go for an agreement without the IMF. That is what proved to be the case in Venezuela in September 1984.

What, then, are the political limits for the economic adjustment process? In the case of the more economically marginal, and highly politically vulnerable, debtor countries such as Peru and the Dominican Republic, the limit has already been reached, if not actually passed in the case of Peru where a limited, but deadly, civil war has already begun in certain isolated regions of the country. Riots in the Dominican Republic have claimed hundreds of lives. These two countries, interestingly, attempted to be very co-operative with their foreign creditors, but were simply economically unable, as opposed to politically unwilling, to continue doing what was demanded of them by foreign creditors in 1984. The Dominican Republic, for example, broke off talks with the IMF in the spring of 1984. Chile, whose domestic situation is comparable to Peru and the Dominican Republic, is also co-operative with its foreign creditors, but is only able to satisfy the demands of its foreign creditors, and the IMF in particular, because it is ruled by a very unpopular and repressive military dictatorship, whose long-term viability is doubtful when one considers the general trend in favour of democracy in South American politics at the present time.

For the two largest debtor countries, Brazil and Mexico, the limits have not yet been reached. Mexico's ostensible political stability (though some observers have called it false, and compared the country to a volcano about to erupt), despite the severe social consequences of its economic adjustment process, is unique, but the big question in 1985 is: how long will it remain stable? The limited economic recovery of 1984 has ameliorated these social tensions, but the indefinite perpetuation of such difficult economic and social conditions is bound to put severe strains on Mexico's political system. The last time Mexico erupted, in the period 1911–18, millions of people died in the first major civil war of this century. Then, as now, an apparent calm concealed social tensions.

Brazil, in complete contrast to Mexico, is in the middle of a highly uncertain political transformation from a military dictatorship to a democracy, which is generating great popular expectations of change, and whose eventual political consequences are of great significance to the whole of South America. These great popular expectations of domestic change have had the inevitable effect of greatly limiting what is politically possible in Brazil at the present time with regard to further economic adjustment. Brazil, whose domestic economic and political problems are far greater than those of Mexico, is the big question mark of 1985: will it decide to attempt co-operation with its foreign creditors, or will it drift into confrontation with them? A great deal rests on this question, given Brazil's prominent geopolitical position in South America.

In Argentina and Venezuela, the two most important second-tier debtor countries, the domestic political limits on economic adjustment have long been reached. For Venezuela, with its unique domestic economic and political strength, the pace of economic adjustment is not dictated by the IMF. Little adjustment is taking place at the present time, and as long as an agreement with the IMF is avoided, Venezuela has genuine freedom of choice as to whether adjustment takes place or not, and if it does take place, it has full control as to the rate for the adjustment process.

The reverse of this situation prevails in Argentina, where great IMF pressure to adjust exists, but where the domestic political limits on the economic adjustment process are even greater than is the case in Venezuela. In fact, Argentina had to give in to pressure in December 1984 after one year of confrontation with its foreign creditors. The Peronist Party, and its control of the trade unions, is the principal political restraint on President Alfonsin's Government.

In Yugoslavia,[14] a communist state, the question of political limits, if looked at in party political terms, does not exist, as no organised political opposition to the communists is allowed. Riots, which have been called protests of the dispossessed and powerless, have taken place. Popular discontent in communist political systems, having no legitimate channels and means to express itself in non-violent forms, tends to build up and then explode with great force. Poland, obviously, is the great example of this process of concealed, though deep, discontent. A Polish-type scenario is unlikely in Yugoslavia at present, but popular discontent is building up. The political system, responsible for the creation of high popular expectations as regards living standards, cannot deliver what it has promised, as co-operation with foreign creditors has always taken precedence over domestic political considerations. The longer this state of affairs continues, the more the legitimacy of the political system—never secure in the best of times in communist political systems—is threatened by popular discontent. How long this state of affairs can continue, without major political turmoil of the Polish variety, is the big question in Yugoslavia at the moment. The political leeway in Yugoslavia, with its relatively high living standards, is far greater than in most of South America, and so the political limits of economic adjustment have not yet been reached. Poverty, and not the real destitution common to South America, is what awaits most Yugoslavs if economic adjustment continues indefinitely. However, because the LYC has told Yugoslavs to think in terms of West European standards of living, then what may be tolerable poverty in

South America may turn out to be unacceptable to many Yugoslavs whose expectations were always higher than was the case for the majority of people in South America. A Polish-type explosion, therefore, cannot be ruled out in the medium and long term.

5.2 Co-operation and confrontation

After two years of economic adjustment, and its attendant social and political complications, the year 1984 marked, in many ways, a turning-point in the politics of debt—domestic and international. By the summer of 1984, many developing countries in the rescheduling process were reaching the limits of the politically possible as regards economic adjustment, while many of the gains of the adjustment process seemed to be threatened by the rise in interest rates at that time. In June 1984, US Prime Rate went up by 2.5 per cent. A combination of unfavourable external economic developments, and a realisation among South American Governments of the potentially disastrous domestic political implications of the economic adjustment process, would seem to be the factors that led to the birth of the Cartagena Process in June 1984.[15]

Although the Mexican President, Lopez Portilo, had initiated secret meetings with his Brazilian and Argentinian counterparts in November 1982 to discuss the possibility of multilateral action by South American Governments to resolve the debt crisis they all faced, his proposals were rejected by the Brazilian Government at that time. From November 1982 to June 1984, the bilateral approach was followed by debtor Governments. Each Government conducted purely bilateral rescheduling negotiations, most Governments were co-operative with their foreign creditors, and all Governments accepted the high-risk premium levied on rescheduled debt and new loans by commercial banks in the period 1982–3. Only with the arrival of the Alfonsin Government in Argentina, and of the Lusinchi Government in Venezuela, in December 1983, did confrontation become a problem in the rescheduling/adjustment processes. The example of these two recalcitrant Governments, and the Argentinian Government in particular, had a potent influence on Governments that remained co-operative with their foreign creditors. Brazil, in particular, was greatly influenced by Argentina. It was this combination of intra-South American politics, domestic politics in all the countries concerned, and unfavourable economic developments in the world economy that led directly to the Cartagena Process.

The Cartagena Process is here taken to cover a number of meetings of the Cartagena Group, the public statements issued after these meetings, and the implications, as interpreted by various commentators, of these meetings and statements (see Appendix 12 for further details). The statements used here are the official English translations of the original Spanish texts issued after the three meetings of the Cartagena Group by the relevant foreign ministries.[16]

The Cartagena Process is at once an opportunity for OECD Governments, and an implied threat to them. It is an opportunity in the sense that the Cartagena Group is asking for a reform of the status quo through direct negotiations with OECD Governments. The document entitled the *Cartagena Consensus*, produced during the first meeting of the Cartagena Group in June 1984, is really just a list of seventeen specific reform proposals for easing South America's debt service burden, and for reorganising its debt repayment system. The most important proposals were as follows:

1. *Interest rates*

As well as urging OECD Governments to cut interest rates, it was proposed that the cost of money to developing countries be no more than what it cost the bank (i.e. LIBOR or Prime Rate). Spreads would, therefore, be abolished.

2. *Fees*

There would be an abolition of all fees during the period of rescheduling, together with all penalty clauses in rescheduled debt and new loan contracts.

3. *Loan maturities*

It was proposed that maturities be significantly extended on new loans and on rescheduled debt, so as to put the rescheduling process into a long-term time-frame.

4. *New loans*

It was proposed that new loan disbursement be restored to pre-1982 levels.

5. *IMF*

It was proposed that there be a considerable easing of IMF conditionality, plus the establishment of a compensatory window for debtor countries at the IMF.

6. *Debt service ratio*

It was proposed that this ratio be 'reasonable'—a word open to many possible interpretations. Argentina's original proposal to set a figure of 20 per cent for the ratio was not put into the final document.

While the reform proposals were put forward in the document, the first meeting also established a formal consultative mechanism, henceforth known as the Cartagena Group (eleven Governments), which agreed to meet on a regular basis in the future. This was the implied threat of the Cartagena Group. If the Group's reform proposals were rejected by OECD Governments, it was implied, then the present Group could evolve into a formal debtors' cartel. Comparisons were made with OPEC by many commentators.[17] Unlike OPEC, which was a cartel to control the production of oil so as to safeguard its high price, the debtors' cartel would threaten to disrupt debt servicing, and even possibly threaten to repudiate debts, if certain demands were not met. Like OPEC, its collective power to disrupt or repudiate, would protect all its members from reprisals by foreign creditors. In the past, if any one debtor country had tried to pursue such extreme policies, it would have been easily isolated and punished by its foreign creditors. If a debtors' cartel existed, however, it would be impossible to isolate and punish the whole of South America.

While the *Cartagena Consensus* was concerned with economic reforms, the *Communiqué* produced after the second meeting of the Cartagena Group in September 1984 in Argentina was explicitly political. Stating that the debt crisis was far too important to be left to the commercial banks and the IMF, the

Cartagena Group called for direct negotiations with OECD Governments to resolve the debt crisis. Though it was not openly said, this demand was unacceptable to OECD Governments, as ever since 1982 they had insisted that the debt crisis was a purely economic phenomenon, which could be adequately resolved between debtors and creditors. Whether this somewhat unrealistic view was held by OECD Governments, or whether it was just a rationale to cover the political unwillingness of such Governments to do anything substantive to help resolve the debt crisis, was hard to tell.

Were the demands of the Cartagena Group met? Though it is hard to say how much the collective pressure of the Cartagena Group affected the behaviour of commercial banks in 1984, not long after the first meeting of the Cartagena Group in June 1984 a number of important rescheduling agreements were signed that did, in fact, go a long way to conceding what the Cartagena Group demanded in June 1984. In the Mexican and Venezuelan rescheduling agreements of September 1984, maturities were significantly extended, spreads were lowered (though not abolished), fees were lowered (though not abolished), and IMF conditionality was eased (in Mexico—the IMF was not involved in Venezuela). However, since these agreements were not concerned with new loans, it was unclear whether new lending would increase significantly as demanded in the Cartagena Consensus. The latter document had also demanded 'reasonable' debt service ratios. This sensitive issue was not mentioned in the agreements of September 1984. Argentina, in its agreement of December 1984, received the same as Mexico and Venezuela as regards maturities, fees, and spreads, but IMF conditionality was not eased. Brazil's negotiations are still not completed (1985), although it seems likely that the terms it receives will be similar to what Argentina received with regard to maturities, spreads, and fees. IMF conditionality, however, will not be eased.

Some countries (Mexico) were granted better terms than others (Argentina), which tended to show that creditors' views of individual countries' economic progress was as important, if not more important, than the collective pressure exerted by the Cartagena Group for better terms for all its members. It was claimed by some commercial banks that the pressure exerted by the Cartagena Group did not affect their decisions on the rescheduling negotiations they had been, or still were, involved in. However, the fact that the largest debtor country, Brazil, was playing the leading diplomatic role behind the scenes in the Cartagena Process was very worrying to foreign creditors. Despite what they said in public on the matter, Brazil, with its large debt, had the most potential to disrupt debt servicing if it so decided. If Brazil decided to become unco-operative towards its foreign creditors, it would be a far more serious threat to those creditors than had been the case with Argentina and Venezuela in 1984.

In the political sphere, and especially after the explicitly political demands made at the second meeting of the Cartagena Group in September 1984, the response of the OECD Governments was distinctly ambiguous. Despite their old insistence that the debt crisis was not a political phenomenon, they did not dismiss or ignore the demands of September 1984 by the Cartagena Group. They proposed that, instead of direct talks between the Cartagena Group and themselves, talks should take place in the Development Committee of the IMF and the World Bank in April 1985. While this proposal was obviously an attempt to avoid direct political negotiations, these indirect talks in the Development Committee were a significant concession to the Cartagena Group. The finance ministers of various OECD Governments would meet with the representatives of the Cartagena Group for the first time in April 1985. This could then lead to more direct political negotiations later in 1985, since the principle of there being an important political side of the debt crisis has been accepted, by virtue of the fact that OECD Governments and representatives of the Cartagena Group will be meeting in a political forum: the Development Committee of the IMF and the World Bank.

The fact that the Cartagena Group agreed to attend the April 1985 meeting, and prepared a common negotiating position for the entire Group at its third meeting in February 1985 in the Dominican Republic, reveals that the Group has made significant progress since its first meeting in June 1984. A consultative mechanism exists, the Group has extracted significant economic and political concessions from foreign creditors, and it has prepared a common negotiating position for the political negotiations of April 1985. The idea of a common negotiating position worries OECD Governments, as it brings the Cartagena Group one step closer to becoming a *de facto* debtors' cartel. In the past, it was almost impossible to get the Governments of South America to agree on anything in such forums as the Organisation of American States (OAS), but the Cartagena Process is a rare example of South American unity. How durable the unity proves to be, only time can tell, but an initial united position makes it far more difficult for OECD Governments to play the divide-and-rule games they are so fond of in future negotiations.

The speed with which the Cartagena Group has established itself as a credible, effective, and united actor in the rescheduling process suggests that its ability to develop from being an implied threat at the present time to an actual threat in the future is considerable. This latter possibility cannot be ignored by foreign creditors, as the speed of the Group's development brings to mind the OPEC example again. OPEC, from its formation in 1960, took over ten years before it established itself as a credible and effective organisation. It was ignored by OECD Governments for most of the 1960s, but during the 1970s its collective power changed the world economy for ever, and nobody ignored it when it had proved its power. Interestingly, one of the founding members of OPEC was Venezuela, which is now one of the more important members of the Cartagena Group. Venezuela, because of its long membership of OPEC, knows the value of collective power. Multilateral action by a group, be it to increase the price of oil or to repudiate debt, protects all concerned from reprisals from those at whom the action is directed, precisely because it is multilateral. Unilateral action, by economically vulnerable and politically weak developing countries, is doomed to failure.

Venezuela also knows that effective pressure, and not polite appeals, can change the basic rules of the present debtor/creditor relationship, to the advantage of the debtor. One of the ironies of the Cartagena Process is that it is the only real leverage that developing countries have over the OECD countries in a wider context of deteriorating terms of trade, increasing protectionism, and high real-interest rates. Moreover, the Cartagena's potential to threaten to disrupt debt servicing or to repudiate debt is a negative leverage which would damage both debtors and creditors alike. The Cartagena Group would like to get the changes it wants in a constructive manner, without having to resort to threats and actions that would be destructive to all concerned. At the beginning of 1985, the desire to co-operate with foreign creditors is still strong in the Cartagena Group, and the Group's potential to be disruptive is only implied, not openly stated. If, however, the OECD Governments do not respond to the Cartagena Group's call for constructive dialogue to reform the *status quo*, then the Cartagena Group could drift, against its will, into open confrontation with foreign creditors in the future.

5.3 International politics

At a conference entitled 'Threats to the Industrial Democracies in the 1980s', held in Washington, DC, at the end of 1982, Henry Kissinger criticised IMF policy in the rescheduling process for 'contracting the economy, increasing unemployment, and reducing consumption in developing countries', and he suggested that the IMF's medicine 'could be a cure worse than the disease'. Finally, after listing these criticisms, he came to his major concern:

At risk here is the internal political evolution of several developing countries, including many important friends of the United States. If the debt crisis winds up spawning radical anti-Western governments, financial issues will be overwhelmed by the political consequences.[18]

Kissinger, an old exponent of *realpolitik*, realised that the commercial banks and the IMF, exclusively concerned with financial issues in the rescheduling process, were in grave danger of becoming the principal cause of a political disaster for OECD Governments, and the US Government in particular. In Kissinger's scenario, IMF-enforced economic adjustment programmes lead to political turmoil, riots, and civil wars of the Central American variety; extreme left-wing regimes come to power, break their links with the United States, and turn to the Soviet Union for assistance. The end result of this scenario is a nightmare for the United States: not one Cuba in South America, but many, and all allied to the Soviet Union. Such regimes would follow the examples set by Cuba and North Korea in the 1970s: they would openly repudiate their foreign debts, and their creditors would be left with nothing.

How, then, is it that prominent Americans such as Henry Kissinger have come to believe such a scenario is not only credible, but increasingly probable? In the 1950s and 1960s, when OECD Governments were the principal creditors of the developing countries,[19] their financial relationships with such countries were direct. More generally, the internal political evolution of such countries was acceptable to, and under the indirect control of, OECD Governments, and the US Government in particular. In South America, for example, the US Government was active in the promotion of various *coups d'état*, most notably the 1964 *coup d'état* in Brazil.[20]

The political evolution of such countries was relatively controllable. In the 1970s, for a whole variety of reasons, that control had begun to break down.[21] One of the major reasons, ironically, was the development of the Euromarkets, and of the growth of lending out of such markets to developing countries during the 1970s. Unlike the official credits of the 1960s, which were conditional, Euromarket credits could be used for anything by the Governments of developing countries. Such credits, disbursed by non-political commercial banks, freed the Governments of developing countries from the political implications of being dependent upon official credits supplied by OECD Governments.

In addition, after the oil price increases of 1973–4, OECD Governments were politically unwilling to increase their credit disbursements to developing countries to the very high levels required by these countries. By reducing their direct financial links with developing countries during the 1970s, though they did not know it at the time, OECD Governments found themselves with progressively less political control over such countries. Increasingly, financial links between OECD Governments and developing countries became very indirect.[22] Those Governments, though the supervisors of the banks concerned, had no control of lending to developing countries by those banks. In addition, the supervision of breakdowns in normal debt servicing in developing countries became the exclusive responsibility of the IMF.

For most of the post-war era the IMF was primarily concerned with the supervision of a regime of fixed but adjustable exchange rates established at Bretton Woods in 1944.[23] With the collapse of the Bretton Woods exchange rate regime in

1971, the IMF's principal task became the provision of conditional, short-term financial assistance to countries experiencing balance-of-payments difficulties.[24] Yet the IMF's economic adjustment programmes, which reached a zenith as regards the number of developing countries involved in the period 1982–4, and which Henry Kissinger criticised, were not under the direct political control of OECD Governments. Though such Governments dominate the IMF's Executive Board through a skewed voting system, and though many left-wing commentators[25] have consequently seen the IMF as a slavish servant of such Governments, it would be misleading to think that the IMF is a mere cipher for state power. It is a genuinely multilateral institution, with its own routinised procedures, and a strong *esprit de corps* among its highly professional staff, who have considerable autonomy in negotiations with developing countries. No one OECD Government, including the US Government, controls the IMF. Such Governments have, on the whole, given unconditional support to the IMF, as it was felt that the economic adjustment process in developing countries was in the interest of OECD Governments.

Is it in the interest of OECD Governments, and especially the long-term political interests, as opposed to the short-term financial interests of commercial banks and the IMF? This conflict between political and economic interests was present in every developing country involved in the rescheduling process. For the United States, which has vital political interests to defend in South América, the possible long-term political consequences of the rescheduling/adjustment processes are extremely serious.

That the United States has vital political interests to defend in South America is undeniable. It is also undeniable that the best way to defend those interests is to ensure that political turmoil does not engulf South America, and that anti-American left-wing regimes do not come to power in that part of the world. In the early days of the emergency response stage (1982–3) of the rescheduling process, the US Government demonstrated its commitment to the economic and political well-being of South America by providing $1.93 billion of financial assistance to Brazil and $2.925 billion to Mexico (see Table 14).

The figures in Table 14, in fact, reveal the political priorities of the US Government in South America. Mexico, which shares a border with the United States, was always the top priority of the US Government. It was in Mexico that the first serious difference emerged between the US Government and Mexico's commercial bank creditors and the IMF.[26] While the Mexican advisory committee and the IMF went constantly for the 'hard' line as regards payments delays, terms on rescheduled debt and new loans, and economic adjustment, the US Government, in order to retain good political relations with the Mexican Government, was more inclined to the 'soft' line on these matters. Sympathetic understanding for Mexico's economic problems, patience with its misdemeanours, and a concern for the long-term political implications of Mexico's economic problems was what characterised US Government policy in Mexico. The US Government, incredible as it may seem in retrospect, was constantly restraining Mexico's creditors from taking an even harder line than they in fact did.

Those creditors, who were competent as bankers but somewhat inadequate as diplomats, talked in terms of 'punishing' Mexico, of making 'demands', and of being 'tough'. They seemed to forget, it seemed, that Mexico was a sovereign state that was very sensitive to the international political implications of its relationship with its creditors during the rescheduling process. Sovereign states cannot be 'punished'—they can be offered positive and negative incentives to act in a particular way. Nor can 'demands' be made of them—they can be persuaded that it is in their national interest to act in a particular way. Such political subtlety, to which all sovereign states attach great importance, was something that bankers knew little about. They seemed not to realise that if, as was often the case, they angered the Mexican Government in the rescheduling negotiations, then this anger would have immediate political implications for US–Mexico state relations, although only an advisory committee dominated by large US banks, and not the US Government, was responsible for the anger that was the cause of worsening state relations between the two countries. The IMF, widely perceived as an American institution, was even worse in these delicate political matters. It made 'demands' all the time, was seen as being dictatorial and arrogant, and seemed to be insensitive to the view that its activities could be interpreted as a gross interference in the internal affairs of sovereign states—such interference being banned by the UN Charter.

In fact, because of these problems in the rescheduling/ adjustment processes, US–Mexican state relations, uneasy at the best of times, deteriorated in the period 1982–3. One result of this is that Mexico has constantly refused to support US policy in Central America, and has appeared to go out of its way to undermine that policy in any way that it could. The US Government, if only because of events in Central America, did not want state relations to worsen, but the behaviour of Mexico's creditor banks and the IMF made it difficult to avoid such a development, since in a free market economy and a democratic political system, as exists in the United States, it was extremely difficult for the US Government to control the behaviour of the Mexican advisory committee and the IMF in their respective negotiations with the Mexican Government.

Persuading commercial banks to act as agents of the US Government was impossible. Their own commercial interests, and not the political priorities of the US Government, guided their behaviour in the rescheduling process. One example will suffice to illustrate the difference between the Government and the banks. Great pressure was exerted by both the US Government and the IMF on the banks to lend more new money to countries like Mexico. If more money was made available by banks, the better relations between Mexico and the United States would be, and the less chance would there be of economic collapse and political turmoil inside Mexico in the future. For many banks, on the other hand, those wider political considerations were irrelevant. They just wanted no part in any new lending to Mexico. In Mexico, as it turned out, this problem was not very serious. In Brazil, however, the problem of new loans was serious enough to threaten the rescue package for that country in 1983.

Brazil, like Mexico, was of great political importance to the United States. In geopolitical terms, Brazil dominated South America, and what happened politically inside Brazil would have profound implications for the political evolution of the rest of South America. During Phase I of Brazil's rescheduling negotiations, a great deal of US Government and IMF pressure failed to persuade many commercial banks to lend new money to Brazil. What was raised in 1983 was far less than what was required by Brazil. The direct result of this failure to increase new lending was a worse economic outlook for Brazil at the end of Phase I, in June 1983, than had prevailed at the beginning of Phase I in the autumn of 1982. Only a massive effort by all concerned, and the Brazilian advisory committee in particular, during Phase II (June 1983–January 1984), reversed the potentially disastrous economic and political situation of mid-1983.

In 1984 the political importance of Brazil had even greater significance for the United States. Brazil was the major diplomatic force behind the organising of the first meeting of the Cartagena Group in June 1984, played the leading role in sustaining the momentum of the Cartagena Process throughout the rest of 1984 and into 1985, and promises to play the leading role in the Cartagena Process in the future. The Brazilian Foreign Ministry, in particular, is a matter for concern to the US Government. It has taken a more radical, South American-orientated foreign policy position, which is far too anti-American for comfort. This is an entirely new development, for since the 1964 *coup d'état*,[27] in which the US Government was heavily involved, Brazil has been a faithful ally of the United States. Since 1982, however, Brazil's tense relations with its foreign, and particularly US, creditors have had an adverse effect on US–Brazil state relations. The debt crisis provided those in the Brazilian Foreign Ministry who wished to end Brazil's subservience (as they saw it) to the United States, and to develop South American unity in the Cartagena Process, with powerful political ammunition to rout those who wished to retain the *status quo ante* as regards relations with the United States. The Economic Planning Minister, Delfim Netto, who was the most faithful friend of the United States in Brazil and against Brazil's participation in the Cartagena process, was the principal political victim of these policy changes. Ostensibly the economic overlord of Brazil, Netto was excluded from the policy-making that led to Brazil's participation in the Cartagena Process. Netto was, in fact, politically dead, and his removal by the new Government in March 1985 was only a formality.

This creeping anti-Americanism was not something unique to Brazil. There is no shortage of virulent anti-American feeling in South America. Historically, this has always been the case, but recent US support for military dictatorships in Brazil (1964), Argentina (1976), Chile (1973), and Uruguay (1973), has caused such popular feelings to become particularly virulent in these four countries. Events since 1982, which saw the collapse of all the old military dictatorships (with the sole exception of Chile), have exacerbated anti-American feelings as they became much more overt in democratic political systems. The role of the IMF, in particular, has attracted a great deal of popular detestation in the whole of South America.

Although the IMF served as a convenient whipping-boy for South American Governments, and although the anti-IMF and anti-American feelings of such Governments were little more than rhetoric for domestic political consumption, popular antagonism towards the IMF and the United States was real enough. More generally, the rescheduling and adjustment processes, with all their attendant consequences, seemed to have been made to order for those who were determined to whip up hatred against the United States. In the past, such people had been confined to the extreme left of the political spectrum, but after the events of 1982–4, the fact that such anti-American feelings were spreading to the various elites of South America was very worrying to the US Government. The old pro-American military dictatorships were leaving the region's political arena, and nationalistic centre–left political parties came to power in Argentina (1983), Uruguay (1985), and Brazil (1985). Similar parties ruled in Bolivia, Ecuador, Colombia, Peru, Venezuela, Mexico, and the Dominican Republic. The general political trend was towards more nationalism, more intra-South American co-operation, and less emphasis on benevolent, intimate ties with the United States.

Although the rescheduling/adjustment processes cannot be entirely blamed for these new political trends, events since 1982 have had the cumulative effect of strengthening nationalism in South America by giving it an issue (the debt crisis) upon which it can constantly feed; of increasing South American co-operation in the Cartagena Process and the OAS; of bringing ever-present anti-American feelings to the boil; and of creating political turmoil in which extreme left-wing political organisations, and the communists in particular, can whip up popular hatred of the United States without fear of punishment in newly democratic political systems. The ironic thing about these developments is that the US Government, and many of the Governments of South America (despite their anti-US rhetoric), do not want a serious worsening of relations, although at the same time they do not want a return to the old sub-servient relationships of the past. With the exceptions of Argentina and Venezuela, the Governments of South America have tried to co-operate with their foreign creditors in the rescheduling process; they ask for constructive dialogue with OECD Governments in the Cartagena Process; they are not destructive in the way that communist regimes are, and would be if they ever came to power in South America. However, domestic economic and political developments in South American countries are forcing the Governments of South America into confrontation with their foreign creditors, and the IMF in particular. On the other side of the table, OECD Governments, and the US Government in particular, seem unwilling, or unable, to restrain the IMF and the advisory committees in the interest of reducing the probability of confrontation with debtor Governments, and of reducing political turmoil in debtor countries.

The IMF, for its part, cannot imagine for one moment that its remedies for the sick patients in the economic adjustment process may not be infallibly correct. It is incapable of thinking in terms of long-term political consequences of its present activities. This is not surprising, as it is run by people from commercial and Central Bank backgrounds who know little of, and have no experience in, the world of practical politics. Living in the heady and rarefied world of economic theory, in which everything regarding economic adjustment is theoretically possible, they have little idea of what is politically possible, in practical terms, in the alien (to them) political systems that exist in developing countries.

While a great debate rages[28] in South America as to whether or not the IMF's remedies will resolve the debt crisis, that debate is mostly conducted in purely economic terms, especially on the part of the IMF. The remedies may, indeed, prove to be efficacious in the long term, but the political turmoil caused by the economic and social consequences of economic adjustment in the short and medium term, could lead to a situation in which there will be 'long-term' for the IMF to worry about. If, as Henry Kissinger fears, radical left-wing regimes come to power in South America as a result of that political turmoil, then the IMF's efforts will not only have been totally futile, but will have been primarily responsible for the political disaster such regimes would turn out to be for OECD Governments, and the US Government in particular.

While Joseph A. Schumpeter may have been correct about *haute finance* not changing the course of history, but rather going along with it,[29] the eventual consequences of the re-scheduling/adjustment processes in South America may prove him wrong in the future. The economic significance of Euro-market credits for developing countries (and South America in particular) is now so great that the long-term political con-sequences of a drastic reduction in such credits, and the con-current IMF-enforced economic adjustment programmes taking place in such countries, could indeed change the course of history in a fundamental way in these countries. The triumph of communism in these countries would be of world-wide historical significance, as it would be one more tactical victory for the Soviet Union in its struggle with the West for mastery of the world.

Indeed, in Yugoslavia the course of its history was very nearly changed, to the advantage of the Soviet Union, during the adjustment/rescheduling processes in that country. Had not the United States exerted great pressure on Yugoslavia's commercial bank creditors to lend new money and on the IMF's conditionality, thereby avoiding internal political tur-moil that could have been exploited by the Soviet Union to its advantage, the historical outcome for Yugoslavia since 1982 might have been very different. After the Polish and Romanian débâcles, and given Yugoslavia's great domestic economic problems, there was great reluctance on the part of commercial banks to lend any new money to Yugoslavia. Even more so than in the case of Brazil and Mexico, lending to Yugoslavia was seen as throwing good money after bad. As regards the IMF, Yugo-slavia's highly decentralised political system and inept macro-economic planning procedures made effective economic adjustment far more difficult than was the case in the highly centralised political systems of the COMECON countries. Great patience on the part of the IMF was required in such a situation. More generally, the country's fragile domestic political stability and its external political neutrality ultimately rested upon its economic well-being.

It was a classic example of a sharp difference between the political interests of the United States and NATO and the economic interests of Yugoslavia's commercial bank creditors and the IMF. Since 1950, when President Truman had said that 'the continued independence of Yugoslavia is of great importance to the security of the United States',[30] the US Government's policy was to ensure that Yugoslavia was not forced into the Warsaw Pact and the COMECON bloc by the Soviet Union. For it to have been so would have been disastrous for NATO's south-eastern flank.[31] The Soviet Union, at a stroke, would have had warm-water ports in the Adriatic Sea for its Mediterranean Fleet and units of the Red Army on the Yugoslav–Italian border. The US Government feared, above all else, that severe economic dislocation would lead to political turmoil, which the Soviet Union, given its known desire to swallow Yugoslavia, would exploit to its own advantage, either by a surprise invasion, or by contriving to have itself 'invited' (more likely) into the country to restore 'socialist order', as it did in Czechoslovakia in 1968 and Afghanistan in 1979.

As early as the spring of 1982, the US Under-Secretary of State for European Affairs, Lawrence Eagleburger, previous US Ambassador to Yugoslavia, 'summoned a group representing US banks to Washington for an unusual and controversial meeting to encourage financial support for Yugosalvia'. The bankers' response, as expressed by one individual present at the 1982 meeting with Eagleburger, was that 'the message he [Eagleburger] should be sending is not that the banks should be lending more to Yugoslavia . . . He should instead tell the Yugoslavs to buckle down and take measures to correct their problems'.[32]

In the Brazilian and Mexican rescheduling negotiations, similar meetings took place between Central Bank officials in OECD countries and representatives of commercial banks for which they had supervisory responsibility. In Yugoslavia, in a totally unprecedented and unique move, a top foreign-policy official of the US Government exerted what seemed to the banks involved to be political interference of the most blatant kind. Indeed, so strong was this political pressure, and so obvious to all concerned, that the Yugoslav Government was embarrassed by it. Sensitive to Soviet charges that Yugoslavia was part of the capitalist world, and that the Yugoslav

Government was too friendly with the United States for its own good, the Yugoslav Government insisted that the neutral Swiss Government act as co-ordinator for the rescue package of 1983.[33] This was only a front, as the US Government played the leading role in presenting the rescue package for Yugoslavia in 1983.

As in Mexico, though to an even greater extent, the US Government pursued a 'soft' line, as opposed to the 'hard' line demanded by the commercial banks and the IMF, during the Yugoslav rescheduling/adjustment processes. The policy was to show a great deal of patience as regards Yugoslavia's numerous economic problems in the short term, so as to avoid internal political instability (the result of any really harsh economic adjustment process) that could benefit the Soviet Union in the long term. And any Soviet gain in Yugoslavia would be a loss for NATO. Even the IMF could see the connection, as the threat to Yugoslavia's continuing neutrality was right on its borders. In South America, on the other hand, the connection between the existing political instability and the possible future coming-to-power of communist regimes was not as clear and direct a threat as was the Soviet Union's proximity to Yugoslavia. Consequently, the IMF showed a great deal of tolerance in Yugoslavia, especially as regards the repeated breaches of the inflation targets agreed with the Yugoslav Government. Ironically, the IMF exhibited more tolerance towards a communist regime than it did to the countries of South America, which were, with the exception of Cuba, part of the free world.

More generally, one of the more significant consequences of the rescheduling/adjustment processes for OECD Governments, and the US Government in particular, was to highlight the political consequences and implications of what was once thought to be an exclusively economic issue: the debt of developing countries. Although a 1977 US Congressional report[34] discussed the political implications for US foreign policy of international debt growth, it was not until the debt crisis began in 1982 that the problem was given the sort of political attention it deserved in the United States. This political neglect was matched by a gap in the literature, which tended to separate the economics and politics of debt, and to give the politics of debt far less attention than the economics of debt.[35]

It became progressively clearer to many people that the US

national interest, with regard to US political interests in developing countries (and South America in particular), and the interests of the commercial banks and the IMF in the rescheduling/adjustment processes in these countries, were not necessarily one and the same thing. There was a great difference between the long-term political interests of the US Government, and the short-term financial interests of US commercial banks and the IMF. In the long term, US foreign policy in South America could not be allowed to become the hostage of short-term financial interests, since the eventual political consequences of allowing the latter to take precedence could turn out to be unmitigated disaster for US foreign-policy interests in South America. The mentality of bankers, competent enough in financial matters but inept in political matters, could not be allowed to dictate the course of US foreign policy in South America.

This ineptitude was shown in action in Eastern Europe. The most naïve political assumptions were made about the supposed altruism of the Soviet Union, which, it was confidently assumed, would act as lender of last resort if East European countries ran into debt problems. Nothing of the sort occurred when Poland, Romania, and Hungary ran into trouble. The Soviet Union, which was ideologically opposed to heavy indebtedness, let is comrades stew in their own juices and let the capitalist institutions bail out their comrades in Eastern Europe: the Paris Club in Poland, the IMF in Romania, and the BIS in Hungary. In South America, during the rescheduling/adjustment processes, it was assumed by the banks that there was no domestic political limits to what could be economically demanded of the region's debtor countries. There are limits, but to somebody who is politically inept and obsessed with short-term financial variables, they are not at all clear.

One of the more positive consequences of the rescheduling process for banks was their efforts radically to improve their political intelligence and sovereign-risk analysis procedures.[36] This was a classic example of dire necessity being the mother of invention, as it became increasingly obvious that economic analysis was of very little use in determining what the Governments of developing countries were really doing and planning to do in the rescheduling process, and in the world at large. Nor did such analysis make it possible to determine how secure was the position of such Governments, the balance of political and social forces in the countries concerned, and the political limits of economic adjustment in these countries.

For the United States, in fact, there was a political backlash against the commercial banks and the IMF. The banks, which have always been unpopular in the United States, were blamed for the mess they found themselves in, and there was great Congressional opposition to the plan to increase the US quota to the IMF in 1983, which was believed to be bailing out US banks with taxpayers' money. These popular perceptions, seized upon by certain US politicians, were understandable; but apportioning blame for the debt crisis was not the most rational or relevant way to resolve it. Apportioning blame or dreaming of a return to the *status quo ante* were both equally futile activities. Since a return to the pre-1982 situation was out of the question, it became clear that new ideas were required to deal with the problem of how best to finance development in developing countries, and how to deal with the debt service burden of the outstanding debt held by such countries. Only such new ideas, coupled with political will to act upon them, would resolve the debt problem of the developing countries.

5.4 Prescriptive proposals and the politically possible

By the end of 1983, with the emergency response phase (1982–3) of the rescheduling process over, the issue of long-term solutions to the problem of debt held by developing countries became more important than that of crisis management. The latter, by its very nature, was *ad hoc*, temporary, and was no real solution to the wider problems faced by developing countries and their foreign creditors alike.

One school of thought, however, believed that muddling through was enough, and that if the limited economy recovery of 1984, in both OECD countries and in selected developing countries such as Mexico, was sustained into 1985, then there was no need to think about long-term solutions. This may, indeed, prove to be the case, but given the potential risks to the stability of the international financial system and to the developing countries' political evolution if this optimistic scenario proves to be incorrect, then speculation about long-term solutions to the problem cannot, nor should, be avoided. Though this optimistic scenario was popular among many bankers, it was a minority view among those who were putting forward prescriptive proposals. Most of the prescriptive proposals were, in fact, based on the assumption that the debt burden of developing countries in the rescheduling process was unmanageable, regardless of whether or not the limited economic recovery of 1984 sustained itself into something more substantial in 1985. Since the debt was assumed to be unmanageable it followed, therefore, that the only way for the stability of the international financial system and of the political systems of the developing countries to be safeguarded was to reduce the debt service burden on outstanding debt, and to increase the amount of new lending in the future by both commercial banks and official creditors.

This assumption of debt unmanageability was challenged by the optimists, who believed that the debt was manageable, and who put their faith in IMF-enforced economic adjustment programmes, economic recovery in the world economy, and the regulatory Central Bank authorities in the OECD countries. The optimists cited the example of Turkey, which was *persona non grata* in the Euromarkets as recently as 1979, but which, after four years of economic adjustment and political order enforced by a military regime, was able to attract voluntary lending by commercial banks in 1983. The optimists, however, failed to mention that Turkey was the only example to back up their point of view. Countries such as Jamaica, Sudan, and Zaïre, which had been in the same position as Turkey in 1979, were in an even bigger shambles in 1983. The sheer number of countries that would have to follow the road followed by Turkey for the rest of the 1980s was such that a big question mark stood against the confident assertions of the optimists.

What, then, were the major prescriptive proposals to resolve the debt problem? Table 20 lists the main proposals. The proposals can be divided into three groups: firstly, those (Kenen, Rohatyn) that seek to reduce the debt service burden on outstanding debt for developing countries; secondly, those (Laulan, Leslie, Mackworth-Young, Lever, Zombanakis) that seek to induce more new lending by banks and official creditors to developing countries in the future; thirdly, one proposal (Kaletsky) that advocates default by developing countries as a

Table 20 Main reform proposals put forward to resolve the debt problems of developing countries, 1983–1985

Source of proposal	Proposal	Views of the proposal		
		Banks	Governments (OECD countries)	Governments (Developing countries)
Peter B. Kenen (University of Princeton)	Establishment of International Debt Discount Corporation, which would buy up debt held by banks at a discount of 10 cents on the $, and pay the banks in long-term bonds against itself.	Deals only with old debt. What about new loans?	Too costly.	Fails to deal with future new loans.
Felix Rohatyn (Lazard Frères)	The IMF, World Bank, or a new agency would do the same as Kenen's IDDC, and then reschedule debt over 30 years, limit interest rate to 6%, and limit debt service ratio to 25%.	Same view as for Kenen plan.	Too costly.	Fails to deal with future new loans.
William Mackworth-Young (Morgan Grenfell)	Future developing countries' deficits to be funded by issuing bonds carrying an	Deals only with new loans. Not	Too costly.	Fails to deal with old debt. Object to being

	international guarantee. Principle to be also applied retrospectively, so as to enable more new lending in the future.	old debts.		part of inter-national guarantee.
Yves Laulan (Société Générale)	Closer consultations between banks, IMF, and World Bank, and more risk-sharing via co-financing agreements with cross-default clauses. New bank loans, would therefore be indirectly guaranteed by the IMF.	IMF rules have to be changed.	Political difficulty of changing IMF rules.	A welcome plan that is the most politically realistic of those on the agenda.
Peter Leslie (Barclays Bank International)	Banks should discount problem loans with Central Banks, thereby removing them from their balance sheets. Such discounted loans would appear as contingent liabilities on balance sheets. The Central Banks would agree to discount on the condition that banks would provide new loans to developing countries to the value of the discounted loans.	Debt issue not a liquidity problem.	Central Banks not sympathetic to the proposal.	Fails to deal with the problem of increasing new lending to developing countries.

Table 20 (*cont.*)

Source of proposal	Proposal	View of the proposal			
		Banks	Governments (OECD countries)	Governments (Developing countries)	
Minos Zombanakis (Financier)	The IMF should make 13-year agreements with developing countries, and after 10 years a country unable to service its debt, despite complete adherence to the IMF programme, would have its payments guaranteed by the IMF for the last three years of the agreement.	How for 10 years? Most developing countries find it difficult to carry out 1-year pro-grammes.	IMF rules do not allow for such a plan.	Fails to deal with old debt.	
Harold Lever (Ex-UK politician)	Official export credit agencies should create an international agency to ensure new bank lending, with IMF advice.	Fails to deal with old debt.	Too costly.	Fails to deal with old debt.	
Anatole Kaletsky (*Financial Times*)	Developing countries should, in a non-aggressive and selective manner, implement a policy of conciliatory default	Totally un-acceptable.	Totally un-acceptable.	An interesting proposal, but risky due to probable reprisals by creditors.	

rational solution to the debt problems faced by the developing countries.

The Kenen and Rohatyn proposals were the most radical, in that they advocated the buying, at a discount, of the commercial bank assets tied up in developing countries with debt problems by a new multilateral agency (Kenen's International Debt Discount Corporation), or by a suitably altered (as regards its Articles of Agreement) IMF (Rohatyn). Such proposals would, in effect, make OECD Governments the only creditors of developing countries with debt problems, and enable the debt owed to them, via the IMF or the IDDC, to be rescheduled over a very long time-frame. Rohatyn, for example, suggested a maturity of thirty years, an interest rate of 6 per cent, and a maximum debt service ratio of 25 per cent in any one year. Even better terms would be offered to all problem debtor countries than was offered to Nicaragua in its exceptional agreement of 1981[37] (see Appendix 5).

These two generalised and overtly political proposals were criticised on the grounds that political willingness even to consider them was simply not present. Among OECD Governments, and the US Government in particular, the perceived potential threat in the debt crisis was not, in the opinion of those Governments, great enough to justify the vast political and economic effort that would be required to turn such radical proposals into reality. Comparisons were made with the Marshall Plan in Western Europe after World War II, where a very real political and military threat posed by the Soviet Union prompted a massive US effort to rebuild and defend Western Europe. Commentators such as Kenen and Rohatyn argued that while the threat to the long-term political interests of the United States in the problem debtor countries was not as visible, tangible, and immediate as the Soviet threat had been to Western Europe in 1945, the future possible political evolution of such countries could turn out to be as serious a threat to the United States as was the Soviet Union to Western Europe in 1945. Since statesmanship, it was argued, is as concerned with the future as it is with the present, then radical political action should be taken now—as it had been in the shape of the Marshall Plan in the 1940s—to ensure that the debt service burden on outstanding debt was reduced, new lending to finance development was resumed, and the political stability of developing countries was thereby safeguarded.

Another criticism, which came from the developing countries themselves, was that the Kenen and Rohatyn proposals did not give enough attention to the problem of new loans. It was assumed that if the debt service burden on outstanding debt was reduced, new lending would then automatically increase. Since these proposals would remove the present negative incentives (assets tied up in developing countries) for commercial banks to provide new money, there was no reason why those banks should lend new money in the future. If this did indeed happen, then debtor countries would find themselves in an even worse position in the future than they did at the present time. The answer to that point was that if the debt service burden on outstanding debt was reduced, the developing countries would find themselves in a better economic position (more disposable income to spend in the future after paying the lower debt service charges), which would in turn make them more creditworthy to commercial banks. The banks would then lend more new money.

The problem of new lending was, in many ways, the most important, and it was not suprising that the Mackworth-Young, Laulan, Leslie, Lever, and Zombanakis proposals were exclusively concerned with it. In the 1970s the commercial banks had implicitly assumed that the high risk of lending to developing countries was something shared, albeit informally and indirectly, between themselves and OECD Governments, both in their roles as official creditors of developing countries and as the supervisors of the banks. After the events of 1982–4, however, more than mere implicit assumptions would be required before commercial banks would be prepared to increase their new lending to developing countries. The risk inherent in the rescheduling process, though it had begun to decrease in 1984, was greater than the risk that had existed during the 1970s. In such high-risk conditions, formal guarantees to protect the security of new assets committed to developing countries by banks would be required in the future. If new lending was to increase substantially, therefore, risk-sharing between commercial banks and official creditors would have to be in a concrete form. The old implicit assumptions of the 1970s were inadequate.

The Mackworth-Young proposal envisaged the funding of future developing countries' borrowing requirements by the issuing of bonds by such countries, which would carry an international guarantee by OECD and developing country Governments. All such Governments would be collectively liable if any developing country defaulted on the bonds it had sold to commercial banks.

The Laulan proposal, which avoided the radical idea road but merely built upon the present-day, World Bank–commercial bank co-financing agreements in developing countries, advocated IMF–commercial bank co-financing agreements, with cross-default clauses written into them. Present World Bank–commercial bank agreements are limited in scope, but the Laulan proposal envisaged multi-billion-dollar agreements involving the IMF and commercial banks. Such agreements would provide a *de facto*, though indirect, guarantee by the IMF for new bank assets so committed to developing countries. The problem with this proposal was that a great deal of political will would be required among OECD Governments to change the IMF's Articles of Agreement, and turn the Fund into something entirely different from what it is at the present time. For the developing countries the proposal was not welcome, as such co-financing agreements involving the World Bank only disbursed conditional credit to be used for specific projects. However, if the credit so provided was made unconditional, the Laulan proposal was welcome to developing countries. The fact that it was relatively politically realistic also made it attractive to developing countries. Another problem of the Laulan proposal (and of the Mackworth-Young proposal) was that it failed to deal with the debt service burden on outstanding debt.

The same criticism was directed at the Zombanakis proposal. Like Laulan, Zombanakis concentrated on the IMF. He advocated thirteen-year agreements between the Fund and developing countries with debt problems. If, after ten years of successful economic adjustment agreed with the IMF, the country concerned was still unable to service its debt normally, then the IMF would guarantee its debt service payments for the last three years of the agreement.[38] The proposal assumed a major change in the IMF's Articles of Agreement. The proposal was rather unrealistic for two further reasons. Firstly, many developing countries found it difficult, or refused, to stick to the targets agreed with the IMF in one-year agreements. Secondly, the idea of ten years of economic adjustment was simply not acceptable to many developing countries. Zombanakis, being a banker, did not even think about the possible political consequences of ten years of IMF-enforced economic adjustment.

The Lever proposal, which substituted the IMF with a new multilateral agency to be created by the various export credit guarantee agencies of the OECD countries, saw new lending by commercial banks in an environment in which such loans would be officially guaranteed in the region of $50 billion per annum.[39] Two American commentators also came up with a similar idea, calling it the Export Development Fund, which would work with the World Bank and would make long-term loans to developing countries to buy capital goods from the OECD countries.[40] Though a good idea, great political will would be required among OECD Governments to set up any such agency.

The Leslie proposal, which is based on the odd assumption that the new loan problem is a liquidity problem as opposed to one of lack of confidence in developing countries, advocates the buying of problem debt, at a discount, from banks by OECD countries' Central Banks. This would, according to Leslie, enable more new loans to be lent to developing countries. Central Banks were against the idea of buying worthless 'assets' with public money, many bankers pointed out that liquidity was not the problem, and anybody who had a view on the subject said that some sort of guarantee would be needed if new bank lending was to increase substantially in the future.

Of these eight proposals, five were made by bankers, and the remainder by an academic, a retired politician, and a journalist. Few proposals were made by people with any real political power. An exception was a controversial proposal made by Norman Bailey, of the US National Security Council, which advocated that developing country debt be replaced with a form of equity asset entitling the holder to a specified share of the developing country's export earnings.[41] Related ideas envisaged developing countries turning over fixed economic assets within their borders to creditors in return for a write-off of outstanding debt. Such ideas, though attractive to some foreign creditors, were unacceptable to the Governments of developing countries, who were extremely sensitive to the political implications of such proposals. This was especially true in South America, where any suggestion of increased US direct foreign investment as a trade-off for less debt was politically unacceptable, given the virulence of anti-US feeling in that part of the world at the time.

The last proposal listed in Table 20, by Kaletsky, was in many ways the most radical and certainly the most interesting for developing countries, and the Cartagena Group in particular, to think about as a possible policy option. Kaletsky proposed[42] that developing countries should, in a non-aggressive and selective manner, implement a policy of conciliatory default. This was not, Kaletsky insisted, debt repudiation (an arguable point), but a *de jure* admission of numerous *de facto* defaults, past, present and future. This could be achieved by, for example, defaulting on long- and medium-term debt, while continuing to service short-term debt owed to banks, the IMF, and the World Bank. Such a move would considerably ease the debt service burden for developing countries on outstanding debt. This idea, which is becoming increasingly popular as a possible option in the Cartagena Group, is anathema to commercial banks, the IMF, and OECD Governments. Developing countries' know that any such move on their part would risk provoking reprisals from commercial bank creditors.

Kaletsky, who argues that the costs of such a move (potential reprisals by creditors) are less than the potential gains (lower debt service costs), is of the opinion that the legal proceedings that banks would begin would not be supported by OECD Governments, and the US Government in particular, for political reasons. The US Government, for example, would not go into all-out political conflict with the whole of South America, in order to support the legal proceedings initiated against the Governments of South America by US banks. If the US Government failed to back up the banks, their reprisals would count for very little, and the banks involved would get little in the way of financial redress through the courts from developing countries they had sued for breach of contract. The courts could only seize assets belonging to such countries outside their borders. The assets so gained would not cover the debt declared to be in default by developing countries.

Although the Cartagena Group is not yet at the stage of actually doing what Kaletsky advocates, it may threaten to do so. Threats to initiate disruptive actions if certain demands are not met are on the agenda of the Cartagena Group at the present time. Future events may, in the last resort, lead the Cartagena Group into such a course of action: threats to default and, if the threats do not obtain the desired response from creditors, default itself. The very fact that such proposals are being made, and are being given serious consideration as possible policy options for the future, indicates the seriousness of the present situation. Interestingly, Kaletsky's study was published by a top US think-tank, the Twentieth Century Fund in New York. If a top US think-tank finds the idea of default reasonable, it would be rash to think that the Cartagena Group does not find it attractive.

In general, these prescriptive proposals attracted more criticism than they did praise.[43] Since politics is the art of the possible, the majority of the proposals have been criticised for being politically unrealistic. The political will and imagination to turn such proposals into real policies simply does not exist among OECD Governments at the present time. Most of the proposals were made at the height of the debt crisis in 1983, and 1984 seemed to indicate that they were not required. This may indeed have been the case, but what of the long-term future? Politics, besides being the art of the possible, is not a static phenomenon, its courses are unpredictable, and the future consequences of present-day events unknown. This is especially true of the volatile and unstable political systems that presently exist in most developing countries. That volatility is not in itself significant, but the debt problem of the developing countries makes it significant for OECD countries, whether they like it or not. Figure 7 shows the relevant connections.

Figure 7 begins and ends with the economic situation of developing countries. A situation of indefinite negative net resource transfer, low GDP growth, and recession increases social tensions, which leads to political turmoil, of which the eventual consequences could turn out to be disastrous for OECD Governments (i.e. communist regimes). In addition, at the purely economic level, such a situation is harmful to the stability of the international financial system, and to the exports of OECD countries to developing countries.

Political turmoil, in turn, leads to confrontation with commercial banks, the IMF, and OECD Governments, as the Governments of developing countries are faced with the choice

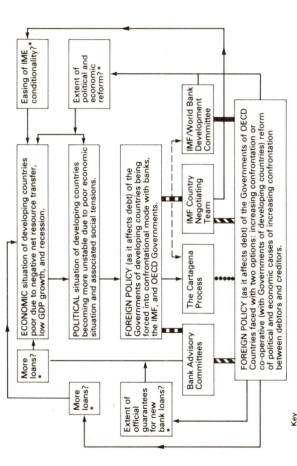

Figure 7 Major political and economic connections between developing countries and OECD countries during the re-scheduling process.

of attempting unconditional co-operation with foreign creditors, with all its attendant political risks due to the very severe economic adjustment such creditors demand, or confrontation with less economic adjustment and less political turmoil. The Cartagena Process is already a vehicle for serious confrontation, based on threats of default, and even (in the most extreme scenario) repudiation of debt. Other forums in which confrontation could take place are meetings with advisory committees and individual IMF country negotiating teams. In the short term, however, the most likely forum for confrontation is via the meetings of the representatives of the Cartagena Group and OECD Government finance ministers in the Development Committee of the IMF and the World Bank. Because of their supervisory responsibilities for commercial banks, their own role as official creditors and guarantors of bank loans through export credit agencies, and their domination of the Executive Board of the IMF, all the connections lead back to OECD Governments.

At present OECD Governments are faced with developing countries' Governments, both bilaterally and in the Cartagena Group, that want to co-operate with their foreign creditors, but are drifting into a confrontational mode with them by adverse domestic and external economic and political factors. OECD Governments, because of those adverse factors, could end up facing unco-operative, hostile, and radical communist regimes if they fail to reform the causes of those adverse factors, and thereby lessen the probability of such regimes coming to power in the future. Their options are either to worsen the cycle of growing confrontation by threatening reprisals if, for example, developing countries threaten to default, or to begin a programme of economic and political reform in co-operation with the Governments of developing countries in order to eradicate the ultimate cause of growing confrontation: the economic situation of developing countries.

The commercial banks will not, and should not be expected to, resolve alone the problem of financing development in the developing countries by increasing new lending. In 1974 the political cowardice of OECD Governments, who refused to increase their lending to developing countries after the oil price increases of 1974, was covered by the willingness of commercial banks to increase their lending to developing countries. Since the events of 1982–4, that willingness no longer exists. OECD Governments will have, therefore, to increase their lending to developing countries, and provide some sort of guarantee (formal or informal) for new lending by banks, before those banks will lend more money to the developing countries. They will, in addition, have to lower world interest rates and reduce the protectionist barriers that impede the exports of developing countries. Most importantly, perhaps, IMF conditionality will have to be eased in the interests of long-term political considerations.

The two big problems, therefore, are how best to finance high-growth economic development in the developing countries with debt problems, and how these countries can be induced to stay within the framework of international financial co-operation, and so avoid the sort of confrontation that would threaten the stability of the international financial system.[44] These problems are political, and can only be resolved through political action by OECD Governments and the Governments of developing countries, acting together in a co-operative manner, to produce mutually beneficial and enduring solutions to these difficult problems.

Notes

1. Delamaide, op. cit., pp. 228-9.
2. The role of these advisers is examined in Tim Anderson, 'The Troika Spawns a Whole New Business', *Euromoney*, August 1982; Quek Peck Lim, 'The Borrower's Trump Card is His Weakness', *Euromoney*, October 1982; Peter Rodgers, 'Troika Takes Banks to Task', *Guardian*, 19 April 1983; Charles Batchelor, 'Price Waterhouse in Debt Advice Venture', *Financial Times*, 4 May 1983; and Arnold Nachmanoff, 'Major Considerations in Advising Sovereign Borrowers on Debt Restructuring', in Group of Thirty, op. cit., pp. 80-3. For the view of an adviser who participated in the Nicaraguan debt rescheduling negotiations of 1980-1, see Weinert, op. cit., pp. 187-94.
3. For general analyses of the politics of debt, both within developing countries and between such countries and their foreign creditors, see Brandt Commission, *North–South* (London: Pan Books, 1980), and *Common Crisis* (London: Pan Books, 1983); Delamaide, op. cit., Chapter 10; Lipson, op. cit.; Emma Rothschild, 'Banks: The Coming Crisis', *The New York Review of Books*, 27 May 1976, and 'Banks:

The Politics of Debt', *The New York Review of Books*, 24 June 1976.

4. The view that no Government will commit domestic political suicide (be it through revolution or elections), if it comes to a choice between political suicide/co-operation with foreign creditors or political survival/confrontation with foreign creditors, in order to retain the confidence of its foreign creditors is a point cogently made in Michael H. Coles, 'Flexibility in Debt Rescheduling: Towards a Solution', in Group of Thirty, op. cit., pp. 62-79. Coles, of Goldman Sachs, was an adviser to many Governments, and it did not take him long to discover that political survival is the top priority of every Government, be it in the developing world or the OECD countries. Unlike the OECD countries, however, many politicians in the developing countries have their physical survival to worry about.

5. For recent analyses of South American politics and the debt question, see Pedro-Pablo Kuczynski, 'Latin American Debt', *Foreign Affairs*, winter 1982/3, and 'Latin American Debt: Act Two', *Foreign Affairs*, Fall 1983; Dallas, op. cit.; and Thomas D. Enders and Richard P. Mattione, *Latin America: The Crisis of Debt and Growth* (Washington, DC: Brookings Institution, 1984).

6. UN Economic Commission for Latin America (ECLA), *Preliminary Balance of the Latin American Economy in 1983* (Santiago: ECLA, 1984).

7. Mike Reid, 'Marines Go on the Mountain Warpath', *Guardian*, 21 September 1984.

8. Enders/Mattione, op. cit., p. 15.

9. Examined in Marko Miliojević, 'Yugoslavia's Security Dilemmas and the West', *The Journal of Strategic Studies*, Vol. 8, No. 3, September 1985.

10. For Mexico, see Kraft, op. cit., and Villarreal, op. cit.

11. For Brazil, see Celso Furtado, *No to Recession and Unemployment: An Examination of the Brazilian Economic Crisis* (London: Third World Foundation for Social and Economic Studies, 1984), and Alan Robinson, 'The IMF vs. The People', *Euromoney*, October 1983.

12. For Argentina, see Andrew Thompson, 'Alfonsin Walks on A Knife Edge', *South*, May 1984.

13. For Venezuela, see Alan Robinson, 'Can Lusinchi Do Without The IMF?', *Euromoney*, January 1984, and Peter Rodgers and Alex Brummer, 'Venezuela's Rescue Deal Without IMF Austerity', *Guardian*, 24 September 1984.

14. For Yugoslavia, see Milivojević (1985), op. cit.

15. For a discussion of the events leading up to the first Cartagena meeting, see Marko Milivojević, 'New Debt Crisis Raises Need for Debtors' Cartel to Fight Banks', *Politics and Profit*, June 1984.

16. The texts used are as follows: *The Cartagena Consensus* (Cartagena, Colombia: Colombian Ministry of Foreign Affairs, 23 June 1984); *Communiqué* (Mar del Plata, Argentina: Argentinian Ministry of Foreign Affiars, 16 September 1984); *Communiqué* (Santo Domingo, The Dominican Republic: Ministry of Foreign Affairs, 10 February 1985).

17. An interesting comparison is made in Peter Rodgers, 'How Many More Insults Will the Latin Americans Accept?', *Guardian*, 26 June 1984.

18. Henry Kissinger's remarks at the 1982 conference quoted in André Gunder Frank, 'A Debt Bomb Primed For The Next Recession', *Guardian*, 12 October 1984, and in Robinson (1983), op. cit., pp. 91 and 93.

19. See Bitterman, op. cit., for this period.

20. Discussed in Jan Knippers Black, *United States Penetration of Brazil* (Manchester: Manchester University Press, 1977).

21. The causes are analysed in Richard E. Feinberg, *The Intemperate Zone: The Third World Challenge To U.S. Foreign Policy* (New York: Norton, 1983).

22. See Kelly, op. cit., and Lipson, op. cit.

23. Discussed in Keith J. Horsefield (ed.), *The International Monetary Fund, 1945-65: Twenty Years of International Monetary Co-operation*, 3 Vols. (Washington, DC: IMF, 1969), and Moffit, op. cit.

24. This change is discussed in Margaret G. De Vries, *The International Monetary Fund, 1966-1971: The System Under Stress* (Washington, DC: IMF, 1976), and John Williamson, *The Failure of International Monetary Reform, 1971-74* (London: Nelson, 1977). See Cline (1976), op. cit., for a discussion of how these changes affected the developing countries.

25. Such as Honeywell, op. cit., and Payer (1974), op. cit.

26. See Stephen D. Bodayla, 'Bankers Versus Diplomats: The Debate Over Mexican Insolvency', *Journal of InterAmerican and World Affairs*, November 1982, pp. 461-82.

27. See Black, op. cit., for further details.

28. See Enders/Mattione, op. cit.; Honeywell, op. cit.; Jansen, op. cit.; Robinson (1983), op. cit.; Villarreal, op. cit.; and, for a theoretical view of the problem, see Mary Sutton, 'Structuralism: The Latin American Record And The New Critique', in Tony Killick (1984), op. cit., pp. 19-67.

29. Joseph A. Schumpeter, *Capitalism, Socialism and Democracy*, 3rd edn. (New York: Harper and Row, 1950), p. 55.

30. Quoted in Dennison Rusinow, *The Yugoslav Experiment, 1948-1974* (London: C. Hurst & Co. for the Royal Institute of International Affairs, 1977), p. 44.

31. See Milivojević (1985), op. cit., for further details.
32. Editorial, 'Yugoslavia's Lenders Apprehensive', *Wall Street Journal*, 7 May 1982.
33. See Milivojević (1983), op. cit.
34. Karin Lissakers, *International Debt, The Banks, and U.S. Foreign Policy*, Staff Report prepared for the use of the Subcommittee on Foreign Economic Policy of the Committee on Foreign Relations, United States Senate (Washington, DC: US Government Printing Office, 1977). In the UK two similar reports appeared in 1983, and caused a great deal of controversy due to their criticisms of the terms demanded of developing countries by UK banks during the emergency response phase (1982–3) of the rescheduling process. See Treasury and Civil Service Committee, House of Commons, *International Monetary Arrangements: Second Special Report of the Treasury and Civil Service Committee, Session 1982-1983, London* (London: HMSO, 1983), and *International Monetary Arrangements: International Lending by Banks—Fourth Report of the Treasury and Civil Service Committee, Session 1982-1983, London* (London: HMSO, 1983).
35. Notable exceptions include Jonathan D. Aronson, *Money and Power: Banks and the World Monetary System* (Beverly Hills, California: Sage, 1977); Cline (1976), op. cit.; Cohen, op. cit.; Charles Kindleberger, *Power and Money: The Economics of International Politics and the Politics of International Economics* (New York: Basic Books, 1970); Moffit, op. cit.; Joan Edelman Spero, *The Politics of International Economic Relations*, 2nd. edn. (London: George Allen & Unwin, 1982); and Susan Strange, 'International Economics and International Relations: A Case of Mutual Nelgect', *International Affairs*, 46, April 1970, pp. 304-15.
36. For a discussion of the inadequate procedures of the 1970s, see Peter Field, 'Meet the New Breed of Banker: The Political Risk Expert', *Euromoney*, July 1980, and S. M. Yassukovich, 'The Growing Political Threat to International Lending', *Euromoney*, April 1976, for an analysis of the political threats faced by banks when lending to developing countries.
37. A point made in Leslie Weinert, 'Banks and Bankruptcy', *Foreign Policy*, No. 50, spring 1983, pp. 138-49.
38. The proposal is fully set out in Minos Zombanakis, 'The International Debt Threat: A Way to Avoid a Crash', *The Economist*, 30 April 1983, pp. 11-14.
39. The proposal is fully set out in *The Economist*, 9 July 1983, pp. 14-16. For Harold Lever's wider views on the debt problem, see Harold Lever *et al.*, *The Lever Group Report* (London: Commonwealth Secretariat, 1984), and 'Drowning in Debt', *Time and Tide*, autumn 1984, pp. 9-12.

40. William H. Bolin and Jorge del Canto, 'LDC Debt: Beyond Crisis Management', *Foreign Affairs*, summer 1983.

41. Norman A. Bailey, 'A Safety Net for Foreign Lending', in T. de Saint Phalle (ed.), *The International Financial Crisis: An Opportunity For Constructive Action* (Washington, DC: Georgetown University Center for Strategic and International Studies, 1983), pp. 27-36.

42. Anatole Kaletsky, *The Costs of Default*, a Twentieth Century Fund paper (New York: Priority Press Publications, 1985).

43. For a critique of them, see Charles Grant, 'Those Debt Proposals: Radical or Just Wrong?', *Euromoney*, July 1983.

44. Cogently argued in Jan Tumlir, 'The World Economy Today: Crisis or New Beginning?', *National Westminster Bank Quarterly Review*, August 1983.

6 Conclusion

6.1 International System

One of the most important developments of the last fifteen years has been the progressive disappearance of the international financial and trading order created by the United States after World War II.[1] In 1973, the system of fixed but adjustable exchange rates created at Bretton Woods in 1944 ended, and was replaced by a non-system of wildly fluctuating exchange rates.[2] By the early 1980s, protectionism (tariff and non-tariff barriers to trade between countries), which the US-created international trading order had lessened in the post-war era in the GATT forum, was on the increase in all OECD countries.[3] In addition, phenomena such as competitive devaluations of currencies, interest-rate wars, and trade wars became significant in all OECD countries.

This rising tide of destabilising systemic disorder, in which the US-created rules of the international financial and trading games were abandoned but not replaced by any other set of mutually acceptable rules, is the wider background against which the rise of developing countries' indebtedness took place in the 1970s and 1980s. This debt growth, and the consequent breakdown of the financing of economic development in the developing countries in the period 1982–4, can be seen as one of the many manifestations of that wider systemic disorder in the international system. This is because the debt problem of the developing countries, along with the concurrent problem of floating exchange rates, is one of the most potentially destabilising forces at work in the international financial system at the present time. Other problems, such as the inflationary consequences of unregulated liquidity creation in the Euromarkets[4] and the erosion of national sovereignty the world over by the creation of a global money market, also exist. As regards the global money market, in which around $200 billion is traded every day,[5] it is clear that it dwarfs world trade. In 1984, for example, total world trade (between countries) amounted to $1.4 trillion. That figure, huge as it is, only represents seven days' trading in the global money market, where money is bought and sold. The cumulative effect of all these developments has been a radical change in the nature of the international financial system.

Some theorists,[6] in recent years, have seen that international financial system as becoming progressively more unstable, bloated, and beyond the political control of OECD Governments. The Euromarkets, which are the core of the international financial system, are beyond the direct control of OECD country Governments, and the operations of banks in such markets in a wider context of floating exchange rates, interest-rate wars, competitive devaluations of currencies, the declining use of exchange controls, and the development of electronic funds transfer systems, have had the effect of eroding the national sovereignty of Governments everywhere.[7] So, while the political need to resolve the problems created by these developments has never been greater, the actual ability of Governments to act to resolve these problems has never been lower.

The position of developing countries, which was once peripheral in the international financial system, became more significant during the 1970s when commercial banks increased their lending to such countries, and when OECD Governments declined in importance as the official creditors of such countries. This change, which connected some of the most economically weak and politically unstable countries in the world with the core of the international financial system, is of great significance for that system. Because of the size of developing countries' debts, and because of the events of 1982–4 in the rescheduling/adjustment process, what happens in such countries in the future has an immediate impact on the stability or otherwise of an already precariously ordered international financial system. That connection means, in effect, that any serious crisis in the debt-servicing capabilities of developing countries is potentially capable of becoming the cause of a wider crisis in the international financial system. Such a development would, in turn, have a detrimental effect on the real productive world economy, whose ability to function efficiently is dependent on the existence of a stable international financial system.

A comparison[8] with the events of the period 1929–33 is unavoidable. During that period a financial crisis in the United States had a calamitous effect on the real economy in that country, causing a severe depression that was not ended until the beginning of World War II. By 1931, when the United States was no longer able to act as creditor to the world as a direct result of its own domestic financial crisis, the effects of events in the United States spread to Europe and the developing countries. An uncontrollable spiral of financial crisis, depression in the real economy, and falling world trade then began in Europe and the developing countries, and South American countries in particular, in the period 1931–3. The eventual economic and political consequences of these developments are too well known to repeat here.[9] Suffice it to say that it was a financial crisis that was the ultimate cause of the world depression of the 1930s. In the opinion of some theorists,[10] the same path could well be taken in the future: from a financial crisis, triggered by a localised event (such as a breakdown in the debt-servicing capabilities of the largest developing country debtors), leading to a general crisis of the real economy all over the capitalist world, which would have the effect of turning the present cyclical recession into a 1930s-type depression.

How probable is such a scenario in the future? If world economic growth picks up, and if developing countries' exports to OECD countries are able to increase substantially, and if interest rates fall, then a crisis of debt-servicing capability among developing countries can probably be avoided. However, real interest rates are still at historically high levels, all the evidence[11] suggests that protectionism is increasing all over the world, and relatively low GDP growth rates are still the norm in most OECD countries. If these present trends continue, the developing countries cannot expect much in the way of lower interest rates or of greater opportunities to increase their exports to OECD countries in the short and medium term. At the same time, they cannot expect a large increase in the amount of new lending, be it from commercial banks or official creditors. Yet without such an increase in new lending such countries cannot get out of the negative net resource transfer and low GDP growth situations they find themselves in at the present time. Such countries, being economically weak and politically instable, find themselves in the position whereby all the major economic variables that most concern them—interest rates, protectionist barriers in OECD countries, low GDP growth in OECD countries, and creditors' projected future lending to developing countries— are beyond their control. They do not, in other words, determine which way these key economic variables will go in the future, but can only react to them.

The big question for the future is how will they react? Their reaction will, in fact, determine whether or not the scenario mentioned above will take place in the future. The possibility exists that if these externally determined economic variables do not improve to the advantage of the developing countries, and if the domestic consequences of adverse economic conditions become such as to create very instable political conditions in these countries, then they could react in a destructive and confrontational manner via the Cartagena Process. This would mean threats to disrupt, or actual disruption of, debt servicing, so as to extract concessions from foreign creditors, and OECD countries in particular. The most extreme act in such a confrontational process with foreign creditors would be the outright repudiation of all foreign debts by the countries involved in the Cartagena Process. The consequences of such developments for foreign creditors, and the commercial banks in particular, is another of the big future question marks. Would such developments, as some theorists suggest, be the 'trigger' needed to begin a general crisis in the international financial system as a whole?

It is a possibility, but it is not an immediate probability due to the international political framework within which commercial bank lending to developing countries takes place. The network of co-operation, and mutual commitment to take remedial measures in the event of crisis, among OECD-country Central Banks, the IMF, and OECD Governments is well developed. The efficacity of that framework was amply demonstrated during the rescheduling process of 1982-4. The present framework is far more developed and effective than was the case during the crisis of 1931-3. Some historians[12] of that earlier period have argued, in a most convincing manner, that had such co-operation between Central Banks and Governments existed at the time, then the spread of the consequences of the US domestic financial crisis to the rest of the world could have been avoided. In addition, such historians also argued that if the US Federal Reserve Board had been more competent than in fact it was, then the purely domestic financial crisis of 1929–31 could have been completely avoided.[13]

A lesson was learned both in the 1930s and during the debt crisis of the 1980s. The market, once it breaks down, cannot by itself resolve the problem of having broken down. Only the political framework within which the market exists can, in the final analysis, resolve the problem of market breakdown through imaginative and efficacious political action.

However, although there is considerable co-operation between OECD-country Central Banks in the forum of the BIS, and although such Central Banks and OECD-country Governments were in agreement as to the need for bold remedial measures in the rescheduling process of 1982–4, there is no political agreement among such Governments as to what should be done to resolve, as opposed to dealing merely with the consequences of, the wider problems that afflict the international financial system, and the developing countries in particular. There is no agreement, for example, on interest rates. The US Government has persistently ignored the calls, from OECD and developing countries alike, that it should take the necessary monetary and fiscal measures to reduce US Prime Rate, and hence world interest rates. As regards exchange rates, which are intimately connected to interest rates, there is no political commitment to a multilateral solution to the problem of wildly fluctuating exchange rates. A bloc mentality prevails with the West Europeans (with the exception of the UK), for example, opting for the protection offered by the European Monetary System (EMS), which brings some order to West European exchange rates, but which offers no protection to the major problem in the present exchange rate regime: the great fluctuations between the US dollar and the other main world currencies such as the German mark and the Japanese yen. Protectionist wrangles continue unabated which threaten to bury the GATT once and for all. In general, instead of a political commitment to finding multilateral solutions to these numerous problems, the trend is towards unilateral acts, with each country acting as it sees fit, and without reference to other countries in the international system.

This is the systemic anarchy that has replaced the US-created international financial and trading orders that existed in the 1950s and 1960s. Although the United States is still the most economically and politically powerful country it is unable, and indeed unwilling, to impose that old order.[14] The old hegemonic world order, in which the United States provided leadership, was relatively easy to manage, but the present multipolar world order is becoming increasingly difficult to manage.[15] It is a non-system of international anarchy, in which unilateralism in international economic affairs reigns supreme. It is not an auspicious time in which a multilateral political solution, among OECD-country Governments and the Governments of the developing countries, to the problem of financing economic development in the developing countries can be easily found. The problem of divisions between OECD-country Governments is further complicated by the major developing countries organised in the Cartagena Group, who are symptomatic of the growing uncontrollability of the developing countries. This contrasts with the situation in the 1950s and 1960s, when such countries were humble supplicants before the OECD countries.[16] Now this is no longer the case. After OPEC's victory in the early 1970s, the tendency was for such countries to be confident, aggressive, and determined to get a New International Economic Order (NIEO), in which more economic and political power would accrue to them. The Cartagena Process is but one manifestation of that trend. How such countries, organised in the Cartagena Process, behave in the future, and what responses (if any) are forthcoming from the OECD countries to their demands, will determine whether or not the debt problems of such countries are resolved in the future.

6.2 Rescheduling process

Morgan Grenfell's William Mackworth-Young, author of one of the prescriptive proposals listed in Table 19, stated, with reference to the rescheduling process, that 'the *ad hoc* system may not work the second time around. We may not be so skilful or so fortunate next time'.[17] The rescheduling process, by its very nature, is a mixture of *ad hoc* and strictly temporary remedial measures intended to return developing countries to normal financial relationships with their foreign creditors in as short a time as is reasonably possible. That rescheduling process cannot in itself, therefore, resolve the wider problem of how best to finance economic development in the developing countries in the future.

However, the main lesson of the rescheduling process offers, in an unintentional way, a clue as to how that wider problem can be best resolved in the future. From 1973 to 1982, the market, and the financial intermediation of Euromarket commercial banks in particular, played the primary role in the financing of the economic development of the developing countries. In 1982, for a whole variety of reasons, normal financial relationships broke down, and the rescheduling process began so as to restore these normal financial relationships in as short a time as possible. From 1982 to 1984, the international political framework within which the market exists played the primary role in the rescheduling process. That framework includes the IMF, Central Banks, and OECD Governments. The primacy of politics, especially via the role of the IMF, was evident in the conditions of crisis that prevailed in the period 1982–4, and the period 1982–3 in particular. The major lesson of the rescheduling process is that only political action can, in the last analysis, resolve the wider problem of how best to finance the economic development of the developing countries in the future.

Yet the paradox of 1984 and 1985 is that while the need for political action on this issue has never been greater, the likelihood of such political action taking place has never been lower. Sharp differences of opinion divide OECD Governments, especially the Governments of Western Europe and the United States, on such issues as exchange rates, interest rates, and protectionism. Aside from these intra-OECD country differences, on issues of great concern to the developing countries, even sharper differences of opinion divide OECD Governments and the Governments of the developing countries. The Cartagena Process is the most important manifestation of these North–South differences at the present time.[18] More generally, although there was a mutual multilateral commitment among

OECD Governments to take remedial measures in the rescheduling process, there is an increasing tendency towards unilateralism in international economic affairs in general. As regards more fundamental issues such as interest and exchange rates, the monetary and fiscal policies of the US Government are the prime example of unilateralism in action—a unilateralism that is seemingly indifferent to the consequences of its own action on other countries in the international system, and that is in sharp contrast to the mutual commitment to multilateralism in international economic affairs that existed in the 1950s and 1960s.

On the issue of the financing of the economic development of the developing countries in the future, there is an ideological aversion to long-term and bold political action, and a belief that the market will, by itself, be able to deal with the problem despite the events of 1982–4. The right-wing swing in politics in the OECD countries, and the United States in particular, have strengthened this belief. Not even the events of 1982–4, nor the statements of commercial banks that they will not go back to the *status quo ante* as regards the future financing of the economic development of the developing countries, seem capable of shaking the faith of those people who believe these ideological dogmas. However, since practical politics has usually more to do with political expediency than to the maintenance of ideological purity, the precedent set by the rescheduling process—extensive political interference by OECD Governments that were ideologically averse to such political interference in the lending process—will probably guide future action by OECD Governments if the circumstances in developing countries warrant such political action.

At the present time, however, OECD Governments, and the US Government in particular, feel that circumstances in developing countries do not warrant such action on their part. Such ideological considerations will not inhibit political action by OECD Governments in conditions of crisis, such as the rescheduling process of 1982–4, but they are presently preventing pre-emptive political action by OECD Governments to avoid the development of economic and political conditions in the developing countries that could lead to yet another crisis in the future. The avoidance of pre-emptive political action by OECD

Governments for purely ideological reasons is the most disturbing aspect of the debt crisis at the present time.

This ideology[19] about the inherently self-correcting abilities of the market is not only dangerous, but it is also largely irrelevant, given the fact that political decisions largely determine which way interest rates, exchange rates, and degrees of protectionism will go in the future. Jan Tumlir, a GATT secretariat economist, after noting that by far the greatest proportion of total OECD countries' GDP derives (directly and indirectly) from the public sector, goes on to note that interest rates (US monetary and fiscal policies), exchange rates (market reactions to differing interest rates), protectionism (political actions by Governments), agriculture (the EEC's CAP and price support in the United States), and oil (OPEC), to take the most important economic variables and economic activities, are all highly politicised.[20] If these things are so highly politicised, and if extensive political interference has characterised the rescheduling process, then it seems incongruous and slightly unreal to pretend that the future financing of the economic development of the developing countries is not a highly politicised question.

This question consists of three related issues: the debt-service burden on outstanding debt, the amount of official lending to developing countries in the future, and the extent of official guarantees of future commercial bank lending to developing countries. Dealing with the first issue would necessarily entail serious consideration of some of the prescriptive proposals listed in Table 20. The second and third issues, like the first, would involve the taking of very important political decisions by OECD Governments. The second issue, as it was perceived by the commercial banks, would have to be resolved in such a way as to create a more equitable distribution of official and commercial bank lending to the developing countries in the future. The third issue, intimately related to the second, would have to be resolved in such a way as to result in some sort of official guarantee by OECD Governments of commercial bank lending to developing countries, if such lending was to increase significantly in the future. Such a guarantee, be it indirect or direct, would create a formalised system of risk-sharing, which was the only circumstance under which commercial banks would lend to developing contries anywhere near the levels of lending during the 1970s.

For the Governments of the developing countries, on the other hand, it seemed obvious—after the highly politicised nature of the rescheduling process—that direct, multilateral, political negotiations take place forthwith between OECD Governments and the Cartagena Group, in order to resolve the problem of how best to finance the economic development of the developing countries in the future. The stakes, both economic (stability of the international financial system) and political (evolution of the political systems of developing countries, and in terms of the political relations between such countries and the OECD countries), were large. Either such negotiations took place now (1985), when the developing countries organised in the Cartagena Process were relatively co-operative, and when the wider economic situation was manageable, or in the future in response to some further crisis, involving confrontation between the Cartagena Group and its foreign creditors, which would be far worse than was the crisis of 1982–4.

The events of 1982–4 have, in their own way, changed the world as radically as did the events of 1973–4, when OPEC increased the price of oil. Darrell Delamaide, in his seminal work on the debt crisis, suggests that

there will be a second debt shock, just as there was a second oil shock in 1979-80. The debt shock is not an economic event any more than the oil shock was. It is political. It is a tremor caused by a massive shift in power. The real issue was not resolved after the first oil shock because it was hardly even recognised.[21]*

Delamaide suggests that since true political statesmanship must recognise the significance of phenomena such as the present debt crisis and must take pre-emptive remedial measures to avert future disasters arising out of that crisis, then political unwillingness even to recognise that a problem exists—such unwillingness characterised the behaviour of OECD Governments in 1983–4—is not only foolish, but is totally self-defeating in the long-term. Such political inertia and unwillingness to recognise and to respond to it is symptomatic of political mediocrities, not true statesmen, who have the intelligence to recognise the significance of particular phenomena, and the political courage and imagination to act. If OECD Governments

* © 1984 Darrell Delamaide. Reproduced by permission from *Debt Shock*.

had acted in such a way during and immediately after the events of 1973–4, with regard to the oil question, then the massive debt growth of the 1970s and the consequent debt crisis of 1982–4 need not have happened. If the entire process of political inactivity, in response to the debt question, is repeated, then the old adage about those who ignore the mistakes of the past are condemned to repeat them in the future will have been shown to be depressingly true yet again.

6.3 Developing countries

Goldman Sachs's Michael Coles, when he said that political survival (not making foreign creditors happy) was the number one priority of every Government in the developing world, was speaking a truth more profound than he perhaps realised when he said it.[22] This priority becomes even more urgent in certain developing countries, where the ruling politicians of such countries also have their physical survival to worry about. For such politicians ruling countries whose social and political systems have been put under great strain by the economic consequences of the rescheduling/adjustment processes, the choice is clear: unconditional bilateral co-operation with foreign creditors, with all the attendant political risks of doing what these creditors demand *ad infinitum*, or progressively more serious multilateral confrontation, in the Cartagena Process, with such creditors, and an attendant lessening of domestic political tensions through the abandonment of economic adjustment as demanded by foreign creditors.

At the beginning of 1985 the developing countries involved in the Cartagena Process were still relatively co-operative with foreign creditors, and were waiting for the latter to reply to their 1984 economic and political demands. What kind of reply they get in 1985 will, in a very real sense, determine whether the relatively co-operative attitude of early 1985 will continue in the future, or whether progressively more serious confrontational attitudes will emerge. Which way the Cartagena Process will go has yet to be decided, and is unclear at the present time. What is clear, however, is that negative net resource transfer, low GDP growth (declining GDP per capital in real terms), domestic recession, and the consequent political turmoil that follows such adverse conditions, cannot be endured by the developing countries concerned without serious damage to their domestic political evolution in the long term.

The Governments of developing countries instinctively know this, as they are directly responsible for trying to control increasingly uncontrollable social and political situations. The situation in the economically weaker countries such as Peru and Bolivia, for example, is already politically explosive. The larger debtor countries, such as Brazil and Mexico, are not as yet in such desperate circumstances, but there is no guarantee that they will not be so within the next five to ten years. OECD Governments and the IMF, on the other hand, are far removed from such practical political problems, and are in danger of dangerously underestimating the great political risks inherent in the rescheduling/adjustment processes in the long term. The IMF, in particular, is in danger of allowing short-term financial considerations to blind it to those long-term political risks. The OECD Governments, though they are the major shareholders of the IMF, have given the Fund a great deal of autonomy in the rescheduling/adjustment processes, in the belief that what the Fund does is in the interests of all concerned—debtors and creditors alike.

While what the IMF does may, indeed, be in the short-term financial interests of the creditor countries, and the commercial banks in particular, there is considerable doubt as to whether what the IMF is doing is in the long-term political interests of OECD Governments, especially the US Government, in areas of great strategic importance such as South America. Such doubts, not surprisingly, are strongest in the developing countries themselves.[23] The issue of IMF-enforced economic adjustment programmes must, therefore, be one of the major problems to be resolved in any multilateral political programme constructed by OECD Governments and the Governments of developing countries in the future.

The major problem at the present time is not the political willingness of the Governemnts of developing countries to participate in the construction of such a political programme, but the political unwillingness of OECD Governments, and the US Government in particular, to recognise that the debt problems of the developing countries justify that construction. The short term, politically unimaginative, and *ad hoc* mentality of OECD Governments is inclined to assume that the debt problem of the developing countries is manageable without the construction of such a political programme. For this sort of mentality, the long-term political evolution of developing countries, though important in purely abstract terms, is not something to justify a major political effort that would be economically costly, unless dire necessity—such as the events of 1982-4—enforced such a political effort.

For the politicians of the developing countries, however, thinking about, and planning to deal with, the future is not an abstract activity, and cannot be avoided. This is especially true of South America. Communist regimes are established in Cuba and Nicaragua, civil wars rage throughout Central America in which communists play a prominent role, civil wars instigated by communists are beginning in countries like Peru, and violent riots have taken place in virtually every country in South America. For politicians in relatively politically stable countries such as Mexico, this spectre of political turmoil and anarchy is one that they wish to avoid at any price. If they do not avoid it, their political survival, and perhaps even their physical survival, is put in grave danger. The avoidance of undergoing such political turmoil is the real *raison d'être* of the Cartagena Process, which aims to exert collective pressure on foreign creditors so as to extract economic and political concessions from them, which would in turn have the effect of lessening the probability of serious political turmoil in the future.

The big question of 1985 is whether OECD Governments, and the US Government in particular, will give these political questions the attention they deserve, and act accordingly before it is too late. If present trends continue, Central America will be communist by the 1980s. The same could be true of Peru. The same scenario of communist victory in the rest of South America is not only a real possibility, but is becoming increasingly probable in the long term. The choice for OECD Governments is simple: political action, to reduce the probability of such a scenario taking place in the future; or political inaction with the consequent risk of facing defeat in the long term, for if such communist regimes do come to power and ally themselves with the Soviet Union, it will be virtually impossible to get rid of them. In such circumstances, as has been the case with Cuba since the early 1960s, any attempt to remove such communist regimes would lead to immediate conflict with the Soviet Union.

6.4 Commercial banks

Despite their traditional abhorrence of political interference in the lending process during normal times (1973–82), the events of 1982–4 have convinced the commercial banks that bold political action by OECD Governments will be required to resolve the problem of how best to finance the economic development of the developing countries in the future. The commercial banks, in other words, are unwilling (and should not be expected) merely to resume the primary role they played in the financing of the economic development of the developing countries in the period 1973–82. The traumatic events of 1982–4 have rendered the *status quo ante* dead as far as the commercial banks are concerned. During the re-scheduling process all lending to developing countries was involuntary, and even by the beginning of 1985 no developing country was yet able to attract voluntary lending from the commercial banks. Only Mexico was anywhere near being able to do so in the short term. OECD Governments would have to make major political decisions on easing the debt service burden on the outstanding debt of the developing countries, and on the provision of official guarantees of new commercial bank lending to such countries in the future, before commercial banks would be willing significantly to increase their new lending.

During the rescheduling process itself, although they played a secondary role to that of the IMF's leadership role, the commercial banks, via the general effectiveness and organisational flexibility of the advisory committees, displayed a quite remarkable ability to act co-operatively to deal with a common crisis. However, despite their organisational strengths, commercial banks, apparently so powerful and influential in more normal times, proved to be very vulnerable, and dependent upon the IMF for leadership in the rescheduling process. Without the IMF, which compelled developing countries to adjust their economies, the advisory committees would not have been able to enforce economic adjustment alone. Similarly, the wider problem of how best to finance the economic development of the developing countries in the future was a matter that the commercial banks could not hope to resolve alone.

As to the future, how much of their assets presently tied up in the developing countries are the commercial banks likely to lose, and how much have they already lost in the rescheduling process? As regards the latter, it was assumed that all assets, rescheduled and unrescheduled, would be repaid— albeit in a delayed manner as far as rescheduled assets were concerned—some time in the future. This assumption, which allowed problem assets (non-performing: actual and potential) to remain on banks' balance sheets, was clearly unrealistic. Though it is virtually impossible to determine what commercial banks regard as worthless, or potentially worthless, assets, it is reasonably clear that a significant proportion of the assets tied up in countries like Poland, Sudan, Zaïre, and the weaker South American countries such as Bolivia and Peru are, in fact, virtually worthless, and will not be repaid in the long term. Assets tied up in such disaster countries will have to be formally written off in the future. Pretending that countries like the Sudan, which are in a total shambles, will ever return to normal debt servicing is totally unrealistic. In the United States, for example, the 1983 International Lending and Supervision Act makes the provision of reserves to offset the losses in certain designated, very high-risk countries (of which Sudan is one) compulsory in law.[24]

With regard to the really big debtors, such as Brazil, Mexico, Argentina, Venezuela, and Yugoslavia, commercial banks are understandably unwilling openly to admit what, if any, of their assets tied up in these countries are regarded as problem assets. Assets that may, some time in the future, become non-performing. Interestingly, despite all the talk about the supposed ending of the debt crisis in 1984 and early 1985, commercial banks, both in the United States and Western Europe, made record provisions to cover possible sovereign bad debts in the developing countries. The long-term prospects, over the next five to ten years, cannot be as optimistic as those public pronouncements on the debt crisis of 1984, for if all was as well as the pronouncements suggested, such record provisions—

which all come out of profits—would not have been made. Whether such problem assets become non-performing because of economic inability to service debt on the part of developing countries, or because of political unwillingness to service such debts on the part of the Governments of the developing countries, is irrelevant to the commercial banks. Whatever the cause of non-performing assets, the possibility exists of large future losses for the commercial banks as a result of the write-off of non-performing assets. The greater the political militancy of the Cartagena Group, and the worse the economic prospects of the countries in that group, the more probable the scenario of debt default by such countries becomes. The expectation, among commercial banks, of very large losses due to non-performing assets in the medium and long term, in conditions of great economic and political uncertainty, is what lies behind the record provisions of late 1984 and early 1985.

Again, the issue goes back to the political attitudes of the OECD Governments. If the demands of the Cartagena Group are accepted, and if political negotiations begin to try to resolve the problem of how best to finance economic development in the developing world in the future, then the probability of large future losses for the commercial banks decreases. The probability of massive losses would be further reduced if a mutually satisfactory solution to the problem was found during those political negotiations. If, on the other hand, nothing politically significant is done, the Governments of the developing countries could find that they were economically unable, or they may decide they were politically unwilling (a far more likely option given the existence of the Cartagena Group), to service their foreign debts. Commercial banks would suffer great losses as a result, especially, as seems most likely given the existence of the Cartagena Group, if debt servicing was stopped in all the major developing countries at one and the same time.

The commercial banks, like the Governments of the developing countries, find themselves waiting for political action by the OECD Governments to resolve the debt problem, both as regards the debt-servicing burden on outstanding debt and the future financing requirements of the developing countries. Whether such political action does, in fact, materalise is the big question of 1985. A great deal, both for the commercial banks and the developing countries, rests upon this important question. The same is true for the OECD Governments, and the US Government in particular, although they seem to be seriously underestimating the political dangers of avoiding political action to resolve the debt problem. Without doubt, 1985 will be the year in which it will be seen whether or not such political action will, in fact, be forthcoming.

Notes

1. For a general discussion of these matters, see Spero, op. cit.
2. See Cohen, op. cit., De Vries, op. cit., Moffit, op. cit., and John Williamson, *The Exchange Rate System* (Washington , DC: Institute for International Economics, 1983).
3. See William R. Cline (ed.), *Trade Policy In The 1980s* (Washington, DC: Institute for International Economics, 1983), for evidence of this increase.
4. See Hogan/Pearce, op. cit., for a discussion of this controversial issue.
5. See Mendelsohn (1980), op. cit., and Versluysen, op. cit., for general discussions of the political implications of the development of global money markets.
6. Most notably, E. A. Brett, *International Money and Capitalist Crisis: The Anatomy of Global Disintegration* (London: Heinemann, 1983), and Hogan/Pearce, op. cit., for a specific discussion of the problems of the Euromarkets.
7. The full political implications of these economic changes are not at all clear. A point made in Derek F. Channon, *British Transnational Bank Strategy: A Report to the UN Centre on Transnational Corporations* (Manchester: Centre for Business Research, Manchester Business School, 1978).
8. See Bareau, op. cit., for a comparative analysis of the events of the 1930s and the 1980s.
9. See Charles P. Kindleberger, *The World in Depression, 1929–1939* (Stanford, California: University of California Press, 1973).
10. Most notably, Brett, op. cit., and (though to a lesser extent) Kindleberger himself in Kindleberger/Laffar-Gue, op. cit. Kindleberger is the leading authority on this very controversial period of twentieth-century economic and political history.
11. See Cline (1983), op. cit., for this evidence.
12. Most notably, Kindleberger, op. cit., and Forrest Capie and Geoffrey E. Wood, 'What Happened in 1931?', in Centre for Banking and

International Finance, The City University, *Financial Crisis and the World Banking System: A Conference held in London, 6 and 7 October, 1983* (London: Centre for Banking and International Finance, The City University, 1983).

13. A point strongly stressed in Kindleberger, op. cit., who notes that the US Central Bank, the US Federal Reserve Board, was only established as recently as 1914. This compares with the Bank of England, which was established in 1694.

14. Cline (1983), op. cit., argues that since a return to the status quo ante is politically impossible, as regards both world trade and exchange rates, the best that can now be achieved in practical political terms is a 'constrained ideal' world order, in which there is a selective adherence to the ideal of avoiding protectionism (for example), but in which the idea of multilateral negotiations (in GATT) to agree on what is politically acceptable to all concerned is still operative.

15. A point discussed at length, from an American perspective, in David P. Calleo and Benjamin M. Rowland, *America and the World Political Economy: Atlantic Dreams and National Realities* (Bloomington, Indiana: Indiana University Press, 1973).

16. See Feinberg, op. cit., for a discussion of these changes, especially as regards US–South American relations in recent years.

17. Grant (1983), op. cit., p. 61.

18. For a wider discussion of these North–South differences as they affect the debt problem, see Brandt Commission (1983), op. cit.

19. For examples of these ideological purists, see Brunner, op. cit., and Vaubel, op. cit.

20. See Tumlir, op. cit.

21. Delamaide, op. cit., p. 242.

22. See Coles in Group of Thirty, op. cit., pp. 62–79.

23. See Villarreal, op. cit., for a South American critique of the IMF.

24. See Bell/Rutledge, op. cit., for further details of this Act.

Appendix 1:
Statistical sources

Since the exact amount of debt owed by the non-oil developing countries is a question over which opinion differs, a word on the statistical sources used in this study is in order. The best analysis of the pros and cons of the various available statistical sources is to be found in Bank for International Settlements, *Manual on Statistics Compiled by International Organisations on Countries' External Indebtedness* (Basle: BIS, 1979). There are three major statistical sources:

1. The World Bank

The World Bank's *World Debt Tables* (annual) give data on long-term public debt for all non-oil developing countries. 'Public debt' is taken to mean debt publicly guaranteed by the Government that holds the debt. The World Bank estimates that around 80 per cent of all long-term debt held by Governments is guaranteed. Around 50 per cent of total non-oil developing country debt is debt held by Governments. The other 50 per cent is held by companies in the private sector, and by state enterprises. Little of this debt is publicly guaranteed. Some of the long-term private debt is mentioned by the World Bank, but most of it is omitted. The main drawback of the World Bank data is that all short-term debt (all private) is omitted.

2. Bank of International Settlements

The BIS produces *The Maturity Distribution of International Bank Lending* quarterly, which gives data on Western bank lending to the developing countries, as reported to the BIS by the banks in question. The main drawbacks of these data are that not all bank lending is reported to the BIS (especially inter-bank facilities), and the data only go back to 1977. However, by combining World Bank and BIS data, a reasonably accurate picture of total debt can be built up, both in the aggregate, and for individual countries.

3. International Monetary Fund

The IMF's *International Financial Statistics, Balance of Payments Yearbook* and *World Economic Outlook* (all annual), provide comprehensive data, by country, on all key economic variables such as imports/exports, reserves, foreign investment, etc. The IMF's *Annual Report* is also useful.

4. Other sources

Lastly, the OECD secretariat produces *OECD Financial Statistics* (annual). The United Nations also produces many publications on the developing countries, both in the aggregate and in terms of individual countries. Of the numerous publications put out by commercial banks, the best is Morgan Guaranty's *World Financial Markets* (monthly).

Appendix 2:
Rescheduled debt, by country, 1956–1982
(millions of dollars)

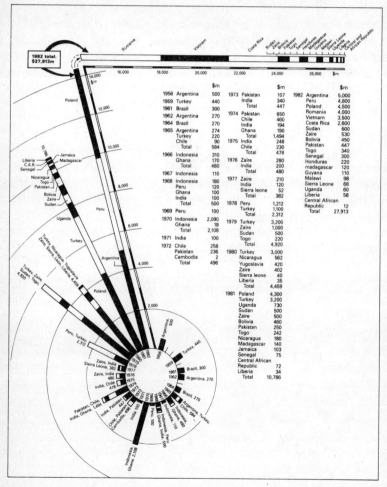

1982 total: $27,913m

	$m
1956 Argentina	500
1959 Turkey	440
1961 Brazil	300
1962 Argentina	270
1964 Brazil	270
1965 Argentina	274
Turkey	220
Chile	90
Total	584
1966 Indonesia	310
Ghana	170
Total	480
1967 Indonesia	110
1968 Indonesia	180
Peru	120
Ghana	100
India	100
Total	500
1969 Peru	100
1970 Indonesia	2,090
Ghana	18
Total	2,108
1971 India	100
1972 Chile	258
Pakistan	236
Cambodia	2
Total	496

	$m
1973 Pakistan	107
India	340
Total	447
1974 Pakistan	650
Chile	460
India	194
Ghana	190
Total	1,494
1975 India	248
Chile	230
Total	478
1976 Zaire	280
India	200
Total	480
1977 Zaire	210
India	120
Sierra leone	52
Total	382
1978 Peru	1,212
Turkey	1,100
Total	2,312
1979 Turkey	3,200
Zaire	1,000
Sudan	500
Togo	220
Total	4,920
1980 Turkey	3,000
Nicaragua	562
Yugoslavia	420
Zaire	402
Sierra leone	40
Liberia	35
Total	4,459
1981 Poland	4,300
Turkey	3,200
Uganda	730
Sudan	500
Zaire	500
Bolivia	460
Pakistan	250
Togo	242
Nicaragua	180
Madagascar	140
Jamaica	103
Senegal	75
Central African Republic	72
Liberia	34
Total	10,786

	$m
1982 Argentina	5,000
Peru	4,800
Poland	4,500
Romania	4,000
Vietnam	3,500
Costa Rica	2,600
Sudan	600
Zaire	530
Bolivia	450
Pakistan	447
Togo	340
Senegal	300
Honduras	220
madagascar	120
Guyana	110
Malawi	98
Sierra Leone	68
Uganda	60
Liberia	58
Central African Republic	12
Total	27,913

Appendix 3:
The Polish debt rescheduling negotiations, 1981–1984

Background

As early as June 1980, it was clear that Poland was in deep trouble, as all its new borrowing in that year was required to service its $26 billion debt. By late 1980, Poland was frozen out of the Euromarkets, as worried banks withdrew short-term credit facilities as they came up for renewal. After the military take-over in December 1981, Western Governments, through the Paris Club, stopped all official debt rescheduling negotiations. The Paris Club had no meeting with Poland until late 1983. Commercial banks continued to meet Polish Government officials, and agreements were signed in 1982, 1983, and 1984. Although Poland ran up huge arrears, failing to pay any interest to Paris Club creditors and only paying commercial banks when it felt like it, the country was never called into default by its creditors.

15 January 1981 (Frankfurt)

Various banks urge Polish Government to reschedule its debts. Polish Government refuses to do so.

31 March 1981 (London)

Newly formed (on initiative of banks) twenty-bank committee tells Polish Government it will be the sole medium for negotiations between the Government and its 501 commercial bank creditors. Polish Government agrees to reschedule $2.4 billion due to banks and $2.4 billion due to Paris Club.

15 April 1981 (London)

At a meeting of the committee, differences emerge between Swiss/US banks, who urge a tough line on the repayment of short-term debt and overdue principal, and West German banks —the most heavily exposed in Poland—who urge a softer line on the above. Softer line advocated by West German banks prevails. *Note*: Committee also agrees to: 1. create five-bank working group to draft memo on rescheduling terms acceptable to banks to be presented to the Polish Government; 2. sets up economic sub-committee to monitor the Polish economy.

20 April 1981 (Paris)

Paris Club meets Polish Government. Sets a historic precedent by agreeing to reschedule interest payments. Agrees to re-schedule $2.4 billion in due principal and interest for 1981.

1 May 1981 (New York)

Banking working group meets Polish Government, which demands that precedent set by Paris Club be followed by banks. Demand rejected by banks, not negotiable for the banks.

20 May 1981 (Frankfurt)

Bank working group presents its memo to the committee. Memo proposes to reschedule $2.4 billion due 1981 over seven and a half years, with spread of 1.75 per cent over LIBOR and penalty clause spread of 2.75 per cent plus rengotiation fee of 1 per cent.

Differences emerge between those (US banks) who want tougher 'conditionality'—economic adjustment and reliable economic data in return for rescheduling agreement, and those (European banks) who wanted to endorse the memo in the interests of a quick agreement with the Polish Government. Decides to refer memo to all 501 creditor banks for final say.

11 June 1981 (New York)

Meeting of major US banks, chaired by Bankers Trust, want

tougher 'conditionality' before they will agree to reschedule their assets in Poland. Meeting rejects memo of 20 May.

30 June 1981 (Paris)

At full meeting of the committee the US banks attack the position of the European banks. An uproar follows. The Europeans say the demands of the Americans are totally unrealistic. Only the IMF, they argue, can impose such demands. Poland was not a member of the IMF. Meeting ends with no agreement.

22 July 1981 (Zurich)

By the time of this meeting, after many informal meetings, a compromise position between the views of US and European banks. A major split is avoided. Memo acceptable to all banks. 10 December 1981 set as the deadline for the signing of a rescheduling agreement based on the memo. The Polish Government is required to provide quarterly reports on its economy.

August/September 1981 (various venues)

Various meetings with the Polish Government. The Government refuses to sign a rescheduling agreement on the terms proposed. Nothing agreed.

28 September 1981 (Vienna)

The July demand that Poland provide reliable economic data is ignored. In particular, the Polish Government refuses to discuss its financial relationships with the Soviet Union. Meeting breaks up in acrimony.

29 September 1981 (Warsaw)

Seven bankers tell the Polish Government that if the memo of 20 May is not signed immediately, then Poland will be declared to be in default by the banks.

30 September 1981 (Warsaw)

Memo signed by Polish Government. Work begins on the drafting of final rescheduling agreement. The memo is only a first draft.

1 December 1981

Poland applies to join the IMF.

April 1982

Due to the fact that the payment of 1981 interest payments that were in arrears was a condition of the final signing of the rescheduling agreement, nothing was signed until April 1982. The position of the banks was made more difficult, due to the refusal of the Paris Club to negotiate with Poland.

6 July 1982 (Vienna)

Committee meets with the Polish Government to begin negotiations on the rescheduling of payments due in 1982. Since Poland is in arrears on its 1982 payments, and due to the boycott of Poland by the Paris Club, only general discussions—not a signed agreement—are possible.

7 November 1982 (Vienna)

Large-scale Soviet aid to Poland enables Poland to make significant inroads into the arrears that built up in 1982. This done, an agreement to reschedule $2.4 billion due in 1982 is signed. The terms are the same as in the 1981 agreement.

2 July 1983 (Paris)

Paris Club reopens negotiations with the Polish Government to reschedule the debts due in 1982 and 1983. Since the Paris Club broke off relations with Poland, it had paid nothing to its official creditors since January 1982.

1 August 1983 (Vienna)

Committee and Polish Government signs a rescheduling agreement for $1.5 billion due in 1983. The terms are an improvement on the 1981 and 1982 agreements. The maturity is ten years, and the spread 1.875 per cent above LIBOR. Under the agreement Poland will have to pay $1.1 billion to clear its arrears of interest payments.

27 April 1984 (Warsaw)

Committee and Polish Government signs an agreement for $1.9 billion due in 1984. In addition, the agreement delays repayment of all Poland's commercial debt falling due before the end of 1987 and completes the rescheduling of its medium-term debt. Unlike the agreements of 1981, 1982, and 1983, the 1984 agreement is the first long-term, multi-year rescheduling agreement. Under the agreement, Poland will have ten years to repay all the debt principal which it incurred before December 1981, and which falls due before the end of 1987. Small interest payments are not being rescheduled. Payments will start after a five-year grace period, and the spread payable will be 1.75 per cent above LIBOR.

14 June 1984 (Vienna)

The committee meets with the Polish Government to discuss the Government's request to reschedule its total $26 billion over twenty years. The request is unrealistic, given the attitude of Western Governments, in the Paris Club, towards the present Polish regime. Western policy is gradually improving political, and hence economic, relations with Poland.

Appendix 4:
The Costa Rican telex

From: Stanislas Yassukovich, Chief Executive, the European Banking Company.
To: The Government of Costa Rica.
Dated: 4 Feburary 1982.

Whilst entirely accepting the fact that you are making every effort to resolve your present situation your telex of January 26 contains evidence of a fundamental and persistent misunderstanding. Until this fundamental misunderstanding is clarified progress towards resolving these present difficulties will be impeded.

You refer to the meeting which took place in London on November 16 between your government's representatives and the lead managers of Costa Rican issues. Whilst this meeting was of course useful, it should have been explained to you by your advisers that the lead managers of Eurobond issues do not represent the noteholders and have no right to commit noteholders to any arrangements or to negotiate on their behalf. The lead managers are not the proper medium of communication with note-holders either, since they are not in a position to ensure that all bearer noteholders are in receipt of any form of communication. In this respect the lead managers of your bond issues are not the same as the committee of creditor banks who have the right to represent all the commercial banks. This is only the beginning of a basic misunderstanding which persists about the nature of the contract your government entered into when it issued its bonds.

You refer to the requirement of your commercial bank creditors that all bonds and FRNS [Floating Rate Note Securities] held by non-natural persons be included in any rescheduling. The commercial banks have no right to make such a requirement since you are not in a position to meet it. This request by the commercial banks is an entirely unreasonable one and is clearly made in ignorance of the legal and technical characteristics of your contractual obligations under the terms of the bond issues.

No distinction exists between so-called natural and non-natural persons since, as any legal adviser will explain to you, the rights of bondholders are uniform, regardless of their nature. It is most unfortunate that this misunderstanding should have arisen because it has placed your government in an invidious position. Whilst you are correctly pursuing negotiations with your commercial bank creditors utilising the legal process called for in the documentation relating to your commercial bank loans, you appear to be neglecting another important group of creditors, namely your bondholders and, what is far worse, you would appear to have been willing to entertain a repudiation of your obligations with respect to some of these bondholders without any attempt to seek their consent.

We are very anxious to do everything to assist Costa Rica in resolving its difficulties as long as its negotiations with creditors proceed according to law and the code of obligations generally accepted as the basis for international financing. However, if your commercial bank creditors insist on forcing you to violate this code of obligations and if you accede to this pressure, we shall campaign vigorously to ensure that you become ineligible for any financing from the multilateral institutions.

We take this view because we believe that the integrity of the international capital market is at stake and this is a more important issue than the difficulties of any single country. [*Euromoney*, August 1982, p. 40.]

Appendix 5:
The Nicaraguan Debt Rescheduling Agreement of 1980

Background

When the Sandinista Government came to power in July 1979, Nicaragua's total debt stood at $1.5 billion, about the same as the country's GNP in 1979. After a bloody civil war the country was bankrupt, and the UN estimated that $2.5 billion was required to repair the destruction caused by the civil war. Though revolutionary, the Government was willing to recognise its foreign debt. Around 40 per cent of that debt was owed to commercial banks. The Government's negotiating team and the bank's advisory committee met six times between December 1979 and August 1980. The first two meetings, in December 1979 and January 1980, were concerned with organisational and logistical questions for the negotiations proper, which were held in Mexico City (four meetings), Managua (one), and Panama City (one).

Opening negotiating positions

These were made in March 1980 at the third meeting in Mexico City. The advisory committee, which did not want to set a precedent by appearing to be 'soft' in Nicaragua, wanted the following: the rescheduled debt was to be repaid over seven years with grace periods of two and three years for different portions of the debt; interest to be paid at LIBOR (then 20 per cent) plus a large spread, plus a fee. In addition, all past due interest was to be paid at the originally contracted rates at the time the agreement was signed. An immediate payment of $100 million was, therefore, demanded to wipe out the arrears on interest payments.

Nicaragua, while ready to co-operate with its creditors but not ready to let debt service costs harm the reconstruction of its wrecked economy, wanted the following: the rescheduled debt was to be repaid over twelve years with a grace period of five years, plus the capitalisation of all past due interest, plus the deferral of all interest payable until after the period of grace was over (i.e. five years); no fee, no dealings with the IMF; no concurrent negotiations with the Paris Club.

These opening positions, though far apart, were forged over the next five months into a mutually satisfactory agreement that was, in every respect, unique and without precedent. The agreement was signed in August 1980.

The Agreement

Total debt involved: $562 million.
Type of debt: owed by the Government, Government entities, and private companies nationalised in 1979 to commercial banks.
Terms of the agreement:

1. *Maturity*

Twelve years with five years grace (1980–92). No repayment of principal until 1985, with more than half of the principal becoming due in 1990–2. The maturity length had no precedent. Most past commercial bank reschedulings had maturities under five years, the longest had been ten years, and the average was around five years. The longest previous grace period was three years.

2. *Past Due Interest (PDI)*

Calculation of PDI at 10.875 per cent and not at the originally contracted rates (around 15 per cent). This was a major concession to Nicaragua. PDI total calculated at $91 million. From 1980 to 1985 Nicaragua would only pay PDI, with 60 per cent of PDI due in 1984 and 1985. Remaining PDI to be paid in 1980, 1981, 1982, and 1983.

This capitalisation of interest had no precedent and was to be refused to many debtor Governments in the future.

3. *Interest Rate*

Rate of LIBOR plus 1 per cent spread until 1985. LIBOR plus 1.75 per cent after 1985. Average spread, on a scale, would be 1.5 per cent over period 1980–92. The lowest spread prior to this agreement was 1.75 per cent. After spreads of 2 per cent and above were the rule. For the period 1980–5 the actual rate payable was 7 per cent. The difference between this rate and the contractually agreed rate (LIBOR plus spread of 1.5 per cent equals 21 per cent) was 14 per cent. This future interest rate difference, in another unprecedented and unrepeated concession by the banks, was capitalised with repayment deferred until after 1985, with repayment as follows: 10 per cent in 1986 and 1987, 35 per cent in 1988 and 1989, and 10 per cent in 1990.

4. *Fees*

No renegotiation fee. Elsewhere the fee payable was 1 per cent of the amount rescheduled.

5. *IMF*

Because the IMF had supported the Samoza Government right up to the very moment of its collapse in 1979, the Nicaraguan Government refused to make an agreement with that organisation a precondition of the rescheduling agreement with the banks. It refused any sort of agreement with the IMF. The issue was not, in fact, negotiable as far as the Government was concerned. The advisory committee, having to decide between insisting on an agreement with the IMF as a precondition of its own rescheduling process or getting no agreement at all given the attitude of the Government towards the IMF, decided not to so insist. Again a concession without precedent. Poland was not a member of the IMF. Nicaragua had been.

Implications of the Agreement

The principle of ability to pay, and avoiding insisting on the view that the debtor should pay the 'market' terms in the rescheduling, was conceded for the first time in Nicaragua. On a total foreign debt of $1.5 billion Nicaragua had, in effect, negotiated for itself a debt service ratio of around 10 per cent for the period 1980–5. On the rescheduled debt of $562 million, the debt service ratio was around 5 per cent for the same period—a quite remarkable ratio bearing in mind what ratios prevailed in other developing countries.

The banks, having made this *de facto* concession (in *de jure* terms they insisted that, allowing for the particular and exceptional circumstances that prevailed in Nicaragua, the final terms were, in fact, 'market' terms), insisted that the Nicaraguan agreement was exceptional. It was not to be repeated in the rest of South America, and was virtually forgotten by 1982. Instead very costly terms were imposed on debtors from 1982 to 1983. Ability to pay was forgotten, and unrealistic costs were imposed. The result was predictable. Instead of a one-off rescheduling agreement (with realistic costs to be paid by the debtor) that settled a country's debt question for the next ten years, as was the case in Nicaragua, the rest of South America was to experience a large number of very short-term, annual, unstable, and seemingly endless rescheduling negotiations from 1982 to 1983. From 1983 to 1984, though the terms of rescheduling agreements improved for some debtor countries, the principle of ability to pay was not conceded in public by the banks, nor in *de facto* terms. The experience of Nicaragua was forgotten.

Appendix 6:
The Mexican debt rescheduling negotiations, 1982–1984

20 August 1982

The Mexican Government invites fourteen banks to form an advisory committee to serve as the sole medium for negotiations between itself and its 1,400 commercial bank creditors. A meeting is proposed in New York where Mexico will ask for a 90-day moratorium on the repayment of $19.5 billion of principal of public sector debt due in 1983.

22 August 1984

The Mexican Government informs the advisory committee that it has received the following emergency loans pending an agreement with the IMF:
1. US Government—$1 billion in prepayment for imports of Mexican oil plus a bridging loan of $925 million.
2. Bank for International Settlements (BIS)—Bridging loan of $925 million.

23 August 1982

90-day moratorium goes into effect.

1 September 1982

The Mexican Government, in an effort to stop capital flight, imposes exchange controls and nationalises the banking system in Mexico. No foreign exchange can go to debt servicing purposes without clearance by the Mexican authorities. *Note*: At this stage the initiative was with Governments. The Mexicans had presented the banks with two *faits accomplis*: the moratorium and the nationalisation decree. The US Government and the BIS provided emergency aid even before the advisory committee was fully operational.

10 November 1982

After prolonged negotiations the Mexican Government sends a letter of intent to the IMF. It is agreed that Mexico will reduce its budget deficit from 16.5 per cent of GNP in 1981 to 8.5 per cent in 1983, foreign borrowing will be cut from $20 billion in 1981 to $5 billion in 1983, and inflation will be cut from 100 per cent in 1982 to 55 per cent in 1983. The price of this adjustment would be a fall in GNP for a few years.

16 November 1982

The Managing Director of the IMF, in an unprecedented move, tells the advisory committee that IMF assistance to Mexico is conditional upon the provision of $5 billion in new loans by the commercial banks to Mexico. The advisory committee is told to obtain written commitments for this amount by 15 December 1982. *Note*: By this move, which infuriated the advisory committee at the time, the concept of involuntary lending was born. Banks had no choice in the matter. The IMF, which had hitherto played a secondary role in commercial bank rescheduling negotiations, was now in charge of the rescheduling process. In its articles of incorporation the IMF is charged with protecting the integrity and stability of the international financial system. That global perspective was far more important than the commercial banks thought.

23 November 1982

The 90-day moratorium is extended to 120-days by the Mexican Government.

8 December 1982

The Mexican Government announces its opening negotiating position for:
1. $5 billion of new loans. Maturity of six years with three years grace, a spread of 2.5 per cent above US Prime Rate, and a 0.5 per cent fee.
2. $19.5 billion rescheduled debt. Maturity of eight years with four years grace, spreads of 1.875 ths. per cent above LIBOR or 1.75 per cent over Prime Rate, and a fee of 1 per cent.

15 December 1982

Deadline for $5 billion passes without any agreement.

20 December 1982

The Mexican Government, having previously refused to take responsibility for the debts of the Mexican private sector, agrees that the private sector companies involved may pay the peso equivalent of external debt service into the Central Bank of Mexico, which will assume the foreign exchange liability to foreign creditors.

23 December 1982

The IMF agrees to lend $3.8 billion over the next three years.

24 February 1983

After long delays caused by the unwillingness of many banks to lend any more money to Mexico, despite the threats of the IMF in 1982, a preliminary draft loan agreement to lend $5 billion to Mexico is produced by the advisory committee. The terms are a maturity of six years with three years grace, spreads of 2.875 ths. per cent over Prime Rate or 2.25 per cent over LIBOR, and a fee of 1.75 per cent. *Note*: The most difficult task of the advisory committee was to persuade the smaller, regional US banks to contribute to the new loan. It was agreed that all banks concerned should lend 7 per cent of their present exposure in Mexico. Even with very profitable terms, many banks refused to lend. The $5 billion was not fully raised until March 1983.

28 February 1983

The Mexican Government proposes a rescheduling of non-guaranteed public and private sector commercial debt as well as of officially guaranteed private sector commercial debt owed to the commercial banks. What is being proposed is that virtually all of Mexico's $80 billion debt be rescheduled by 1984. As regards the $19.5 billion due in 1983, a preliminary draft agreement has been drawn up. The terms are a maturity of eight years with four years grace, spreads of 1.875 ths. per cent over LIBOR or 1.75 per cent over Prime Rate, and a fee of 1 per cent. *Note*: As with the new loan the main problem of the advisory committee was to sell the deal to all 1,400 banks concerned. The final signing of the agreement, therefore, could not come about until August 1983.

17 March 1983

The Mexican Government asks for a further extension of the moratorium of 23 November 1982 until 15 August 1983, or until a rescheduling agreement is signed. The agreement comes in August 1983.

23 March 1983

The advisory committee tells the Mexican Government that $5 billion of new money has been raised from 526 banks.

6 April 1983

The Mexican Government announces that schemes to cover a total of $15 billion of private sector external debt to banks and other foreign creditors will apply if all concerned creditors agree to reschedule the principal of such debt over a maturity of six years with three years grace. Service on this debt, as stated in December 1982, will be paid in pesos by debtors to the Mexican Central Bank and the foreign exchange risk is to be covered by a Mexican Government trust fund pending a final rescheduling of private sector debt. A deadline of 25 October 1983 is set for applications to join this scheme.

6 May 1983

The Mexican Government begins negotiations with the Paris Club to reschedule all officially guaranteed private sector debt outstanding on 20 December 1982. The minimum maturity acceptable to Mexico is six years.

23 May 1983

The IMF formally declares that Mexico has fully complied with all first-quarter targets agreed with the IMF. This news is well received among all Mexico's foreign creditors.

1 August 1983

Nearly one year after the crisis broke in 1982 the final rescheduling agreement is signed, incorporating the terms agreed in February 1983.

24 October 1983

The Mexican Government, having drastically cut new borrowing in 1983 as part of its agreement with the IMF, asks the advisory committee for $3.8 billion for 1984. Mexico wants a maturity of nine years with five years grace, and a lower spread. *Note*: Despite improvements in Mexico's economic position, many banks were still wary of lending to Mexico. It was now proposed that banks contribute 5 per cent of present exposure in Mexico to the 1984 loan. The advisory committee still found it difficult to raise the $3.8 billion.

27 April 1984

$3.8 billion loan signed with a maturity of nine years with five years grace, a spread of 1.5 per cent above LIBOR, and 0.5 per cent fee. This is a considerable improvement on the terms obtained in 1983.

9 September 1984

After prolonged negotiations a unique rescheduling agreement is reached between the Mexican Government and the advisory committee. It is an agreement without precedent and is bound to influence other rescheduling negotiations in South America. $49 billion, which is over half of Mexico's total debt, is to be rescheduled over fourteen years. Of this figure, $43 billion is to be transferred from US Prime Rate (13 per cent) to LIBOR (12 per cent). This was a major concession to Mexico. The spread above LIBOR is to be 1.11 per cent. The spread is a great improvement on the spread paid in the 1983 rescheduling (1.875 per cent). *Note*: As was to be expected, Brazil, Venezuela, and Argentina demanded the terms that Mexico got. It seems probable that they will get them in 1985.

Appendix 7:
The Brazilian debt rescheduling negotiations, 1982–1984

June 1982

Brazil fails to meet the terms of an economic adjustment programme agreed with the IMF in February 1982. The consequent lack of IMF support makes it virtually impossible for Brazil to raise new money from its commercial bank creditors.

27 August 1982

The Brazilian Government meets the fourteen-bank advisory committee, set up in June 1982 at the initiative of the banks in order to advise Brazil on its borrowing requirements for 1983, and is told that any new disbursements by the banks is conditional upon an agreement between Brazil and the IMF. Following the Mexican crisis of 20 August 1982, Brazilian banks begin to lose deposits in the interbank market.

1 September 1982

Brazil's reserves sink to $2 billion due to unfavourable developments in the interbank market.

25 October 1982

The Brazilian Government announces that after the federal assembly elections, on 15 November 1982, it will seek conditional IMF assistance and a large loan from the banks. *Note*: This policy irritates Brazil's creditors. Unlike Mexico, whose policies were honest (admitting it had a problem) and decisive (dealing with them), Brazil pretended that it did not need to reschedule. It pretended that it could borrow from the banks as usual—a totally wrong view. In addition, knowing that it would be politically unpopular, it negotiated an agreement with the IMF. Yet such an agreement was the foundation upon which everything else would rest. Despite a large build-up in arrears, no bank would lend Brazil anything until that agreement was in place.

30 November 1982

The Brazilian Government asks for $2.4 billion of bridging finance to cover the period to the end of 1982. There is no favourable response from the advisory committee.

1 December 1982

The US Government provides $1.1 billion of bridging finance, pending the agreement of a programme by Brazil with the IMF.

17 December 1982

Letter of intent to the IMF is published in Brazil indicating that the Brazilian Government is looking for $5 billion from the IMF.

20 December 1982

The Brazilian Government, with the support of the IMF, makes the following demands of the advisory committee:
1. New loans. Provision of $4.4 billion of new money for 1983. The proposed terms were a maturity of eight years with two and a half years grace, a spread of 2.5 per cent over LIBOR or 2.25 per cent over Prime Rate, plus a fee of 1 per cent.
2. Rescheduled Debt. Rescheduling of $4 billion of principal due in 1983 on public and private sector external debt, with the proposed terms being the same as the terms for the new loan.

3. Short-term credit. Restoration of trade-related, short-term credit lines to $10 billion, representing their level at 30 June 1982.
4. Inter-bank deposits. Restoration of inter-bank deposits to their level at 30 June 1982 ($10 billion).

Note: While the first two demands were acceptable to banks, the last two were not, especially the fourth. The inter-bank question was to cause the most acrimony in the negotiations. Banks refused to provide inter-bank loans to Brazil. By June 1983, Brazil had only $6 billion in inter-bank deposits.

24 December 1982

The BIS approves $1.2 billion of bridging finance to be repaid in equal instalments at the end of February, May, and August 1983.

31 December 1982

The advisory committee approves a bridging loan of $2.2 billion, originally requested by Brazil in November 1982, with a maturity of ninety days, and a spread of 1 per cent over LIBOR or 0.75 per cent over Prime Rate.

3 January 1983

The Brazilian Government announces that it will henceforth suspend all repayments of principal on public medium- and long-term debt due in 1983. This unexpected move angers Brazil's creditors.

6 January 1983

Letter of intent signed by Brazil and the IMF.

24 January 1983

The advisory committee meets, and reports that all the targets for sections 1, 2, and 3 of the 20 December meeting have been met. The target for the inter-bank lines (section 4) has not been met. In an unprecedented move, the committee decides that the names of recalcitrant banks will be published if they persist in refusing to extend inter-bank facilities to Brazil. This move later infuriates the banks involved—mostly smaller, regional US banks.

25 January 1983

The IMF declares that its assistance to Brazil is conditional on the provision of $10 billion in inter-bank lines to Brazil.

18 February 1983

Being well aware of the refusal of many banks to provide inter-bank facilities, the advisory committee announces that only $8.7 billion is now required.

25 February 1983

Brazil and the banks sign two important agreements: firstly, one for a new loan of $4.4 billion for 1983; secondly, another for the rescheduling of $4.7 billion of principal due in 1983. The terms for both agreements are a maturity of eight years with two and a half years grace, spreads of 2.5 per cent over LIBOR or 2.25 per cent over Prime Rate, plus a fee of 1.5 per cent. *Note*: The terms are more expensive than those Mexico had to pay in its 1983 rescheduling agreement.

28 February 1983

The IMF approves $4.8 billion of financing under its Extended Finance Facility, plus another $550 million under its Supplementary Financing Facility.

10 March 1983

Brazil makes its first drawing of $2.5 billion on the $4.4 billion arranged with commercial banks on 25 February 1983. At the same time, the advisory committee agrees to defer repayment of the $2.2 billion bridging loan, agreed 31 December 1982, until the end of 1983.

15 March 1983

The first repayment of $400 million on the $1.2 billion BIS bridging loan, agreed on 24 December 1982, is made. $800 million is outstanding.

6 May 1983

After much speculation, it is admitted by the Brazilian Government and the IMF that the programme targets agreed in the letter of intent signed on 6 January 1983 have not been complied with.

18 May 1983

The IMF announces that the second tranche of IMF funds, totalling some $400 million and due on 31 May 1983, will be delayed due to Brazil's failure to comply with its agreement with the IMF.

24 May 1983

The banks decide to postpone a further disbursement of $634 million of their $4.4 billion loan, in the light of what the IMF decided to do.

June 1983

The advisory committee decides that Brazil will have to make do with only $6 billion in inter-bank deposits. No more can be raised, despite all the long efforts of the committee.

August 1983

Under heavy pressure from the advisory committee, the Brazilian Government begins negotiations with the Paris Club to reschedule $2 billion of official government debt due in 1983 and 1984. *Note*: By the summer of 1983, in sharp contrast to the situation in Mexico, Brazil was in a worse position than it had ever been in. It was unable to keep within the targets of its agreement with the IMF, which meant that disbursement of IMF and bank loans was delayed. This, in turn, only worsened Brazil's ability to service its debts. On top of everything else, the country's export earnings were worse than expected in 1983.

1 September 1983

It is reported that the Brazilian Government has drafted a new letter of intent for the IMF, which approves of its intention to cut the budget deficit, cut inflation, and boost exports, but experience suggests—as was the case with the first letter of intent of 6 January 1983—that the Government will be politically unable to implement the agreement agreed with the IMF.

21 September 1983

The IMF, having agreed that a $11.5 billion rescue package will be required for Brazil in 1984, insists that its contribution to the package (the IMF and Paris Club will provide $4.5 billion) is conditional on the advisory committee raising $7 billion from the banks. The committee, for its part, suggests that raising $5 billion will prove very difficult. Brazil is, and is perceived to be, in a far worse condition than Mexico, hence the reluctance to lend.

20 October 1983

The IMF, in a move that is clearly more conciliatory towards the recalcitrant banks, suggests that only 80 per cent of the $7 billion demanded from the banks by the IMF on 21 September 1983 will be sufficient to satisfy the IMF, and so make possible an IMF agreement with Brazil.

24 November 1983

The IMF announces an agreement with Brazil, whereby $1.1 billion will be disbursed to Brazil, which will then immediately pay it to the BIS, which it owes $1.1 billion. The BIS bridging loan was extended many times during 1983. The advisory committee announces that it has raised $6.5 billion, of which around $3 billion will be disbursed in 1983. That will then make a significant inroad into Brazil's $6 billion debt service and unpaid imports arrears. The Paris Club announces that it will reschedule $3.8 billion of Government debt, and not the $2 billion originally envisaged in August 1983.

28 January 1984

The advisory committee signs a $6.5 billion loan agreement with the Brazilian Government. However, disbursement is delayed because of doubts about the contribution of Paris Club Governments ($2.5 billion in new loans plus the rescheduling of $3.8 billion). A clause is written into the bank loan agreement, which has no precedent, that disbursement is conditional upon the concurrent disbursement of the loans provided by Paris Club Governments. In addition, Brazil has failed to stay within the targets of its September 1983 letter of intent to the IMF.

February 1984

Another letter of intent is being drafted by Brazil. The main problem is an inflation rate of 220 per cent per annum. *Note*: Despite all the problems, the commercial bank, Paris Club and IMF parts of the rescue package fall into place, but once the arrears are cleared Brazil is still left with only $5 billion of reserves by the summer of 1984.

21 June 1984

The Brazilian President, in a joint statement with his Argentinian, Mexican, and Colombian counterparts, issues a statement protesting against the increase in interest rates and the development of protectionism in developed countries. The statement reads: 'We have demonstrated our goodwill in servicing the debt and re-adjusting our economies, but we cannot accept any more the forceful paralysis of our economies'. The Brazilian Government is particularly angered by the fact that the terms of the 1984 rescheduling agreement are exactly the same as those of the 1983 agreement, whereas Mexico has obtained better terms in 1984 than it did in 1983. The precedent set by the Mexican 1984 deal deeply influences the Brazilian Government as it prepares its negotiating position for the 1985 rescheduling.

1 August 1984

The Brazilian Government meets the advisory committee and suggests a cut in the spread of 1 per cent, a lower fee, and a long-term maturity structure rescheduling agreement to cover $20 billion due in the period 1985-7. The committee is in agreement about the need for a long-term agreement, but only wants spreads cut by 0.5 per cent. *Note*: These negotiations continued for the rest of 1984 and are still continuing (1985). The election of a new Government, ending twenty years of military rule, at the end of 1984 complicated the negotiations. The statements of President Elect Tancredo Neves, suggested the absolute minimum that Brazil would accept in the 1985 agreement was what Mexico received in September 1984.

Appendix 8:
The Yugoslavian debt rescheduling negotiations, 1982–1984

August 1982

Because of the Polish debt crisis Yugoslavia had been frozen out of the Euromarkets since 1980. Negotiations under way with American banks, led by Manufacturers Hanover, to borrow $300 million over two years. Concurrent negotiations with the BIS to borrow $500 million over three years. The BIS insists that a maturity of one year is the only one it can consider.

1 October 1982

The Yugoslav Government, in an effort to avoid a rescheduling, imposes a draconian adjustment programme, supported by the IMF, on its economy. Like Brazil at the very same time, Yugoslavia, for reasons of national pride, dealed rescheduling, although it could not be avoided.

20 December 1982

Yugoslavia meets with the Paris Club to discuss the rescheduling of Governemnt debt due in 1983. The Swiss Government agrees to act as co-ordinator of Government's contributions to the Yugoslav rescue package.

17 January 1983

An advisory committee is formed (on the initiative of the banks), Yugoslavia is advised to reschedule, and the first meeting of the committee is chaired by an IMF official. The IMF sets a deadline of 25 February 1983 for the committee to decide how to help Yugoslavia. It is stressed that commercial bank assistance is a precondition of the disbursement of $600 million by the IMF. The latter is the third tranche of $1.8 billion facility granted to Yugoslavia by the IMF in 1981. Yugoslavia's good relations with the IMF greatly helped its position in relation to the commercial banks.

19 January 1983

Paris Club Governments agree to lend a total of $1.3 billion in the form of export credits. The BIS agrees to consider lending $300 million to Yugoslavia for around six months.

21 January 1983

The advisory committee agrees with the Yugoslav Government to reschedule $1 billion of principal due in 1983 and to begin talks about a $1 billion loan. The terms are a maturity of five years with two years grace, a spread of 1.75 per cent above LIBOR, and a fee of 1 per cent. The Yugoslav Government feels that the terms are too costly. The committee sets a deadline of 25 March 1983 for Yugoslavia to accept the terms. The Yugoslav Government also objects to the committee's insistence that the new loans be 'joint and severally' in the names of the National Bank of Yugoslavia and the Socialist Federal Republic. *Note*: The unusual demand for the exact legal status of the Yugoslav entities that would borrow, and hence be liable for, the loan arose out of the confused situation caused by the high degree of political decentralisation that exists in Yugoslavia. The supreme political entity, the Socialist Federal Republic, had never actually borrowed in its own name in the past. Legislation was required for it to be able to do so. The entire issue, which looked unimportant, became the most contentious issue in the negotiations.

25 March 1983

Committee-set deadline passes without agreement on the bank package, now only worth $1.8 billion, as many banks refuse to lend to Yugoslavia despite great IMF and Paris Club pressure to do so. BIS lends $300 million for six months, the World Bank lends $250 million, the IMF lends $600 million, and $1.3 billion is made available in the form of export credits by Paris Club Governments.

14 September 1983

After months of difficult negotiations a $1.8 billion package is signed by the banks and the Yugoslav Government. The terms are more or less those demanded by the advisory committee in January 1983. Taking all the sources of assistance together, the Yugoslav rescue package for 1983 is worth $4.5 billion. The BIS includes a further $200 million in September 1983. *Note*: The package just covers the $4 billion required for debt servicing in 1983. $5 billion will be required in 1984.

26 January 1984

The advisory committee, recognising Yugoslavia's success at economic adjustment, offers better terms on the $1.5 billion of commercial bank debt to be rescheduled in 1984.

4 March 1984

The Yugoslav Government drafts a letter of intent to the IMF. An IMF credit of $500 million is being negotiated. The success of the IMF agreement with Yugoslavia is the precondition for the provision of the $1.5 billion package of the banks and the provision of around $1 billion from other Governments. A total package of $3 billion is being negotiated for 1984.

1 June 1984

First instalment of IMF credit disbursed. Some problems with some parts of the agreement. Notably the reluctance of the Yugslav Government to deregulate prices as demanded by the IMF.

19 November 1984

The Yugoslav Government begins further talks with the IMF with the object of initiating long-term rescheduling negotiations for payments due in the period 1985-8. The precedent set by Mexico in September 1984 greatly influences the requests of the Yugoslav Government. The Mexican agreement involved minimal IMF supervision, whereas the IMF feels that Yugoslavia should be kept under strict control. It insisted, therefore, on a further IMF standby programme (with full conditionality) after the current programme expires on 31 March 1985.

Appendix 9:
Structure of the Mexican Advisory Committee, 1982–1984

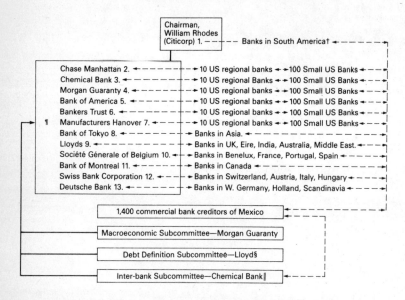

Chairman,
William Rhodes
(Citicorp) 1. —— —— —— Banks in South America†

Chase Manhattan 2.	10 US regional banks	100 Small US Banks
Chemical Bank 3.	10 US regional Banks	100 Small US Banks
Morgan Guaranty 4.	10 US regional banks	100 Small US Banks
Bank of America 5.	10 US regional banks	100 Small US Banks
Bankers Trust 6.	10 US regional banks	100 Small US Banks
Manufacturers Hanover 7.	10 US regional banks	100 Small US Banks

Bank of Tokyo 8. — Banks in Asia.
Lloyds 9. — Banks in UK, Eire, India, Australia, Middle East.
Société Génerale of Belgium 10. — Banks in Benelux, France, Portugal, Spain
Bank of Montreal 11. — Banks in Canada
Swiss Bank Corporation 12. — Banks in Switzerland, Austria, Italy, Hungary
Deutsche Bank 13. — Banks in W. Germany, Holland, Scandinavia

1,400 commercial bank creditors of Mexico

Macroeconomic Subcommittee—Morgan Guaranty

Debt Definition Subcommittee—Lloyds§

Inter-bank Subcommittee—Chemical Bank‖

Key

* By mid-1983 William Rhodes was also chairman of the advisory committees for Argentina, Peru, Uruguay, and Brazil. For Rhodes, rescheduling became a full-time activity. Since 1980 Rhodes had been Senior Vice-President for South America. He had been involved in the Nicaraguan and Jamaican debt rescheduling negotiations in 1980 and 1981. This background experience gave Rhodes good contacts with officials of the South American Division of the IMF. He was also well connected to members of the Mexican Government.

† Other than Mexico.

‡ Monitors the Mexcian economy and reports regularly to the advisory committee.

§ Discovering who (in Mexico) owes what to whom (banks). Because of the large amount of debt, and the poor debt monitoring record of the Mexican Government (a problem in other debtor countries as well), discovering the true total debt figure proved to be a difficult and prolonged job for Lloyds. Once that was done, it was a matter of coming to some agreement, after talks with representatives of the Mexican Government, as to which debts would be included in the rescheduling negotiations.

‖ Since inter-bank lines extended to Mexcian banks had to be rolled over every week, it was the job of this subcommittee to ensure that all the lines were, in fact, rolled over. Also keeping the advisory committee informed of the interbank position.

¶ The advisory committee had to evaluate the information provided by its subcommittees, present an opening negotiating position as regards terms for rescheduled debt/new loans, persuade all banks involved to lend new money and discover what terms were acceptable to them via the regional communications networks, come to a final agreement as regards terms with the Mexcian Government, and draft the texts of the final agreements.

◄– – ► Communications Network

◄——— Flow of information to the advisory committee

Appendix 10:
The Institute of International Finance
(Ditchley Institute)

Origins

The Institute of International Finance, also known as the Ditchley Institute, was initially conceived at a meeting of thirty-five senior bankers in Ditchley Park, Surrey in August 1982. The second meeting of the Ditchley group, in New York, October 1982, formally agreed to form an institute of international finance within two or three months of the second meeting. In January 1983, the Institute was formally established in Washington, DC, a governing interim board was elected, and B. Ogden was appointed as chairman of the interim board, who, having retired as vice-chairman of Chase Manhattan Bank in early 1983, played the leading role in obtaining support for the Institute among banks. Finally, in June 1983, the interim board chose André de Lattre, a former deputy governor of the Banque de France, to be the Institute's first managing director.

Organisation

The thirty-five founder banks of the Institute included the top ten US banks, the four UK clearing banks, the top three Swiss banks, plus leading banks from West Germany, Italy, France, Canada, Japan, and Brazil. About five hundred banks were expected to join the Institute, and the annual charges were set as follows: $100,000 for large banks, around $15,000 for medium-sized banks, and $7,000 for small banks. The Institute was particularly interested in attracting second-tier banks, which do not have large research departments, and which might be less hesitant to lend to developing countries as a result of their membership of the Institute. An eventual staff of around eighty people was envisaged. The Institute was fully operational by the end of 1983.

Objectives

In the press release issued at the time the Institute was established, it was said that the Institute's primary objective was 'to promote a better understanding of international lending transactions by improving the availability and quality of financial and economic information on major country borrowers' via the collection, collation, and dissemination of economic and political information. Another objective was to improve liaison between commercial banks and the IMF and Central Banks. The IMF would not, however, make economic data on developing countries available to the Institute. Finally, the Institute aimed to engage in dialogue with borrowing countries on a voluntary basis. In addition to stating its objectives the Institute made it clear what it was not. To avoid breaking US anti-trust laws and alienating developing countries, the Institute stressed that it was not a 'banker's cartel'. It was not a credit-rating agency, nor a bargaining agent for representatives of member banks in their dealings with developing countries.

Criticisms

Even before it was operational, the Institute was being criticised in some quarters. Among some European and regional US banks, it was cynically suggested that the Institute was created by, and would be run in the interests of, the top ten US banks. It certainly was true that the Institute was the brainchild of these banks, but in order to reassure the cynics the first managing director was a French banker. Other observers suggested that while the basic idea was a good one, it was five years too late. The debt crisis was almost over when the Institute became operational. It was also suggested that since the IMF would not be providing any information to the Institute, there was no guarantee that the information it would be providing would be any better than the information banks had had before the Institute existed.

Performance

Although the Institute has only been operational for one year, and it is hard to judge its effectiveness in so short a time, it is clear that virtually all major banks have agreed to become members. The Deutsche Bank was the only major bank to decline the invitation to join the Institute. B. Ogden, one of its founding fathers, in a 1983 interview with *Euromoney* (July 1983), commented that 'we'll only be able to test how successful the Institute has been in five to ten years from now. Its major task is to prevent these sorts of crises from happening again'. In the short term, it is suggested that if the Institute is able to increase co-operation between banks in the area of lending to developing countries, then it will have served a useful purpose.

Appendix 11:
Merchant/investment bank advisers to the Governments of developing countries in the rescheduling process, 1982–1984

Origins

Although banks such as Baring Brothers, Merrill Lynch, and Schroders had long been employed as advisers to the Central Banks of OECD countries, it was not until the formation of the so-called 'troika' of Lehman Brothers Kuhn Loeb (USA), Maison Lazard (France), and S. G. Warburg (UK) in 1975, at the behest of the Indonesian Government (which wanted a representative selection of bank advisers to sort out the financial problems of the state oil company, Pertamina), that the business of advising the Governments of developing countries began to grow. From 1975 to 1982, the 'troika' acted as advisers to the Governments of Indonesia, Panama, Gabon, Sri Lanka, Senegal, Ivory Coast, Togo, Benin, Upper Volta, Niger, Zaïre, and Turkey.

In 1981, with the beginning of the South American debt crisis in Central America, Leslie, Weinert and Yohai (USA) advised Nicaragua, the 'troika' advised Costa Rica, and Samuel Montagu (UK) advised Jamaica. In other parts of the world, and again in 1981, Morgan Grenfell (UK) advised Sudan, Uganda, and Zimbabwe, and Samuel Montagu advised Zambia. In 1982 Saloman Brothers (USA) was advising Bolivia, Merrill Lynch (USA) advised Peru, and Samuel Montagu advised the Dominican Republic.

Although Leslie, Weinert and Yohai, Samuel Montagu, Morgan Grenfell, Saloman Brothers and Merrill Lynch made an impact, Governments seemed to be more impressed by the greater experience and expertise offered by the 'troika', which was advising fifteen Governments by 1982. Its unique combination of banks from different countries gave it a knowledge base no one merchant/investment bank could possibly rival.

These sorts of combinations proved the most popular point to sell to Governments when looking for new business. In 1983, for example, Price Waterhouse, the international accountancy group, formed a company with four bankers (French, British, Swiss, and US), and went into the advisory business. The company was headed by Michael Coates, chairman of Price Waterhouse.

Fees

The number of banks that wanted to enter the advisory business was a direct consequence of the large fees to be had for comparatively little effort. Costa Rica, for example, paid $500,000, in advance, for six months' advice from the 'troika'. This seemed to be the going rate, although fees of up to $1 million were reported to have been paid by the more important Governments in 1982 and 1983.

Objectives

Although the bank advisers gave general financial advice, their major function in the 1981–3 period was to advise Governments involved in the rescheduling process, and to be actually present during their negotiations with advisory committees and the Paris Club. Being experienced bankers, with an intimate knowledge of international banking issues and the debtor country in question, they claimed to be able to get a better deal for the country concerned than if the country had faced its foreign creditors alone.

The *modus operandi* of the advisers was well planned, detailed, and thorough, and is best explained in a brief note submitted to a 1983 conference on rescheduling techniques by Arnold Nachmanoff,* a senior director of a 'troika' member bank, S. G. Warburg. The note is as follows.

* Arnold Nachmanoff, 'Major Considerations in Advising Sovereign Borrowers on Debt Restructuring', in Group of Thirty, *Rescheduling Techniques, Papers Presented*

**Major Considerations in Advising Sovereign Borrowers
on Debt Restructuring**

Outline

1. *The role of advisers*

— Added experience and skilled manpower for the debtor.
— Source of independent, professional and confidential advice.
— Can facilitate communication and understanding between debtor and creditors.

2. *Objectives of debt restructuring*

— Alleviation of liquidity problem.
— Stabilisation of external flows.
— Return to normal financing and economic growth.

3. *Defining and analysing the problem*

— Causes of the problem.
— Availability of economic and financial data.
— Nature of the debt; breakdown by class, debtor, creditor maturity, interest rate structure, currency, etc.
— Analysis of debt service requirements within context of debtor's capacity to service debt.
— Domestic adjustment measures available to alleviate illiquidity, e.g. budget actions, exchange rate policy, capital controls.
— Scope and nature of required debt restructuring.

4. *Communication with creditors*

— Importance of communication between debtor and creditor to restore climate of confidence and co-operation.
— Provision of information to creditors on a regular basis regarding (1) the debtor's financial and economic situation, (2) efforts to deal with the problem, and (3) commitment to

to an International Conference on Sovereign Debt, London, 3 and 4 November 1983
(London: OYEZ IBC Ltd. for the Group of Thirty, New York), pp. 80–3.
    © 1984 Group of Thirty, Consultative Group on International Economic & Monetary Affairs, Inc. Reproduced by permission from *Rescheduling Techniques: Papers Presented to an International Conference on Sovereign Debt*, London, 3 & 4 November 1983.

honour obligations to maximum extent possible, in particular with respect to keeping interest current.
— Establishment of clear intention to negotiate a mutually satisfactory solution in reasonable time-frame, discouraging disruptive litigation.

5. *Formulating a restructuring plan*

— No two restructuring operations exactly the same.
— Definition of elements to be included in a restructuring package: stabilisation programme, IMF assistance, bridging finance, official debt rescheduling, commercial debt rescheduling, mobilisation of new inflows.
— Relationship among individual elements of package; co-ordinating sequence of events, and negotiations with international agencies and different classes of creditors.

Major factors to be considered

— Economic and financial feasibility: is the package service-able by debtor in the context of projections of its available foreign exchange resources and its current and projected economic situations?
— Political feasibility: acceptability to debtor in terms of the political and social consequences of the economic constraints which the package will impose on the country; requirements for legislative approval.
— Acceptability from creditors' point of view: (e.g. regulatory restrictions, balance sheet considerations of private creditors).
— Fair and equitable treatment of creditors: comparability among the various creditor classes.
— Issue of inclusion of private sector debt.
— Legal issues: settlement of suits, analysis of documentation: availability of competent legal counsel.
— Medium- and longer-term prospects for return to normal financing facilities.

6. *Negotiation*

— Clarification of objectives, priorities.
— Timing imperatives or constraints.

— Realistic financial and political parameters.
— Precedents set in previous restructuring operations.
— Current market situation (market terms, other restructurings in progress).
— Linkage between elements of the package: rescheduling and new money facilities.
— Establishing credibility of negotiating positions.
— Durability of agreements.

7. *Post-negotiation*

— Assurance that documentation reflects agreements achieved and does not unduly circumscribe future actions of the debtor.
— Maximum effort to ensure that signed agreements are adhered to. Monitoring of cash flow to ensure that the agreed repayment schedules are sustainable.

The above note, as well as offering a fascinating insight into how an adviser thinks and works, is also as fine a view of the major issues in the rescheduling process as has ever been produced in the literature. The note reveals that the objectives were: to ask all the right questions relevant to the rescheduling; to obtain reliable answers to all such questions; to draw up an overall strategic plan for the Government concerned to resolve its debt problems, and to monitor all aspects of the strategic plan to ensure that set objectives were, in fact, achieved.

Performance

It would be fair to say that the performance of inexperienced bank interlopers, who had just entered the advisory business for the fees, soon resulted in their dismissal. Salomon Brothers, for example, was dismissed by the Bolivian Government after only one year. The 'troika', on the other hand, did not suffer such an indignity.

The most successful performances, it seems, were in the smaller debtor countries—Leslie, Weinert and Yohai, for example, helped to obtain very favourable terms for Nicaragua (see Appendix 5 for full details of this agreement). Elsewhere, however, only relatively small concessions were extracted from advisory committees. In the Sudan, for example, Morgan

Grenfell helped convince the advisory committee for that country to accept the suggestion that the Sudan pay no re-negotiation fee in its rescheduling agreement.

For the countries with very large debt problems, however, performance was not very impressive, as the larger the debt problem in any particular country the more insistent the relevant advisory committee (especially in the period 1982–3) became that the country accept what the market wanted, i.e. a high-risk premium in the terms on rescheduled debt and new loans.

More generally, advisers helped debtor Governments to think more clearly about all aspects of the debt problems they faced, and about the rescheduling process in which they found themselves as a result of those debt problems. In the case of developing countries with little experience of international finance (especially in Africa), such assistance by their advisers was of great importance.

Criticism

Had the advisers been totally ineffective, they would not have attracted the strong criticisms of advisory committees, the Paris Club, and the IMF. Advisory committees, in particular, seemed very irritated by the presence of advisers during their negotiations with the Governments of developing countries. They accused them, among other things, of only being interested in collecting fees, of giving bad and unrealistic advice to Governments as regards their initial negotiating positions in their negotiations with their creditors, and for giving too much confidence to Governments. Governments came to regard rescheduling as a right to be demanded, and not a favour to be granted by advisory committees. They soon realised that the position of creditors was far weaker than the arrogant antics of advisory committees would have at first suggested.

Criticism also came from the 'troika', and what really infuriated advisory committees was that such criticism was made in the form of a public statement—an entirely unprecedented development. The 'troika', in its 1983 statement, stated:

that a small number of short-sighted commercial bankers at middle management level resist the appointment of professional financial advisers by sovereign governments, as it might hinder efforts to impose directly unrealistic [my emphasis] rescheduling terms without due regard to the exposure of all categories of creditors and the relevant country's potential long-term financial rehabilitation. [Quoted by Peter Rodgers, 'Troika Takes Banks to Task', *Guardian*, 19 April 1983.]

The 'troika' pointed out that commercial banks' insistence on market terms, in rescheduling and new loan agreements (1982–3), were unrealistic, since just when developing countries were the least able to pay, more was being demanded of them by advisory committees. The effect of the high-risk premium so levied, in the view of the 'troika', was to increase the overall risk in the long term by making unrealistic demands in the short term.

Appendix 12:
The Cartagena Process:
chronology of events, 1984–1985

November 1982

The Mexican President, Lopez Portilo, initiates secret meetings with his Brazilian and Argentinian counterparts to discuss the possibility of a multilateral response to the debt crisis by South American countries. His plan is rejected by the Brazilian Government.

March 1984

A number of powerful Governments meet in Quito, Ecuador. Brazil, Mexico, and Argentina are the most important Governments present. All agree to organise, and drum up wider support for, a formal summit of debtor Governments within the next few months.

May 1984

A joint letter, signed by the Presidents of Argentina, Brazil, Colombia, Ecuador, Peru and Venezuela, is sent to the 1984 London Summit of OECD Governments. The letter protests against rising interest rates. Mexico, which declined to sign the letter, is singled out for praise by the London summiteers. No specific proposals are forthcoming from the London Summit to deal with the debt problem.

21/23 June 1984

The Governments of Argentina, Bolivia, Brazil, Chile, Colombia, the Dominican Republic, Ecuador, Mexico, Peru, Uruguay, and Venezuela (eleven in all) meet at Cartagena, Colombia for three days of talks. A formal consultative mechanism, henceforth known as the Cartagena Group, is established, agrees to meet on a regular basis in the future, and issues a document entitled *The Cartagena Consensus*. The document offers an analysis of the causes of the debt crisis, and offers seventeen specific proposals for easing South America's debt service burden and for reorganising its debt repayment system. The debtors' summit, so as not to alarm foreign creditors unduly, insists that it is not a debtors' cartel, but it is clear that it is an informal group whose aim is to put collective pressure on foreign creditors in the debt rescheduling process.

14/15 December 1984

The second meeting of the Cartagena Group takes place at Mar del Plata, Argentina. A communiqué is issued, which calls for direct talks between debtor Governments and OECD Governments within six months of the present meeting. The debt crisis, the communiqué insists, is far too serious to be left to commercial banks and the IMF. Reports suggest that the US Government would not be prepared to agree to attending any such talks, as to do so would be to admit the debt crisis is political. Since 1982 the line taken among foreign creditors was that the debt crisis was merely an economic problem to be resolved between debtors and creditors.

22 September 1984

At the annual meetings of the IMF and the World Bank it is suggested, by the US and other OECD Governments, that the talks proposed by the Cartagena Group take place in the Development Committee of the IMF and the World Bank. Though an obvious attempt to avoid direct talks, it is a significant concession. The first meeting of the Development Committee is set for April 1985.

15 November 1984

While not dismissing the proposals about talks in the Development Committee, the Cartagena Group at a meeting of the Organisation of American States (OAS) in Brazil, makes it clear that its final goal is direct talks with OECD Governments and sees the talks in the Development Committee as an important step on the road to that final goal. Significantly, the Brazilian Foreign Minister delivers a speech on behalf of the Cartagena Group at the OAS meeting, which confirms what has been suspected for a few months: Brazil is playing the leading diplomatic role in the Cartagena Process.

8/10 February 1985

The third meeting of the Cartagena Group meets at Santo Domingo in the Dominican Republic. The final communiqué agrees to meet Western finance ministers in the Development Committee of the IMF and the World Bank in April 1985, but avoids making another call for direct political talks with OECD Governments so as to give the April talks a chance before repeating (if necessary) the call for direct talks. A common negotiating position is agreed for the April meeting, which worries many OECD Governments, as having a common line in such a meeting brings the Cartagena Group one step nearer to a *de facto* debtors' cartel. A common line also makes divide-and-rule tactics, on the part of OECD Governments, almost impossible in the April meeting.

Bibliography

George Abbot, *International Indebtedness and the Developing Countries* (London: Croom Helm, 1979).

American Express International Banking Corporation, *International Debt: Banks and the LDCs*, AMEX Bank Review Special Paper No. 10 (London: American Express International Banking Corporation, 1984).

Tim Anderson, 'The Troika Spawns a Whole New Business', *Euromoney*, August 1982.

Anthony Angelini, *International Lending, Risk and the Euromarkets* (New York: Halstead Press, 1979).

Kaj Areskoug, *External Public Borrowing: Its Role in Economic Development* (New York: Praeger, 1969).

Jonathan D. Aronson, *Money and Power: Banks and the World Monetary System* (Beverly Hills, California: Sage, 1977).

Jonathan D. Aronson (ed.), *Debt and the Less Developed Countries* (Boulder, Colorado: Westview Press, 1979).

Dragoslav Avramović, *Economic Growth and External Debt* (Baltimore: Johns Hopkins University Press, 1964).

Edmar Lisboa Bacha and Carlos F. Diaz Alejandro, *International Financial Intermediation: A Long and Topical View*, Princeton Essays in International Finance No. 147 (Princeton, NJ: Princeton University Press, May 1982).

Norman A. Bailey, 'A Safety Net for Foreign Lending', in T. de Saint Phalle (ed.), *The International Financial Crisis: An Opportunity for Constructive Action* (Washington, DC: Georgetown University Center for Strategic and International Studies, 1983).

A. D. Bain, 'International Lenders and World Debt', *Midland Bank Review*, winter 1984.

Bank of International Settlements, Committee on Banking Regulations and Supervisory Practices (the Cooke Committee), *Report on the Supervision of Banks' Foreign Establishments* (the Basle Concordat) (Basle: BIS, 1975).

Bank of International Settlements, Committee on Banking Regulations and Supervisory Practices (the Cooke Committee), *Principles for the Supervision of Banks' Foreign Establishments* (the revised Basle Concordat) (Basle: BIS, 1983).

Paul Bareau, 'The Lessons of an Earlier International Debt Crisis', *The Banker*, December 1983.

Charles Batchelor, 'Price Waterhouse in Debt Advice Venture', *Financial Times*, 4 May 1983

Geoffrey Bell and Graeme Rutledge, 'How to Account for Problem Loans', *Euromoney*, January 1984.

Graham Bird, *The International Monetary System and the Less Developed Countries* (London: Macmillan, 1978).

Graham Bird, 'A Role for the IMF in Economic Development', *Banca Nazionale de Lavoro Quarterly Review*, December 1982.

Graham Bird, 'The Banks and the IMF: Division of Labour', *Lloyds Bank Review*, No. 150, October 1983.

Henry J. Bitterman, *The Refunding of International Debt* (Durham, North Carolina: Duke University Press, 1973).

Jan Knippers Black, *United States Penetration of Brazil* (Manchester: Manchester University Press, 1977).

Stephen D. Bodyala, 'Bankers Versus Diplomats: The Debate Over Mexican Insolvency', *Journal of Interamerican and World Affairs*, November 1982.

William H. Bolin and Jorge del Canto, 'LDC Debt: Beyond Crisis Management', *Foreign Affairs*, summer 1983.

Brandt Commission, *North–South* (London: Pan Books, 1980).

Brandt Commission, *Common Crisis* (London: Pan Books, 1983).

E. A. Brett, *International Money and Capitalist Crisis: The Anatomy of Global Disintegration* (London: Heinemann, 1983).

W. H. Bruce Brittain, 'Developing Countries' External Debt and the Private Banks', *Banca Nazionale de Lavoro Quarterly Review*, No. 123, December 1977.

Colin Brown, 'The Problem of Provision Against Sovereign Debt', *The Banker*, February 1983.

Karl Brunner, 'International Debt, Insolvency and Illiquidity', *Journal of Economic Affairs*, Vol. 3, No. 3, April 1983.

David Buchan and Alexander Lebt, 'Yugoslavia Battles to Keep the IMF at Bay', *Financial Times*, 20 November 1984.

David P. Calleo and Benjamin M. Rowland, *America and the World Political Economy: Atlantic Dreams and National Realities* (Bloomington, Indiana: Indiana University Press, 1973).

Forrest Capie and Geoffrey E. Wood, 'What Happened in 1931?', in Centre for Banking and International Finance, The City University, *Financial Crisis and the World Banking System: A Conference held in London, 6 and 7 October, 1983* (London: Centre for Banking and International Finance, The City University, 1983).

Cartagena Group, *The Cartagena Consensus* (Cartagena, Colombia: Colombian Ministry of Foreign Affairs, 23 June 1984).

Cartagena Group, *Communiqué*, (Mar del Plata, Argentina: Argentinian Ministry of Foreign Affairs, 16 September 1984).

Cartagena Group, *Communiqué* (Santo Domingo, The Dominican Republic: Dominican Republic of Ministry of Foreign Affairs, 10 February 1985).

Derek F. Channon, *British Transnational Bank Strategy: A Report to the UN Centre on Transnational Corporations* (Manchester: Centre for Business Research, Manchester Business School, 1978).

Hollis B. Chenery, 'Foreign Assistance and Economic Development', *American Economic Review*, Vol. LVI, September 1966.

William R. Cline, *International Monetary Reform and the Developing Countries* (Washington, DC: Brookings Institute, 1976).

William R. Cline, *International Debt and the Stability of the World Economy* (Washington, DC: Institute for International Economics, 1983).

William R. Cline (ed.), *Trade Policy in the 1980s* (Washington, DC: Institute for International Economics, 1983).

Jerry Coakley and Laurence Harris, *The City of Capital: London's Role as a Financial Centre* (Oxford: Basil Blackwell, 1983).

Benjamin J. Cohen, *Organizing The World's Money: The Political Economy of International Monetary Relations* (London: Macmillan, 1977).

Michael H. Coles, 'Flexibility in Debt Rescheduling: Towards a Solution', in Group of Thirty, *Rescheduling Techniques: Papers Presented to an International Conference on Sovereign Debt, London, 3 and 4 November, 1983* (London: OYEZ IBC Ltd. for the Group of Thirty, New York).

Peter Cooke, 'Developments in Co-operation Among Banking Supervisory Authorities', *Bank of England Quarterly Bulletin*, Vol. 21, No. 2, June 1981.

Peter Cooke, 'The International Banking Scene: A Supervisory Perspective', *Bank of England Quarterly Bulletin*, Vol. 23, No. 1, March 1983.

Roland, Dallas, 'Democracy and Debt in Latin America', *World Today*, April 1984.

Stephen I. Davis, 'How Risky is International Lending?', *Harvard Business Review*, January/February 1977.

Darrell Delamaide, *Debt Shock* (London: Weidenfeld & Nicolson, 1984).

Sidney Dell, *On Being Grandmotherly: The Evolution of IMF Conditionality*, Princeton Essays in International Finance No. 144 (Princeton, NJ: Princeton University Press, 1981).

Pierre Dhonte, *Clockwork Debt: Trade and the External Debt of Developing Countries* (Lexington, Mass.: Lexington Books, 1979).

John W. Dizard, 'International Banking: The End of Let's Pretend', *Fortune*, 29 November 1982.

Jonathan Eaton and Mark Gersovitz, *Poor-Country Borrowing in Private Financial Markets and the Repudiation Issue*, Princeton Studies in

International Finance No. 47 (Princeton, NJ: Princeton University Press, June 1981).

Economist Survey, 'A Nightmare of Debt: A Survey of International Banking', *The Economist*, 20 March 1982.

A. F. Ehrbar, 'Oil and Trouble at Continental Illinois', *Fortune*, 7 February 1982.

Jessica P. Einhorn, 'International Bank Lending: Expanding the Dialogue', *Columbia Journal of World Business*, Fall 1978.

Jessica P. Einhorn, 'Co-operation Between Public and Private Lenders to the Third World', *World Economy*, May 1979.

Thomas O. Enders and Richard P. Mattione, *Latin America: The Crisis of Debt and Growth* (Washington, DC: Brookings Institute, 1984).

Padriac Fallon and David Shirreff, 'The Betrayal of Eastern Europe', *Euromoney*, September 1982.

G. Feder and R. E. Just, 'A Study of Debt Servicing Capacity Applying Logit Analysis', *Journal of Development Economics*, Vol. 4, March 1977.

G. Feder, R. E. Just, and K. Ross, 'Projecting Debt Servicing Capacity of Developing Countries', *Journal of Financial and Quantitative Analysis*, Vol. 16, December 1981.

Richard E. Feinberg, *The Intemperate Zone: The Third World Challenge to U.S. Foreign Policy* (New York: Norton, 1983).

Peter Field, 'Meet the New Breed of Banker: The Political Risk Expert', *Euromoney*, July 1980.

Peter Field, 'The IMF and Central Banks Flex Their Muscles', *Euromoney*, January 1983.

André Gunder Frank, *Capitalism and Underdevelopment in Latin America* (New York: Monthly Review Press, 1967).

André Gunder Frank, 'A Debt Bomb Primed for the Next Recession', *Guardian*, 12 October 1984.

L. G. Franko and M. J. Seiber (eds), *Developing Country Debt* (New York: Pergamon Press, 1979).

Jeff Frieden, 'Third World Indebted Industrialization: International Finance and State Capitalism in Mexico, Brazil, Algeria and South Korea', *International Organisation*, Vol. 35, No. 3, summer 1981.

Irving S. Friedman, *The Emerging Role of Private Banks in the Developing World* (New York: Citicorp, 1977).

Irving S. Friedman, 'Country Risk: The Lessons of Zaïre', *The Banker*, February 1978.

Celso Furtado, *The Economic Development of Latin America: Historical Background and Contemporary Problems* (Cambridge: Cambridge University Press, 1976).

Celso Furtado, *No to Recession and Unemployment: An Examination of the Brazilian Economic Crisis* (London: Third World Foundation for Social and Economic Studies, 1984).

Jeffrey E. Garten, 'Rescheduling Sovereign Debt: Is There a Better Approach?', *World Economy*, Vol. 5, No. 3, November 1982.

Ian Giddy and Russ Ray, 'The Eurodollar Market and the Third World', *University of Michigan Business Review*, March 1976.

L. S. Goodman, 'Bank Lending to Non-OPEC LDCs: Are Risks Diversifiable?', *Federal Reserve Board of New York Quarterly Review*, Summer 1981.

Charles Grant, 'How the Ditchley Initiative is Becoming Reality', *Euromoney*, July 1983.

Charles Grant, 'Those Debt Proposals: Radical or Just Wrong?', *Euromoney*, July 1983.

J. M. Gray and H. P. Gray, 'The Multinational Bank: A Financial MNC?', *Journal of Banking and Finance*, No. 5, 1981.

Group of Thirty, *Rescheduling Techniques: Papers Presented to an International Conference on Sovereign Debt, London, 3 and 4 November 1983* (London: OYEZ IBC Ltd. for the Group of Thirty, New York).

Jack Gutentag and Richard Herring, *The Lender-of-Last-Resort-Function in an International Context*, Princeton Essays in International Finance No. 151 (Princeton, NJ: Princeton University Press, May 1983).

William Hall, 'The Ditchley Institute: Search for the Right Man as Leader', *World Banking Survey (Part 1), Financial Times*, 9 May 1983.

Chandra S. Hardy, 'Commercial Bank Lending to Developing Countries: Supply Constraints', *World Development*, Vol. 7, No. 2, February 1979 (Special Issue on International Indebtedness and World Economic Stagnation).

Chandra S. Hardy, *Rescheduling Developing-Country Debts, 1956–1981: Lessons and Recommendations* (Washington, DC: Overseas Development Council, 1982).

W. P. Hogan and I. F. Pearce, *The Incredible Eurodollar: Or Why the World's Money System is Collapsing* (London: Unwin Paperbacks, 1982).

Martin Honeywell (ed.), *The Poverty Brokers: The IMF and Latin America* (London: Latin American Bureau, 1983).

Keith J. Horsefield (ed.), *The International Monetary Fund, 1945–65: Twenty Years of International Monetary Co-operation*, 3 Vols. (Washington, DC: IMF, 1969).

Helen Hughes, 'Debt and Development: The Role of Foreign Capital in Economic Growth', *World Development*, Vol. 7, No. 2, February 1979 (Special Issue on International Indebtedness and World Economic Stagnation).

Institute of Bankers, *The Financing of Long-Term-Development: Papers Presented to the 32nd International Banking School, Cambridge, August 1979* (London: Institute of Bankers, 1979).

Karel Jansen (ed.), *Monetarism, Economic Crisis and the Third World* (London: Frank Cass, 1983).

Antonio Jorge (ed.), *Foreign Debt and Latin American Economic Development* (New York: Pergamon Press, 1983).

Anatole Kaletsky, *The Costs of Default*, a Twentieth Century Fund Paper (New York: Priority Press Publications, 1985).

Ishan Kapur, 'An Analysis of the Supply of Eurocurrency Finance to Developing Countries', *Oxford Bulletin of Economics and Statistics*, Vol. 39, No. 3, August 1977.

Janet Kelly, 'International Capital Markets: Power and Security in the International System', *Orbis*, winter 1978.

Tony Killick (ed.), *Adjustment and Financing in the Developing World: The Role of the IMF* (London/Washington, DC: Overseas Development Institute/IMF, 1982).

Tony Killick, *The Quest for Economic Stabilization: The IMF and the Third World* (London: Heinemann, 1984).

Charles Kindleberger, *Power and Money: The Economics of International Politics and the Politics of International Economics* (New York: Basic Books, 1970).

Charles Kindleberger, *The World in Depression, 1929–1939* (Stanford, California: University of California Press, 1973).

Joseph Kraft, *The Mexican Rescue* (New York: Group of Thirty, 1984).

Pedro-Pablo Kuczynski, 'Latin American Debt', *Foreign Affairs*, winter 1982/83.

Pedro-Pablo Kuczynski, 'Latin American Debt: Act Two', *Foreign Affairs*, fall 1983.

Harold Lever, 'The Lever Plan', *The Economist*, 9 July 1983.

Harold Lever, 'Drowning in Debt', *Time and Tide*, autumn 1984.

Harold Lever *et al.*, *The Lever Group Report* (London: Commonwealth Secretariat, 1984).

Peter E. Leslie, 'The Techniques for Debt Rescheduling', in *The Euromarkets in 1983: Papers Presented to an International Conference on the Euromarkets, London, 8 and 9 March 1983* (London: Financial Times Conferences, 1983).

Quek Peck Lim, 'The Borrower's Trump Card is His Weakness', *Euromoney*, October 1982.

Charles Lipson, 'The International Organization of Third World Debt', *Orbis*, Vol. 35, No. 4, autumn 1981.

Karin Lissakers, *International Debt, The Banks, and U.S. Foreign Policy*, Staff Report prepared for the Use of the Subcommittee on Foreign Policy of the Committee on Foreign Relations, United States Senate (Washington, DC: US Government Printing Office, 1977).

D. C. McDonald, 'Debt Capacity and Developing Country Borrowing: A Survey', *IMF Staff Papers*, September 1983.

John Mathis, 'Lessons Learned From International Debt Reschedulings', *Journal of Commercial Bank Lending*, January 1983.

M. S. Mendelsohn, *Money On The Move: The Modern International Capital Market* (New York: McGraw Hill, 1980).

M. S. Mendelsohn, *Commercial Banks and the Restructuring of Cross-Border Debt* (New York: Group of Thirty, 1983).

Marko Milivojević, 'Anatomy of a Rescheduling: Yugoslavia, 1982–1983', *South Slav Journal*, Vol. 6, No. 2(20), summer 1983.

Marko Milivojević, 'New Debt Crisis Raises Need for Debtors' Cartel to Fight Banks', *Politics & Profit*, June 1984.

Marko Milivojević, *The Yugoslav Hard Currency Debt and the Process of Economic Reform Since 1948*, Bradford Studies on Yugoslavia No. 9 (Bradford: Postgraduate School of Yugoslav Studies, 1985).

Marko Milivojević, 'Yugoslavia's Security Dilemmas and the West', *The Journal of Strategic Studies*, Vol. 8, No. 3, September 1985.

Azizali F. Mohammed and Fabrizio Saccomanni, 'Short-term Banking and Euro-Currency Credits to Developing Countries', *IMF Staff Papers*, September 1973.

Michael Moffit, *The World's Money: International Banking from Bretton Woods to the Brink of Insolvency* (London: Michael Joseph, 1984).

Morgan Guaranty, 'Global Debt: Assessment and Long-Term Strategy', *World Financial Markets*, June 1983.

Morgan Guaranty, 'Korea: Adjustment Model For The 1980s', *World Financial Markets*, March 1984.

Morgan Guaranty, 'The LDC Debt Problem—at the Midpoint?', *World Financial Markets*, October/November 1984.

Arnold Nachmanoff, 'Major Considerations in Advising Sovereign Borrowers on Debt Restructuring', in Group of Thirty, *Rescheduling Techniques: Papers Presented to an International Conference on Sovereign Debt, London, 3 and 4 November 1983* (London: OYEZ IBC Ltd. for the Group of Thirty, New York).

Mancur Olson, *The Logic of Collective Action* (Harvard, Mass.: Harvard University Press, 1965, 2nd edn., 1971).

Neil Osborn, 'The Rhodes Show Goes On and On', *Euromoney*, March 1984.

Gustav F. Papanek, 'The Effect of Aid and other Resource Transfers on Savings and Growth in Less Developed Countries', *Economic Journal*, 82, September 1972.

Gustav F. Papanek, 'Aid, Foreign Private Investment, Savings, and Growth in Less Developed Countries', *Journal of Political Economy*, January/February 1973.

Cherly Payer, *The Debt Trap: The IMF and the Third World* (Harmondsworth: Penguin, 1974).

Cheryl Payer, *The World Bank* (New York: Monthly Review Press, 1982).

Corrado Pirzio-Biroli, 'Making Sense of the IMF Conditionality Debate', *Journal of World Trade Law*, October 1983.

Richard Portes, 'East Europe's Debt: Interdependence is a Two-Way Street', *Foreign Affairs*, Vol. 55, No. 4, July 1977.

Mike Reid, 'Marines Go on the Mountain Warpath', *Guardian*, 21 September 1984.

Walter E. Robichek, 'Official Borrowing Abroad: Some Reflections', *Finance and Development*, March 1980.

Alan Robinson, 'The IMF vs. the People', *Euromoney*, October 1983.

Alan Robinson, 'Can Lusinchi Do Without the IMF?', *Euromoney*, January, 1984.

Alan Robinson, 'One by One, They Come to Terms', *Euromoney*, March 1984.

Peter Rodgers, 'Troika Takes Banks to Task', *Guardian*, 19 April 1983.

Peter Rodgers, 'How Many More Insults Will the Latin Americans Accept?', *Guardian*, 26 June 1984.

Peter Rodgers, 'British Bulldog that Faced Argentina', *Guardian*, 17 December 1984.

Emma Rothschild, 'Banks: The Coming Crisis', *The New York Review of Books*, 27 May 1976.

Emma Rothschild, 'Banks: The Politics of Debt', *The New York Review of Books*, 24 June 1976.

Dennison Rusinow, *The Yugoslav Experiment, 1948-1974* (London: C. Hurst & Co. for the Royal Institute of International Affairs, 1977).

Anthony Sampson, *The Money Lenders: Bankers in a Dangerous World* (London: Hodder & Stoughton, 1981).

J. C. Sánchez (ed.), *Debt and Development* (New York: Praeger, 1982).

Joseph A. Schumpeter, *Capitalism, Socialism and Democracy*, 3rd edn. (New York: Harper & Row, 1950).

Marilyn Seiber, *International Borrowing By Developing Countries* (New York: Pergamon Press, 1982).

Gordon W. Smith, *The External Debt Prospects of the Non-oil Developing Countries: An Econometric Analysis*, New International Economic Order Series Monograph No. 10 (Washington, DC: Overseas Development Council, 1977).

Robert M. Solow, 'On The Lender of Last Resort', in Charles P. Kindleberger and Jean-Pierre Laffar-Gue (eds), *Financial Crises* (Cambridge: Cambridge University Press, 1982).

Joan Edelman·Spero, *The Politics of International Economic Relations*, 2nd edn. (London: George Allen & Unwin, 1982).

Barbara Stallings and Julian Martel, 'Public Debt and Private Profit: International Finance in Peru and Argentina', *NACLA Report*, Vol. XII, No. 4, July/August 1978 (New York: North American Congress on Latin America).

Susan Strange, 'International Economics and International Relations: A Case of Mutual Neglect', *International Affairs*, 46, April 1970.

Mary Sutton, 'Structuralism: The Latin American Record and the New

Critique', in Tony Killick, *The Quest For Economic Stabilization: The IMF And The Third World* (London: Heinemann, 1984).

Andrew Thompson, 'Alfonsin Walks on a Knife Edge', *South*, May 1984.

Treasury and Civil Service Committee, House of Commons, *International Monetary Arrangements: Second Special Report of the Treasury and Civil Service Committee, House of Commons, Session 1982–1983* (London: HMSO, 1983).

Treasury and Civil Service Committee, House of Commons, *International Monetary Arrangements: International Lending by Banks—Fourth Report of the Treasury and Civil Service Committee, House of Commons, Session 1982–1983* (London: HMSO, 1983).

Jan Tumlir, 'The World Economy Today: Crisis or New Beginning?', *National Westminster Bank Quarterly Review*, August 1983.

UN Economic Commission for Latin America (ECLA), *Preliminary Balance of the Latin American Economy in 1983* (Santiago: ECLA, 1984).

Roland Vaubel, 'The Moral Hazard of IMF Lending', *World Economy*, September 1983.

Eugene L. Versluysen, *The Political Economy of International Finance* (Farnborough: Gower, 1981).

Réne Villarreal, *The Monetarist Counter-Revolution* (Mexico City: El Colegio de Mexico, 1983).

Margaret G. De Vries, *The International Monetary Fund, 1966–1971: The System Under Stress* (Washington, DC: IMF, 1976).

Howard Wachtel, *The New Gnomes: Multinational Banks in the Third World* (Washington, DC: Transnational Institute, 1977).

Henry C. Wallich, 'Banks, LDC's Share Concern for Viable System', *Journal of Commerce*, 30 July 1981.

Henry C. Wallich, 'Rescheduling as Seen by the Supervisor and the Lender of Last Resort', in Henry C. Wallich (ed.), *Crisis in Economic and Financial Structure* (Lexington, Mass.: Lexington Books, 1982).

Leslie Weinert, 'Banks and Bankruptcy', *Foreign Policy*, No. 50, Spring 1983.

Richard S. Weinert, 'Nicaragua's Debt Renegotiations', Cambridge *Journal of Economics*, 5, 1981.

WSJ Editorial, 'Yugoslavia's Lenders Apprehensive', *Wall Street Journal*, 7 May 1982.

Sidney Weintraub and William R. Cline (eds), *Economic Stabilization in Developing Countries* (Washington, DC: Brookings Institute, 1981).

Thomas E. Weisskopf, 'The Impact of Foreign Capital Inflow on Domestic Savings in Underdeveloped Countries', *Journal of International Economics*, 2, 1972.

Paul A. Wellons, *Borrowing By Developing Countries in the Euro-Currency Market* (Paris: OECD, 1977).

W. G. Wickersham, 'Rescheduling of Sovereign Debt', *International Financial Law Review*, September 1982.

John Williamson, *The Failure of International Monetary Reform, 1971–74* (London: Nelson, 1977).

John Williamson, *The Lending Policies of the IMF* (Washington, DC: Institute for International Economics, 1982).

John Williamson, *IMF Conditionality* (Washington, DC: Institute for International Economics, 1983).

John Williamson, 'Keynes and the International Economic Order', in David Worswick and James Trevithick (eds), *Keynes and the Modern World* (Cambridge: Cambridge University Press, 1983).

John Williamson, *The Exchange Rate System* (Washington, DC: Institute for International Economics, 1983).

Miguel S. Wionczek (ed.), *LDC External Debt and the World Economy* (Mexico City: El Colegio de Mexico, 1978).

S. M. Yassukovich, 'The Growing Political Threat to International Lending', *Euromoney*, April 1976.

Yoon-Dae Euh, *Commercial Banks and the Creditworthiness of Less Developed Countries* (Ann Arbor, Michigan: Michigan University Micro-Films International Research Press, 1978).

Minos Zombanakis, 'The International Debt Threat: A Way to Avoid a Crash', *The Economist*, 30 April 1983.

Index

(NOTE: *passim* means that the subject so annotated is referred to in scattered passages throughout these pages of text.)